# RIOTS AND MARTIAL LAW IN CEYLON, 1915

*Photo by Pâté*

THE GREAT ESALA PERAHERA

(procession in the month of August every year), with the Tooth Relic on the elephant under a canopy, headed by musicians and dancers, going round Kandy from the Daladá Máligawe.

A similar annual procession in Gampola was abandoned, owing to the opposition of the Muhammadans, which was the earliest of the causes of the riots.

# RIOTS AND MARTIAL LAW IN CEYLON, 1915

P. RAMANATHAN

WITH A MAP AND ILLUSTRATIONS

GYAN

*Published by*

Gyan Publishing House
5, Ansari Road
Daryaganj, New Delhi-110002
Phone: 011-47034999, 9811692060
E-mail: books@gyanbooks.com

*Distribution Network*
gyanbooks.com
India, USA, Canada, UK, Australia, France



ISBN: 9788121239615 (PB)
First Published, London1916

2nd Impression 2020

*Printed at:* Gyan Press, Delhi.



**Riots and Martial Law in Ceylon, 1915**
Author: P. Ramanathan

# Riots and Martial Law in Ceylon, 1915

BY

P. RÁMANÁTHAN, K.C., C.M.G.

*Elected Member of the Legislative Council of Ceylon representing the Educated Ceylonese.*

---

"Civil and Political Liberty can never flourish in a country which has no veneration for Justice, and does not cultivate the Sense of Justice; in which the people do not protest then and there against acts of oppression, and take up the cause of the down-trodden as their own cause, and work constitutionally for redress."

---

"Believing the British Empire to stand for Justice, Freedom and Good Government, we pledge ourselves, as citizens of the greatest empire in the world, to maintain the heritage handed down to us by our fathers."

---

LONDON:

ST. MARTIN'S PRESS, 15 CRAVEN STREET, STRAND

1916

# PREFACE.

I BEG to call the attention of the sympathetic reader to the following extract from *The Ceylon Legislative Council Debates* of the 14th of October last, in explanation of the need for this book,—to obtain through the Rt. Hon. the Secretary of State for the Colonies and the British Parliament the redress which I failed to get from the Government of Ceylon on behalf of the Sinhalese :

"The non-official Members of Council, Sir, dare not turn a deaf ear to the lamentations of the people as expressed in their petitions before us. If we do, we shall lay ourselves open to the charge of betraying the trust reposed upon us by His Majesty the King and the people alike. I believe, Sir, the Legislative Council has received about 350 petitions already, and I know not how many more have reached Your Excellency. I have a heap of them here on the table addressed to you, which I have not yet presented.

"When I read these petitions, Sir, I feel very sorry. I feel that I must do something for the people who are groaning under the misfortunes which they have suffered for no fault of their own. And I expect you, Sir, who have been so sympathetic and have extended to me your private friendship, to try and do something for the people on this extraordinary occasion. I have gone amongst them, and I have seen grown-up men and women weeping bitter tears owing to the untold sufferings that have been imposed on them by the atrocities of the martial law, and by the illegal and unrighteous acts of the Commissioners appointed by Your Excellency, not knowing how inexperienced, and how wanting in the sense of justice—

"His Excellency the Governor :—Mr. Rámanáthan, there are three of them here, and I am sure your words do not apply to them.

"The Hon. Mr. Rámanáthan :—I wish them to stand up and answer, Sir.

"His Excellency the Governor :—I am sure you do not mean to make any imputations against any member.

"The Hon. Mr. Rámanáthan :—Sir, I have seen the work of the Special Commissioners, I have heard of their doings—

"His Excellency the Governor :—I take it that your remarks do not apply to any members of this Council.

"The Hon Mr. Rámanáthan :—Private friendship, Sir, has nothing to do with public duty. That is my creed, and this is a most uncomfortable day for me. I have been called upon to do a duty that is most unpleasant, but which I must do at any cost, because the just cries of the people are dear unto God, and to the British throne, and to you, Sir. If any Honourable Members who have been charged with the duty of administering the Government have done wrong, it is for them to rise and say, in the presence of this assembly, 'I have done wrong; I desire that my work should be thrown away, and that others better advised than I have been should do the work in the manner in which it should be done.'

"I beg Your Excellency's forgiveness, and the forgiveness of my honourable friends who are sitting round this table, if, in the discharge of my duty, I have to say some things painful to them, but far more painful to myself. I will ask them to bear with me, because in the complicated circumstances of the case there should not be a pronouncement upon only the official side of it, but there should be a careful consideration of, and an unbiassed pronouncement on, the other side of the case too, which is the case of the people that I am trying to lay before Your Excellency.

"I believe that those who have been called by the King to do their duty to the people will do it when their eyes are opened, and make the contentment of the people their greatest concern. We may reasonably expect them to see that the rights and liberties of the people are conserved, and that nothing will be done to shake their confidence in the righteousness of the British Government."

P. RÁMANÁTHAN.

THE ATHENÆUM,
PALL MALL.

# CONTENTS.

Photo by Platé

KANDY (chief town in the Central Province), where the disturbances began.

# CHAPTER I.

## THE CAUSES, AND THE COURSE, OF THE RIOTS.

The earliest of the causes of the riots were the intolerance and aggression of the "Hambaya" Muhammadans towards the Buddhists.

THE intolerance and aggressiveness of a small section of the Muhammadans known to the Sinhalese as "Hambayas" (boatmen), and their insistence on the religious processions of the Sinhalese Buddhists passing in silence before their mosques in Gampola and Kandy, were the earliest of the causes of the recent riots in Ceylon, which began on the 29th May and ended on the 5th of June, 1915.

Who are the Hambaya Muhammadans?

The Hambayas are Muhammadan immigrants from the east coast of South India. They are not permanently settled in Ceylon. They do not as a rule bring their wives and families to the Island. Sojourning in it for a year or two at a time for purposes of trade, they return periodically with their savings to South India. They do not intermarry with any of the other Muhammadan communities of Ceylon, the largest of which consists of those who have been settled in the Island for several centuries, and who from the days of the Portuguese Government have been known to the Europeans as the "Moors." They number about 235,000 souls. But the Hambayas do not count more than 33,000, and of this number it is well to bear in mind that those who opposed the issue of licenses to conduct the Buddhist processions in Gampola and Kandy were principally the trustees of the mosques in those towns and their immediate supporters. If other Hambayas were drawn into the affray, it was only through party spirit, or the desire to make common cause with those who appeared to be the leaders of that community. In Gampola and Kandy many of these Muhammadans have prospered in trade, and have generously met the religious requirements of their brethren by enlarging and rebuilding the mosques in those places. But, unlike the Moors, who had learnt in the course of centuries the necessity of living in peace with their Sinhalese fellow-subjects and being tolerant to their religious observances, the Hambayas sought for their mosques in the Kandyan territory greater respect from the Kandyan Buddhists than the Moors have been in the habit of claiming for their own mosques.

Their opposition to the Buddhist Procession in Gampola in August, 1912.

When the Buddhists were preparing to celebrate in Gampola their greatest national festival, called the Esala Perahera, in August, 1912, by conducting the procession through all the streets of that town to the river Mahaweli-ganga and back, the Hambayas intimated to the police that they objected to the perahera passing their newly-built mosque with the beating of drums, the blowing of horns, and the cheering of the crowds.

The hasty and imprudent action of the Government Agent.

The obvious duty of the Government Agent, as the head of the police in the Central Province, was to send for the trustees of the Hambaya mosque and point out to them that none of tne trustees of the three mosques of the Moors on the same road had raised similar objections; that it was not customary in the Kandyan Provinces to impose silence on

Buddhist processions; and that, if the Hambayas persisted in their objection and intended to obstruct the perahera by force, it would be necessary to bind them over to keep the peace. But the Government Agent (Mr. Saxton) rashly directed the police officer to mark off by signposts a hundred yards alongside of the Hambayas' mosque, and directed him to inform the Basnayake Nilame of the Buddhist temple, from which the Esala Perahera was to start, that in taking the procession through the town no drum or other musical instrument should be played within the hundred yards indicated by the signposts.

The Basnayake Nilame, astonished at the order of the Government Agent, stopped all preparation for the perahera, and sought the advice of the other Nilames of the Kandyan country, who knew that the religious processions of the Buddhists in the Kandyan country stood on a different footing to those of the maritime country.

Continued tension between the Buddhists and the Hambaya Muhammadans during pendency of case in court.

The hasty action of the Government Agent forced the trustee of the Buddhist temple at Gampola to seek redress in the District Court of Kandy. He complained that the order made by the Government Agent was against the fifth article of the Convention of 2nd March, 1815, entered into in Kandy between the British Sovereign and certain chiefs of the Kandyan kingdom, whereby the religion of Buddha, professed by the chiefs and other inhabitants of the Kandyan Provinces, was declared inviolable, and its rites, ministers, and places of worship were to be maintained and protected by the British Government.

Very acute was the tension of feeling throughout the Sinhalese districts from the time of the Government Agent's order of August, 1912, to the day of the determination of Basnayake Nilame's suit by the Supreme Court in February, 1915.

The District Judge of Kandy (Mr. Paul E. Pieris, M.A., LL.M., Barrister-at-law, C.C.S.), having heard many witnesses and considered a large number of documents, held by his judgment, pronounced on 4th June, 1914, that the Esala Perahera was a rite of the religion of Buddha, which was undertaken to be maintained and protected under the Convention of 1815; that the accustomed route of the perahera and the continuance of the music was an essential part of the rite; that the Kandyan Convention constituted a binding compact unalterable in all following times; that the plaintiff, as Basnayake Nilame and trustee of the Walahagoda Devale, was entitled to conduct the procession with elephants to the accompaniment of drums and other musical instruments through all the streets of Gampola, including that portion of Ambagomuwa Street where the Hambayas had built in recent years a mosque; and that the acts of the Government Agent were a violation of the right conferred upon the plaintiff by the Kandyan Convention.

The Buddhists of Ceylon felt deeply thankful that they could thereafter hold their national festivals as of old without obstruction, in the Kandyan districts at least. But when they heard that, at the instance of the Government Agent, the Attorney-General had filed a petition of appeal to the Supreme Court against the judgment of the District Court, they became as depressed and downcast as the Hambayas grew in buoyancy and defiance.

After the case had been argued in the Supreme Court, and during the period its judgment was

Audacious attack of Muhammadans in January, 1915, on a Buddhist procession in Kurunegala, before decision of case in appeal.

reserved, the Muhammadans had the courage to attack, on the 27th of January, 1915, a religious procession of the Buddhists undertaken to dedicate an image of Buddha to a *vihára* situate a few miles from Kurunegala, on the road to Kandy. The procession had to pass through the village Telliagomuwa, where the majority of the inhabitants were Muhammadans. On the perahera approaching a school, which the Muhammadans from want of means used also as a place of worship, they attacked the Buddhists and caused some damage to the image of Buddha, as reported in the daily newspaper called *The Ceylonese* of 2nd February, 1915, according to which the Kurunegala police were immediately summoned, an Inspector arresting fourteen Muhammadans, who were produced before the Police Magistrate, charged with rioting and with being members of an unlawful assembly. Evidence for the prosecution was recorded on the 28th and 29th of January, and the further hearing of the case fixed for the 2nd of February.

Keen disappointment of the Buddhists and their fears, consequent on the reversal of the judgment of the District Court by the Supreme Court.

On that very day (2nd February) the Supreme Court, consisting of Shaw, J., and Sampayo, Acting J., delivered its judgment, reversing the decree of the District Judge of Kandy in favour of the plaintiff.

Mr. Justice Shaw was of opinion that the words of the Convention—" the religion of Buddha professed by the chiefs and other inhabitants of these Provinces is declared inviolable, and its rites, ministers, and places of worship are to be maintained and protected "—were not intended to give this particular perahera any right to be conducted in a manner different to other religious processions in the Colony, nor to be for ever conducted apart from the ordinary police supervision for the protection of the public peace and safety which may appear to the Government to be necessary; and his lordship held that, even supposing that the particular right claimed was reserved by the Convention to this particular perahera, such right was now controlled and varied by the provisions of the Police and Local Boards Ordinance. And Mr. Justice Sampayo was of opinion that, if the provisions of the Police Ordinance of 1865 and the Local Boards Ordinance of 1898 in respect of licenses for processions and tom-toms in any way contravened the Kandyan Convention, neither the District Court nor the Supreme Court had jurisdiction to enforce the Convention as against the Ordinances.

The Kandyan Buddhists were in utter despair when they perused the judgments of the Supreme Court Judges, delivered on the 2nd February, 1915. "How shall we hereafter celebrate our national and religious festivals in our own country without molestation? Who has ever opposed us in our own Kandyan Provinces except the newly arrived Hambayas?" they cried.

**Muhammadans again insult and attack with stones a Buddhist procession in Kandy in May, 1915.**

The time for the celebration of another great Buddhist festival—the anniversary of the birthday of Buddha—fell on the 28th of May, 1915. With much trepidation of heart, those who had hitherto conducted the carol processions in Kandy applied to the Government Agent, Central Province, for the usual license, but the Hambayas of Kandy, who owned the mosque at Castle Hill Street, objected to its issue. The elected members of the Municipal Council unanimously recommended the issue of the license. The Government Agent, having ascertained from the trustees of the Castle Hill Street mosque that the hour for closing it on Friday, the 28th May, was twelve midnight, issued the license subject to the condition that the procession should not enter Castle Hill Street before midnight.

Failure of the Police to nip the riotous spirit of the Muhammadans in time.

He, however, neglected to take the precaution, suggested by the District Judge of Kandy, in the Walahagoda Devale case, of having the aggressive Hambayas bound over to keep the peace. He also failed, as the head of the police in the Central Province, to have a sufficient number of properly armed police officers and constables in the streets of Kandy, so as to prevent any sudden outbreak of riot.

It was about 1 a.m. when the first carol procession with a band of musicians in a decorated cart turned from King Street into Castle Hill Street. The Sinhalese crowd were amazed to see the Hambayas' mosque open and lit up, and a crowd of Muhammadans, including Afghans, standing on either side of the street. Inspector Cooray, observing from the junction of King Street this defiant attitude of the Muhammadans, desired the carol party not to go forward, but to pass into a cross street so as to avoid the mosque altogether. The conductors of the procession obediently turned the carol cart into the street indicated. Just then the Hambayas and the Afghans clapped hands, jeered and boohed, which was more than the Sinhalese could bear. They halted indecisively, looking towards the mosque, when a still larger crowd, headed by another party of carol-singers in a second cart, came and entered Castle Hill Street. The first party then followed the second party.

As they advanced, a number of stones and empty bottles fell on the people, hurled from the upper

The fury of the Sinhalese at the attack of the Muhammadans.

storeys of two boutiques near the mosque and from the platform of the mosque. The Sinhalese crowd were infuriated. They rushed forward, picked up the stones lying on the street, pelted them at the boutique and mosque, chased the Muhammadans, who fled into the mosque, pulled down its iron bars and smashed its glass panes, broke into the adjoining boutiques and flung into the streets the boxes of grain and groceries.

During all this disturbance there were no more than one Inspector and six constables, who, of course, could not control the crowd. Mr. Cooray sent for help from the Police Station, and a squad of police who arrived seized about twenty-five men on charges of riot and housebreaking.

The surging crowd passed into other streets about 2 p.m., and disappeared with their battered cars. Thus ended the national Wesak festival of the Buddhists in 1915, undertaken in all piety and reverence to celebrate the birthday of the great peacemaker, named Goutama Buddha.

Now we come to another cause of the riots. The good people of Kandy, who next morning heard of this disturbance in Castle Hill Street, did not consider the collision between the Muhammadans and the Buddhists to be anything but a local incident. They thought that, as the inhabitants of Kandy Town consisted less of Kandyan Sinhalese and more of the people who had come from the maritime country as sojourners for a livelihood, the affray of the previous night would soon be forgotten. But the Kandyan villagers, as staunch Buddhists, were of a different opinion. In the attack of the Hambayas and the

*Photo by Pláté*

KANDY: *DALADÁ MÁLIGAWE*

(the Temple of the Tooth Relic on the left, with the Octagon containing the sacred books in Pali and Sinhalese), which the Buddhists feared would be attacked by the Muhammadans. A Dagoba (or relic monument) is on the right.

hired Afghans they saw clear signs of permanent danger to their religious practices and the unfettered celebration of their national festivals. They could not make light of the blind bigotry of the "upstart Hambayas," or of their natural desire for reprisal on the great temple of the Tooth Relic, called the Daladá Máligáwa.

The unprovoked murder of an innocent Sinhalese youth by a Hambaya Muhammadan, in the presence of a well-behaved crowd.

On Saturday morning (29th May), Kandyan villagers streamed into the town of Kandy from the neighbouring hamlets for worship at Daladá Máligáwa, and hung about the streets, having heard from the Hambayas themselves that they were expecting a band of fighters from Colombo to attack and wreck their holy temple. On being asked by some of the leading men of the town, they said, "We hear the Máligáwa is in danger. What is the good of our living, if it is going to be wrecked?"

But though the streets were thronged with a mixed population of Kandyans and Low-country people, no disturbance of any kind occurred during the day on Saturday, 29th May.

At nightfall the people collected opposite the shop of one of the principal Hambaya traders of Kandy, and seemed interested in what was going on within. One of the inmates, intending perhaps to disperse the crowd, fired a revolver at about 8 p.m. from the upper storey and killed a Sinhalese youth of about eighteen years, who was only a sightseer, being a servant at the Hillwood College, Kandy, for girls. The few constables who were standing about did not arrest the murderer.

The crowd cried out, "There is the man upstairs who killed the boy. Why don't the police seize him?" The gross indifference of the police astonished

The supineness of the Police in not arresting the murderer impels the Sinhalese to revenge themselves on the Muhammadans.

the Sinhalese. The police seemed to connive with the Muhammadans. Some of the more indignant Sinhalese entered the shop and threw out the goods into the street, which the people set fire to and burnt in the middle of the street. The inmates fled and the police made themselves scarce.

Emboldened by the passivity of the police, the crowd moved on to Trincomalee Street and attacked a jeweller's shop after the best part of the jewels had been removed by the owner. Some forty constables with two superintendents (Messrs. Thornhill and Tranchell) arrived and stood at the Castle Hill Street junction, as if they feared another attack on the mosque. The Police Magistrate of Kandy (Mr. Stace) and some constables came in time to take into custody three or four Sinhalese men who were in the jeweller's shop. A few other Muhammadan boutiques were attempted to be forced, but the mere presence of the police, who were unarmed, prevented the ruffians from effecting their object.

The corpse of the boy remained on the pavement till the early hours of the morning, when it was removed to the mortuary.

Arrival of rowdy Muhammadans by night train from Colombo to attack the Buddhists.

About ten o'clock the same night (29th May), the railway Station Superintendent received a message from the Government Agent to stop at Kadugannawa the night mail train coming from Colombo to Kandy, as a large body of rowdy Muhammadans was coming in that train to join hands with the Hambayas in Kandy and work against the Buddhists; and the Inspector-General of Police was also requested to come up to Kandy with fifty soldiers by a special train. Starting from Colombo at 11 p.m. on the 29th May, he arrived with the Panjábis at Kandy at 3 a.m. on

# Map of CEYLON

The coloured portion shows the Provinces brought under Martial Law. The parts affected by the Riots are towns and villages mostly along or near the railways, or principal and minor roads.

*(The railways are indicated in red)*

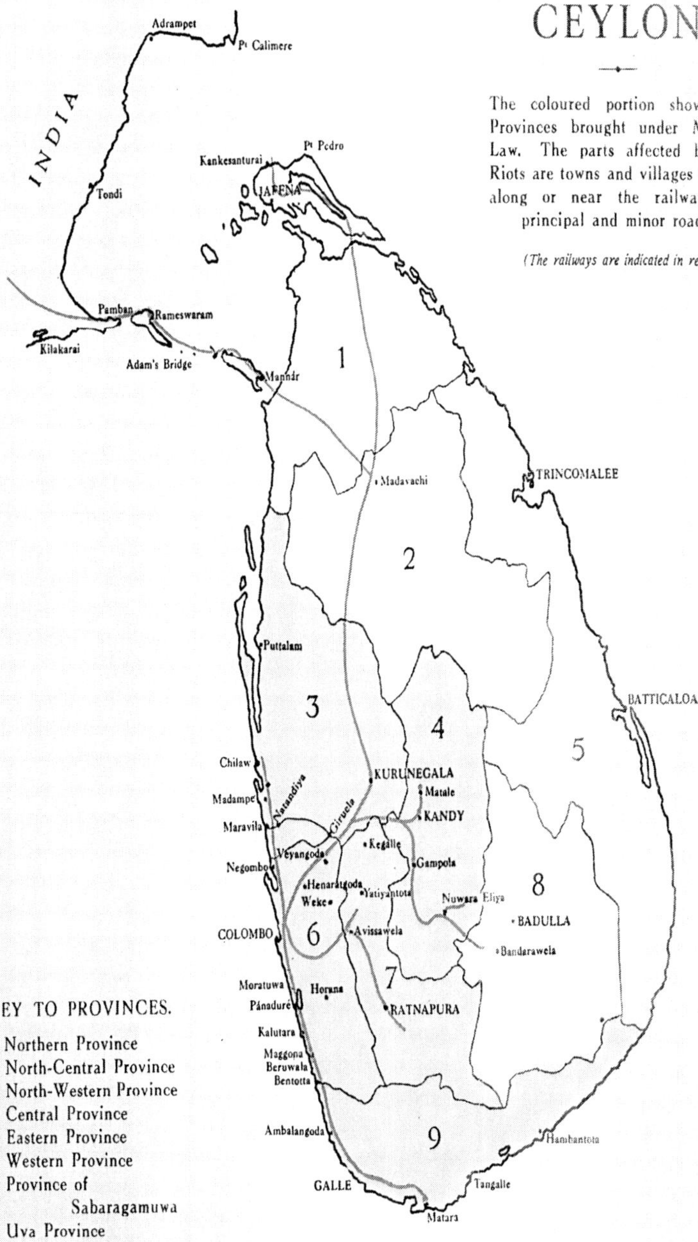


KEY TO PROVINCES.

1. Northern Province
2. North-Central Province
3. North-Western Province
4. Central Province
5. Eastern Province
6. Western Province
7. Province of Sabaragamuwa
8. Uva Province
9. Southern Province

the 30th. The Station Superintendent telephoned to the Stationmaster at Kadugannawa, as ordered, and he caused the carriage in which the Muhammadans were travelling to be detached from the train, and allowed the rest of the train to go to Kandy. On the following morning (Sunday), the carriage containing the Muhammadans was brought to Kandy, and a crowd of Sinhalese, who had heard of this move of the Hambayas, was waiting outside the station gates; but the Station Superintendent had the gates shut, and the police gave the Muhammadans the option of remaining in the carriage and returning to Colombo by the next train, or being marched to the Police Station as men bent on riot. They preferred to go back, and were despatched to Colombo.

On Sunday morning (30th May) the Sinhalese grew more alarmed about the safety of the holy Daladá Máligáwa, and gathered again in the streets in larger numbers. The leading men of the town, Sinhalese (Buddhists and Christians), Burghers, and Tamils, and even Muhammadans, who did not know of the arrival of the Panjábis at 3 a.m., began to get anxious about the safety of the city, owing to the helplessness of the police, and the ignorance of the exact situation and the palpable indecision of the local authorities.

Clamour of the Sinhalese in Kandy to meet the Government Agent and place before him their fears and grievances.

Certain of the leading inhabitants of the town called on the Government Agent (Mr. Vaughan) at 8 a.m., but were told he was in bed. They went about the town collecting as much information as possible, so as to devise some measures for the abatement of the ferment that prevailed throughout the town. They found there was a universal desire on the part of the people to meet the Government Agent, and to place before him their fears and grievances, and obtain from him an assurance that they would be inquired into. A deputation was formed to interview the Government Agent. Mr. Dissáwa Dunuwilla, Mr. Advocate Arthur Pereira, Mr. Ratwatte (the cashier of the Mercantile Bank), Mr. Proctor Weerasurya, and some others, went to the Government Agent's house at noon. Mr. Dissáwa Dunuwilla introduced the deputation. In the course of the conference it was submitted to the Government Agent that the indifference and inefficiency of the police left the city in a most unprotected state; that the murderer of the Sinhalese youth was still at large, though he could have been arrested then and there; that the looters were gaining a preponderance in the town; that the good people of all classes, including Muhammadans, were anxious that the trouble between the Buddhists and the Muhammadans should be amicably settled; and that no settlement of any kind could be brought about except in the presence of the Government Agent as the accredited authority of the Government of Ceylon. They told him that the principal Muhammadans would not attend any meeting in which the Government Agent was not present. They therefore begged him to meet the crowd near the Town Hall, or the principal men to be selected by the crowd in the Town Hall itself, and they said that, if at this conference he promised to inquire into the case of the people, and find a remedy in due course, the whole crowd would quietly disperse. They invited him to address the crowd and give them an assurance of inquiry and redress.

The Government Agent, however, declined to meet the crowd in the streets, or the men whom they named

The refusal of the Government Agent to meet and appease the people.

in the Town Hall. He proposed to give the deputation a letter to his Mudaliyár, Mr. H. P. Jayawardane, to go and speak to the people. On the deputation pointing out the utter uselessness of anybody but the Government Agent himself addressing the people, he directed the gentlemen present to see the Inspector-General of Police at the Police Station, and said he would himself be there. He did not inform them that that Officer had arrived in Kandy before dawn with Panjábi soldiers, and the people need not fear for the safety of the city. He was evidently afraid of meeting the crowd, or hesitating to assume any responsibility.

The deputation then went to the Inspector-General of Police and waited long for the Government Agent to arrive, feeling that most valuable time was being lost at the Police Station, when everybody ought to have gone among the crowd and to be doing their best to disperse it.

A street fight between some Muhammadans and Sinhalese, while the crowd was waiting for the Government Agent.

The crowd grew more and more impatient at the indifference and inefficiency of the police and the neglect of the Government Agent to respond to their call for a conference with them or with their nominated leaders, and presently someone kicked at the door of a Muhammadan tailor, when the door opened, and out came an elderly Muhammadan with a club in his hand. He got into the street and whirled the club fiercely among the crowd, when he was struck down. His two nephews rushed in defence of their uncle and stabbed three Sinhalese men, one of them being an innocent passer-by, viz., Mr. Dissanayaka, a clerk at the Government Kachcheri. One of the Sinhalese men who was stabbed expired while being conveyed to the hospital. It may be mentioned here that the two Muhammadans who wounded the three Sinhalese were afterwards tried by Court Martial and sentenced to penal servitude.

Arrival of armed soldiers and retirement of the crowd, without a single shot fired.

At the time this collision took place, the Cadet Corps of Trinity College, who were part of the Cadet Battalion of the Ceylon Light Infantry, were returning from the Police Station together with their Principal (the Rev. Mr. Fraser) and other teachers, after being sworn in as special constables. While at the station; they saw some of the members of the deputation speaking to the Inspector-General of Police. Though the Cadet Corps wore civil suits and were unarmed, they went into the crowd and helped in the arrest of the Muhammadans who had stabbed the three Sinhalese men and run back into their house. At the sight of the Cadet Corps, which numbered about 60, the crowd fell back and retired towards the Town Hall.

The Inspector-General of Police (Mr. Dowbiggin) and the Government Agent (Mr. Vaughan) came on the scene in their motor-car, and alighted on the pavement of Trincomalee Street. The Inspector-General and the Government Agent seemed disconcerted at the crowd not dispersing on their arrival. The crowd, on the other hand, expected to hear them speak and allay their fears and grievances. When they saw the Government Agent get amongst the Cadet Corps and enter into conversation with Mr. Fraser, and the Inspector-General jump into the car and drive away, they thought the latter was beating a hasty retreat, and the Government Agent had not the courage to address them. But Mr. Dowbiggin returned on foot with about 50 Panjábi soldiers and some constables, and asked them to disperse the crowd. The Panjábis went up to the crowd and pushed them back with the butt end of their rifles, without firing a single shot, and they all went away in different directions. Thus ended the much-talked-of riot in Kandy Town. The Government Agent and the Inspector-General of Police set the Cadet Corps on patrol duty from 6 p.m. to 2 a.m. from that night for several nights, and the Panjábis were picketed at different centres.

The true dimensions of the disturbances in Kandy Town.

We may pause here for a moment to outline the true dimensions of the disturbances in Kandy Town.

The first riot occurred between 1 and 2 on the morning of the 29th May, 1915, in consequence of the intolerance and aggression of the Hambayas and Afghan Muhammadans assembled in and about the mosque in Castle Hill Street. No lives were lost, nor any serious bodily injury inflicted. Some boutiques were damaged and their contents turned out, which were mostly made a bonfire of in the streets, and the glass shutters of the mosque and some iron bars were also damaged.

The second riot took place between 8 and 10 p.m. on the same day (29th May), provoked directly by the failure of the police to arrest the murderer of an innocent Sinhalese youth, whom a Hambaya brought down with a bullet from a revolver fired from the upper storey of his master's shop. No other persons were killed. Some shops and boutiques were damaged, and their contents thrown into the streets to be burnt.

The third disturbance occurred between 3 and 4 p.m. on the following day (30th May). It was not a riot, but a street fight between three Muhammadans and a few Sinhalese in the presence of a large crowd of people, brought together by a natural interest in the stirring social events that had developed during the last three years, as stated in pp. 1—14.

These events, standing out linked together in the minds of the Buddhists, have operated as causes for the attack on the Muhammadans in various parts of the Island during the one week that began on the 29th May and ended on the 5th June, 1915.

The effect of the disturbances in Kandy, and of the supineness of the Police, on the Buddhists in other parts of the country.

The riots in Kandy Town, comparatively speaking, were not serious, but the example set there as regards the manner in which the avengers of the insult to Buddhism should treat the aggressive Hambayas proved most infectious, especially as the police, the protectors of the public peace, were generally believed to be conniving with them. It was said that many of the Panjábi soldiers brought to Kandy to control the situation were Muhammadans, and that the Hambayas were expecting reinforcements from the Muhammadans of Colombo and South India. The property, the honour, and the lives of Sinhalese men and women were felt to be in imminent danger if they did not immediately defend themselves by forcing the Hambayas to leave the villages. In this state of passion and panic among the Sinhalese, and the irresolution and inactivity of the local authorities, the rowdies, gamblers, thieves and robbers of each village saw a rare opportunity for their own aggrandizement. They emphasized the stories of desecration and disruption of the religious processions of the Buddhists, and spread false reports of the destruction of the Daladá Máligáwa, of the rape and mutilation of Sinhalese women, and of the desire of the British Government not to arrest or punish the opponents of the Muham-

The clever intrusion of thieves and robbers, and the spreading of false reports.

madans, as it was at war with Turkey. With lightning rapidity all these tales were carried from village to village, and thus arose a tremendous ferment in the country, which manifested itself as anti-Muhammadan riots.

The work of excited stragglers from the Kandy crowd.

When the disturbances in Kandy Town ceased by the presence of the Panjábi soldiers, the more energetic of the men in the crowd, who loved excitement and revenge, sped quickly on foot and by bicycle and railway train in different directions, such as Gampola, Kadugannawa, and Matale, to rouse up the people. Many were the tricks practised on them. In Gampola, for instance, the villagers living beyond the limits of that town were asked by some of these rowdy stragglers from Kandy to go quickly to Gampola, as a grand *pinkama* (or procession of gifts to the Vihare and priests) was coming to Gampola. So saying, they returned to Gampola and awaited the arrival of the villagers. When a large crowd had gathered, they were told that the *pinkama* was obstructed by the wicked Hambayas, and that their mosque must be pulled down. The rowdies led the attack and the people helped in the work of destruction. Similarly, all along the railway line at Rambukkam, Polgahawela, Alawwa, Ambepussa, Mirigama, Veyangoda, Henaratgoda and Kelaniya, it was the rowdies that inveigled the people into the affray, and made a cat's-paw of them for their own sport and aggrandizement.

Motives for the spread of the riots.

The desire for vengeance in some, and the thirst for excitement and the greed for loot in others, and the assurance of all these classes that the rural police would not arrest them, helped the progress of the riot wherever the boutiques of unpopular Hambayas were. For kind-hearted and righteous Hambayas always found defenders among the Sinhalese.

Want of sympathy between the paid and unpaid police.

The rural police in Ceylon consists mostly of those who are called "unpaid headmen," and of a small fraction of paid constables stationed at great distances along some of the main thoroughfares. Generally speaking, the paid constables domineer over the unpaid headmen, and do not hesitate to implicate them in trouble with the Government Agents or Police Magistrates. There is no sympathy or appreciative co-operation between the two classes of the police.

The state of the ordinary police constable.

The ordinary policeman is drawn from the scum of society on a pay of about five shillings per week, is put through a course of drill, including rifle practice, made to wear boots, trousers and hats supplied free, and then set on beats for several hours in populous towns. During all this training they come to know the art of getting on in the Police Force by methods none too clean or scrupulous, in order to save themselves from fines and dismissals or win the favour of Sergeants, Sub-Inspectors, and Inspectors for purposes of promotion.

The condition of the rural police, called unpaid headmen.

The unpaid rural headman comes of the proprietary peasant class, having a stake in the country and anxious to maintain the fair name of the family to which he belongs and of himself. His duties, concerned with the peace of one or more contiguous villages, are onerous, and the expenses he has to incur, while dancing attendance on the Muhándiram or the Mudaliyár of the district, or the Police Magistrate, or the Assistant Government Agent, or the Government Agent himself, in connection with the collection of revenue, the making of inquiries into complaints and crimes, the writing out of reports and taking them to the Mudaliyár, etc., are often beyond his resources.

Necessity of paying and better organizing the rural police.

The Government of Ceylon have not yet thought it proper to formulate a scheme for paying these minor headmen sufficiently to avoid the temptations of bribery and the seductions of slackness, though it has often gone to the Legislative Council for the sanction of schemes for raising the salaries of already well-paid officers from the Governor down to the lowest civil servant. The danger of allowing unpaid headmen to do duty as peace or police officers has been demonstrated in the recent riots. There was no motive strong enough to dissociate them from the errors of the people, nor an organization behind them sufficiently powerful to pull them up promptly when they were caught in the vortex of popular frenzy.

Criminal misconduct of the paid and unpaid police in certain places.

As an instance of how the paid and unpaid police combined together in the very outskirts of Colombo to help in the looting of Muhammadans, because the moral force of proper supervision was not in existence then or before, I may quote the statement in writing of a boatman, Seena Saibu Lebbe, of Attulugama, in Rayigam Korale, who came from Panadure to Colombo in his own barge (or " padda " boat) to deliver goods at Colombo and carry other goods from Colombo to Palanthe, near Ratnapura. He says :—

The case of an unfortunate Muhammadan boatman, in an outskirt of Colombo.

" On the 30th of May last, about 10 a.m., I started from Colombo, near the new bridge, Dangaha Totopala, in Skinner's Road, in my boat with six other boatmen. It was loaded with 22 bags of rice, cloth, and sundries, which I intended to take to Palanthe, in Kukulu Korale, about 80 miles from Ratnapura. We reached Kittanpahuwa, at Urugodawatta (Colombo), at 11 a.m., cooked and finished our meal, and started again at noon. When we had gone about half a mile, about ten persons came to the side of the canal and asked me whether I would transport some things they had to Kalutara. I said I could not, because the way in which they came down and spoke to me meant mischief. We went on rowing the boat, and I saw the men, followed by about 100 other Sinhalese men, stalking us. Some of them were also pelting stones at us. To avoid the stones I and my boatmen got under cover of the roof of the boat. For want of rowing, the boat stopped. Then about fifteen men walked into the canal and scrambled into the boat and poled it onwards. A furlong higher up they took the boat towards the shore and moored it. Then about forty men stepped into the boat and looked here and there for my goods. I asked my men to go to the Police Station, which was about half a mile ahead, and they quietly left the boat. Finding me helpless, and yet suspecting that my men would complain to the police, they began to carry off a bag of rice, a bundle of cloth, and some of our wearing apparel, and then ordered me to open my box, which I was obliged to do. They removed from it Rs. 50 in notes and silver, and quickly departed. A little while afterwards one sergeant, one constable, and one headman (unpaid peace officer) came up. I complained to them of the loot. They left the policeman in the boat and asked me and my men, who had returned, to row the boat to the Police Station, and went away. I reached the bridge near the Police

Station and tied up the boat about 5 p.m. The sergeant and headman came into my boat and asked me to stay there for the night, and the policeman to continue to stay in the boat.

"At dawn on the 31st, a *vidáne* (unpaid headmar), whom the people there called *áráchchi*, and two others, came to my boat and asked me to untie the boat and row it onwards. I said the country was too disturbed to take the boat on, and that it would be better if I remained near the station. The *áráchchi*, who lived close by the station, said I must not remain there, but must go on. He would not listen to my remonstrances. Just then the sergeant arrived and said, 'You can go safely now; nothing will happen to you.' I refused to go, and begged him to take charge of my goods, and said that then only would I move on with my boat. The sergeant thought a little, and asked me to measure out rice in different quantities to five men. The sergeant himself took four measures of rice, four pots and pans, 2 lbs. of potatoes, and 2 lbs. of Bombay onions, and told me, 'Now you can safely go.' It was then 10 a.m. I was obliged to go. It was no use being under the protection of such a set of police officers. I had not gone beyond a third of a mile when a large number of Sinhalese men, coming from both sides of the canal, jumped into my boat and looted all my property, which was of the value of Rs. 1,073.50 (about £70), including the Rs. 50 already removed from my box and the Rs. 120 which I had secreted round my waist, together with the license of my boat and other papers. This looting occurred at noon. No policeman or headman came to my help. My men ran away when the looters got into my boat, and I was beaten because I did not disclose the money I had round my waist.

"With the empty boat I started at midnight and reached my village, Attulugama, on the 7th June, and found that my house there had been broken into and everything in it looted."

The beginning of riots in Colombo.

All that happened in Kandy—the desecration and disruption of the Wesak Procession between 1 and 2 a.m. on the 29th May, the murder of the Sinhalese youth on the evening of that day, and the indifference and inefficiency of the police and the consequent intrusion of looters on the platform of religious animosity—were known in Colombo and the outlying villages on the morning of the 30th May, by means of thousands of pilgrims who had returned to their homes, and some newspapers published morning and evening. While the rowdies in Colombo were held in check by the sight of policemen moving on their beats as usual, the rowdies outside the gravets of Colombo had no such fear. They allowed themselves early in the morning of the 30th May to indulge in the spirit of mischief and loot. Following the example of the village guardians of the peace, the rowdies of Urugodawatte and Kolannawe seized and wholly plundered the unfortunate boatman whom the police sergeant and the unpaid headman had partly plundered before.

After this successful loot in the midday of the 31st May, the vagabonds went into Colombo by the Urugodawatte Road, through Grandpass and Dematagodde, to see how things were getting on in the city.

*Photo by Plâté*

COLOMBO: QUEEN'S STREET

Post Office on the left. The Governor's residence ("Queen's House") on the right.

A pretty kettle was boiling there. But the men at the fire were not vagabonds. They were the artizans and labourers employed at the railway yard of the Ceylon Government at Maradana, quite close to the Headquarters of the Metropolitan Police.

Quarrel between some workmen of the Government Railway Department and a Muhammadan about a cup of tea.

During the interval of one hour allowed for their midday meal, about five or six of these men went to a tea-shop just opposite to the railway workshop, and were charged by the Muhammadan serving tea there one farthing more than the usual rate. An altercation ensued. Excited words led to rough handling and a call for the police. The railway men hurried back to the Government yard, closed the gates, and from behind the high wall they pelted stones at the boutique, and so broke a few pots and bottles of aerated water standing on the shelves. The inmates quickly closed the boutique and informed the police. The workmen returned to the workshop and reported to their brethren, who were mostly Sinhalese, the cause of the row, and also their fear that at the end of the day there would be an inquiry. At 4.30 p.m. they were asked to go in single file through the wicket gate in order that the Muhammadan boutique-keeper might identify the men who had altercated with him in the forenoon. They refused to go in single file. Standing together in a body, they made for the large gates which opened into the high road, but the gates were securely fastened. They resented this treatment and threatened to go on strike the next morning.

This meant a serious dislocation of business and loss of revenue for the railway department. Its chief officers tried to argue with the men as to the propriety of picking out the men complained against. The workmen remained obdurate.

The Government Agent, W.P. (Mr. Fraser), accompanied by the Attapattu Mudaliyar (Mr. H. A. Pereira) and the Colombo Gravets Mudaliyar (Mr. W. L. Bandaranayaka), arrived at the workshop; and many gentlemen, seeing a crowd assembled on the road opposite the barred gate of the railway premises, gained entrance by the side door and were asked to speak to the workmen. Mr. E. C. Jayawardane (M.M.C. for the Maradana Ward) and Mr. Barrister Batuwantudawa addressed them and succeeded in persuading the railway authorities to throw open the principal gates. The workmen went out and found a great crowd of wayfarers blocking the high road. As they pushed their way across the junction, there was shouting and hooting, which stirred up the spirit of fun and frolic in the younger members of the crowd, who picked up the stones from the heaps of road metal lying handy and hurled them aimlessly. Several persons were hit, including an Assistant Superintendent and Inspector of Police. The shops and boutiques along Maradana Road and Skinner's Road were immediately closed. The constables arrested about eight men and brought them to the Maradana Station, followed by a crowd of Sinhalese clamouring for their release, and Mr. J. H. Daniel, the Superintendent of Police, ordered them to be set free.

Spread of the riotous spirit by street rowdies in Colombo.

The crowd, observing the disinclination of the police authorities to come into conflict with them, lingered at the junction, as did also the police, and a squad of armed constables under two Inspectors marched up and down and were called back. The tramcar service was interrupted. About 7 p.m. someone in the crowd could not resist the temptation of setting fire to a large cadjan shed, adjoining the tea-

Photo by Plâté

COLOMBO: ST. JOHN'S ROAD

Boutiques on either side, some of which were looted.

shop where the trouble first began. It was erected by a Sinhalese man for the exhibition of curios. The whole building was quickly burnt down, and the Fire Brigade arrived in time to prevent the extension of the fire to other buildings. The crowd was alarmed at the unexpected development, and required little persuasion to disperse. The tramway service was resumed.

The ways of the looters.

But the looters had seen enough of the indecision and impotence of the police to hurry on with their work of plunder, especially in places where constables were not to be seen. The procedure of the rowdies was to send forward a batch of boys to raise the cry of "Kollé, kollé" (loot, loot) near a Muhammadan boutique, hearing which the owner and his assistant would in panic jump out and see a crowd of fiercely growling Sinhalese with sticks and clubs raised high in their hands. Then the rowdies would shout and run forward, making the Muhammadans take to their heels. The ruffians would then enter the shop and throw the goods on to the pavement or the street in bags, boxes, bottles or parcels, just as they were piled on the tables and shelves, and needy men and women who were about would carry the things away.

The work of the habitual criminals and their henchmen.

The vagabonds, who deserted the junction of streets near the Maradana railway bridge, went in different directions and joined hands with others, saying, "Now or never." There are in Colombo about 1,500 habitual criminals prowling about daily for prey.* Allowing six active henchmen to each of these

* Statistics tabled at a meeting of the Colombo Municipal Council in August last show that there are 5,066 habitual criminals in the Island, and that out of these

habituals, we have an army of 9,000 sturdy ruffians among a population of 230,000 men, women and children in the city. To this corps, versed in wily methods, we must add a larger number of impoverished artizans and labourers, whose desire to live peacefully and honestly has been blunted by the ravages of the present war in Europe. Employers of labour have been obliged to reduce their establishments, and the distress among workmen of all classes has been very severe since August. 1914. The necessitous condition of such people forced them to accept the lead of the criminals of the city. The two classes of rowdies did not seem to forget that their attention should be confined mainly to the boutiques of the Muhammadans, so as not to awaken the suspicions of the populace.

Extension of loot to different parts of the town.

Dispersing from the railway bridge junction at Maradana, some hurried westwards to Darley Road, opposite St. Joseph's College, and, after looting two boutiques there, pushed on to Union Place, where a number of boutiques were rifled and their contents either set fire to in the public thoroughfare or boldly removed. An hour later, at 9 p.m., another great mob entered Bankshall Street, Pettah, where the Hambayas mustered strong, as most of the boutiques there belonged to them. A free fight ensued, and many a boutique was wrecked and many men were wounded. Another set of ruffians came with the

incorrigibly wicked fellows there live in Colombo 1,455, being distributed as follows:—Pettah Ward, 539; Kotahena Ward, 296; Maradana Ward, 114; Cinnamon Gardens, 107; Slave Island, 99; Wellewatta and Bambalapitiya, 76; Grandpass, 74; Modera, 57; Fort, 55; Kollupitiya, 36.

*Photo by Plâté*

COLOMBO: GALLE ROAD

Boutiques on the right.

cry of "Kollé, kollé," and attacked a tea boutique in Front Street, opposite the Y.M.C.A. buildings, and a boutique in Prince Street. Here, too, a free fight occurred between the Muhammadans and the Sinhalese, and the police patrol who came on the scene carried five wounded persons to the Pettah Police Station, and thence to the General Hospital. None of the men were seriously injured.

Report of an Inspector of Police on the *impassé* condition of supervision at the Headquarters, and the audacity of the roughs.

The party of rowdies who went southwards from the Maradana Bridge towards Borella at 7 p.m. is well described by Mr. Inspector W. E. de Silva, who was then in charge of the Police Station of Borella. His statement shows clearly the *impassé* condition of the Police Force and the audacity of the roughs. He says :—

"On the 31st May last, when I was doing my duty at Borella Junction, I observed a tramcar full of passengers coming from Maradana towards Borella, shouting and screaming, at about 7 p.m. I had heard about six o'clock the same evening that some Moor boutiques near the Maradana Railway Station had been looted and a cadjan shed set fire to. So I was prepared for a possible looting in my division, bounded on the east by the Jail Road Junction, on the other side by Cotta Road Toll Bar, on the third side by Timbirigasyaya, and on the fourth side by the railway level crossing on the Base Line Road. I had only sixteen men under me. *No orders whatever were issued to me about the treatment of the rioters.* I had to act on my own discretion. For want of orders, I did not allow my sergeants and constables to be armed with anything more than batons. When the tramcar passed my station and stopped at the junction, all the men in it landed, and I went up to them with my force. I found there Mr. D. V. Altendorf, the Superintendent of the Police Headquarters. He came from his residence near my station. The men who landed did not do anything at first. Not being the residents of my division, they seemed to wait for developments, and I observed the poorer classes of the residents in the neighbourhood, including Sinhalese fishmongers, dhobies and rowdies, making for the junction. Some of the Moors, seeing the crowd coming, closed their boutiques and kept themselves within, and I myself advised the Moors who had not closed the boutiques to close them. While I was so doing, Superintendent Altendorf came on the scene. At this time there were in all about 100 persons at the junction. Some of them began to break open and loot the boutiques, *not minding us a bit*. It was the men who came in the tramcar that broke open the boutiques, and immediately the resident rowdies rushed in and looted the goods. I and my force seized about twelve of the looters, while they were carrying rice bags and other provisions. Mr. Altendorf was wounded in the forehead by a stone pelted at him. He had to retire to his house to dress his wound, and he came back in half an hour. The looting was then over, and the crowd quickly dispersed in different directions, some along Cotta Road, some towards Timbirigasyaya.

"I heard that another tramcar load of rowdies had got down at the Jail Road Junction about 8 p.m., and ran off towards Demettagodde or Base Line Road, damaging the Moor boutiques skirting that road. While the looting was going on at Borella Road Junction, *I telephoned to Headquarters, reporting that looting was taking place and asking for assistance*. I was told by the operator there that *there was no Commanding Officer or Assistant there,* because they had all gone out to suppress looting in Maradana and the Pettah. *I could have done better work than I did, had I received assistance.*

"Things were quiet in the whole of my division from 8 p.m. on the 31st May to 4 p.m. on the 1st of June, when a crowd of about 100 came down from the street from Maradana with yellow and white flags at the head of the procession, while some of the leaders had clubs in their hands. The road was straight, and I saw the procession coming from afar. I was surprised that it had not been arrested before it came into my division. *I rang up Headquarters, stating that a procession of rioters was coming towards my station, and that I wanted immediate help.* The operator replied that *the Superintendent and his assistants were all out,* and no one could be sent to reinforce me.

"I went back to the street with my force and saw looting was going on; and as I was making my way to the looters I saw Superintendent Attygalle and Mr. T. W. Roberts, the Commissioner of the Court of Requests, Colombo, coming in a motor-car along Cotta Road. Mr. Attygalle got down and told me to give my men carbines and swords. I ran up to the station with my men, got them armed, and led them to the place where looting was taking place, following the Superintendent and the Commissioner. *The crowd did not mind them at all.* We rushed up, and tried to disperse the rioters, and in the effort to disperse them, two carbines went off, and two men who were at the muzzle end got burnt in their chest, and blood also trickled down. The carbines were not loaded with ball. I had ordered the men to take from the station guns and bayonets, and only blank cartridges, because *I was not requested by Superintendent Attygalle to issue ball cartridges.* Mr. Attygalle immediately asked me who gave the order to fire. I said I did not, and the constables whose guns went off said that they did not fire, but that the guns went off accidentally. *On hearing the guns go off, the crowd immediately dispersed.* I sent the two wounded men to my station, and from there they went in rickshaws to the hospital.

"There was no disturbance of any kind in my division after 5 p.m. on the 1st.

"On the 2nd, about 9 a.m., Inspector Ekanayake came with an armed force of about fifteen constables from the Headquarters to my station, and told me he had been asked to patrol the streets, and that Mr. Wait, the Police Magistrate of Colombo, had given him verbal orders to shoot rioters when necessary. While we were talking, Mr. J. Ludovici, the Acting Assistant Superintendent of Police (who was my immediate superior), and Inspector Elayatamby came up. We were then informed that a riotous crowd of Moors was making its way to Colombo from the direction of Cotta. Mr. Ekanayake and his men went to meet that crowd, and we three followed. We found that the crowd was not one of Moors at all, but Sinhalese, and they had come into my division midway between the old toll-bar and my station, and were breaking into a bungalow belonging to a Moorman, who had taken the precaution to close it and go away on the previous evening. *Mr. Ekanayake ordered his men to load and fire from a distance of* 100 *yards.* One shot took effect on Mr. R. A. Mirando, a plumbago merchant, who, having left his own bungalow 150 yards away, came into the street to observe the looting that was going on in front of him. Another man was wounded in his leg. *The crowd fled* chiefly through a narrow road leading towards the Kelani Valley railway line. We pushed on towards the Cotta Railway Station, and, finding no further disturbance, returned. We all came back to the Borella Junction, where we found Superintendent J. H. Daniel, who, having heard of the death of Mr. Mirando, inquired on whose orders we fired. He was told that Mr. Ekanayake had authority from the Police Magistrate of Colombo to give such an order, and that it was Mr. Ekanayake who gave the order to fire. Mr. Daniel took him to the spot, and, returning, asked Mr. Ludovici to hold an inquiry and report proceedings to him. Mr. Elayatamby and I gave evidence, and I said to myself how fortunate it was that I had not armed my men with ball cartridge on the 31st and 1st!

"Besides this disturbance in the early part of the 2nd of June, there was no more disturbance during the rest of the day.

"I was informed by telephone message from Headquarters, between 9 and 10 a.m. on the 2nd, that the military had taken charge of Colombo, and that the police had only to assist them. Between 9.30 and 10 o'clock about fifteen Town Guardsmen came to my station, and four of them at a time kept watch at the junction till the first batch was relieved by a second batch of the Town Guard.

"No disturbance occurred in my division on the 3rd or 4th, or thereafter.

"About 7 p.m. on the 4th I received a telephone message from Mr. Superintendent Daniel to place an armed Police guard consisting of one inspector, one sergeant, and seven men at Borella Junction. I immediately marched the men and made an entry in my information book. I gave the men three rounds of blank ammunition, carbines and fixed swords.

"I had been on duty from the 31st May to the 3rd June, 12 midnight, without any relief at all. On the 4th, not having had my dinner at the usual time, because of my attendance at the Borella Junction with the Town Guard, I thought at 12 midnight I would go to the station, make an entry in my information book that I had been on duty from 7.15 p.m. to 12 midnight, and then go to my house for dinner. But having made this entry, I went back to the Borella Junction, remained with my men for over one hour and a half, and went home for dinner. As soon as I finished it, a constable arrived and told me that the Inspector-General of Police was at the junction and wanted me there.

"He blamed me for issuing blank cartridges to my men, and for not being with my men when he arrived. On these two grounds of alleged neglect of duty I was convicted on the 6th June by the Police Magistrate of Colombo on my own foolish admission of the charges, prompted by my friends, and condemned to three months' simple imprisonment; and, on the day preceding my discharge from jail, I was taken to the Maradana Headquarters and drummed out of the Police Force in disgrace, in the manner that I have set forth in my petition to His Excellency the Governor."*

* The petition of this unfortunate Inspector, whose past record was very good, but who nevertheless was made a

Two other eye-witnesses, going in rickshaws through the 2nd division of Maradana Road towards the Post Office at 9.15 p.m. (31st May), found at the Regent Street Junction two constables and a Town Guardsman. Passing them, *they saw several persons preparing to force open the boards of a boutique. They* returned to the junction and *requested the two Police Constables who were there to go and arrest the men*, who had just began to loot the boutique. *The constables* looked in that direction, but *did not go forward at all.* The eye-witness then proceeded and saw the looting carried on vigorously.

The passivity of the police and the activity of the looters.

On the next day, too (1st June), the inefficiency and muddled condition of the police were the talk of the town everywhere. The Rev. G. A. F. Senaratne, of the Wesleyan Methodist Mission in Colombo, proceeded from his residence, "Sweden Bank," in Alexandra Place, on Tuesday morning to the Young Men's Christian Association Buildings in the Pettah, and found that the rioting had begun there again. He went to Dam Street, near the Government Kachcheri, and found "the rickshaw coolies and other Sinhalese of the lower classes" in a state of excitement. He pacified them, and stood watching on the steps of "The Rest," where the missionaries meet. In the lengthy statement he has sent to me, he has underlined many words, and I give below a few extracts. He says :—

The story of the Rev. Mr. Senaratne.

"I saw several wounded, mostly Sinhalese, were being brought from the Fort end of Dam Street. I

scapegoat of to cover deficiencies in higher places, brought the usual answer: "His Excellency the Governor sees no reason to interfere!"

was told that they were coming from Bankshall Street and Wolfendahl, *where the Moors took the offensive.* Another thing I observed was *police lenience*, which perhaps was caused by a sense of helplessness. Two Sinhalese men were brought under arrest by four constables. At the very gate of the Police Station a gang of rowdies got round the policemen and demanded the release of the two men, and *the police shamefully gave in to the mob.* Then, when I saw that crowds were forming all round in the streets near the Police Station, I asked a sergeant to disperse these groups. *The police simply kept gazing, as if they were mesmerized.*

"At about 12.30 p.m. I went back towards the Y.M.C.A. In the Racquet Court there was a gang of rowdies headed by one Noor (a Muhammadan), who for all purposes appeared like a Sinhalese. They were marching along Front Street with clubs and iron bars in their hands. Most of them were the well-known Pettah rowdies and habituals. . . .

"A little later we saw scores of people going through the Racquet Court with looted goods, especially from the Crystal Palace (stores). Noor and his friends, too, brought some booty, and they began to demand from every looter who crossed the Racquet Court a share of the things that were being carried away. *There were four constables in Front Street, who kept on watching and doing nothing.* This inaction of the police encouraged the riff-raff, and *even street boys began to run* towards Keyzer Street, *and they brought loads of crockery, etc.* . . .

"I walked towards Price Park. . . . Here I heard from the people *stories of Moor atrocities* towards Sinhalese women in Moor Street and Wolfendahl

*Photo by Plâté*

COLOMBO: PETTAH· MAIN STREET

The kind of boutiques (or small shops), on the left, that were looted. The Town Hall on the right.

Street. I did not want to believe any of them, and said, 'They can't be true.'

"I went back to Dam Street and saw a large number of women and children within the Police Station premises. I inquired why they came there. They said they came from Wolfendahl, Siripina Lane, New Moor Street, Silversmith Lane and Alutkade. *The Moors,* who were quite strong in these places, *had driven them away from their tenements.* I made enquiries whether they were ill-treated. They said that, except for a hit or two, they had not been badly handled. *These people, numbering between* 150 *and* 200, *sought refuge in the Police Station premises, but in a little while they were all turned out.* This I thought was most cruel. Then I invited them to "The Rest," and made arrangements for them to cook their meals. In the evening a good many of them moved themselves to a godown of a Sinhalese merchant close by.

"In the afternoon a number of Moor women and children came rushing from the side of Price Park under police protection. They were housed in the verandah of the Girls' School. In the evening this company was escorted to the Old Moor Street by their co-religionist. . ."

Another gentleman records :—" On Tuesday (the 1st of June) I went to the Front Street, Pettah, at 7.30 a.m. and turned into the street where the old Volunteer Headquarters stood. A crowd of about 200 persons were there, and five or six men, with sticks in their hands, were at the head of the mob. My rickshaw man got alarmed and refused to go forward, so I sent him with the rickshaw to stay near the

Accounts of other eye-witnesses.

Racquet Court, and I walked through the crowd, who seemed to know me. Thirty yards away about *twenty-five constables, with batons only, headed by two inspectors, sauntered leisurely, and did nothing at all to disperse the crowd.* Mr. Hay de Saram, Inspector of Police, warned me of the danger of going amongst the crowd, which he said was ' hostile.' The men in the crowd appeared to be the worst characters resident in the Pettah, annoyed with the police and yet afraid to collide with them, just as the unarmed police were afraid to order them to disperse. There was no means of enforcing such an order. I passed on to other parts of the Pettah, observing the wreck here and there. Muhammadans stood looking on from the outer verandahs of their houses, their doors being partly shut.

" At 10.30 a.m. I returned to my rickshaw, which I found near the Fort Railway Station, and proceeded towards the Pettah Railway Station, where I saw a very large crowd of the Sinhalese filling the whole road. Most of the men were witnessing the proceedings of a band of ruffians engaged in looting the boutiques. Stones were flying about, and it was dangerous and even impossible to go through the crowd in a rickshaw. So I stood at a distance and saw the work of the ruffians. They were throwing high the goods stored in the boutiques, and people of all sorts were carrying them away as they fell in the street. *I did not see any police there.*

" Not being able to go through the crowd, I turned back and went by another road to the Reclamation Road, and from there to Kochchikadde, and then returned to the Fort, and heard of the looting of the shop called the Crystal Palace."

Captain E. W. Jayawardene, Ceylon Light Infantry (sometime Acting District Judge of Colombo), says :—

"The Volunteers were mobilized at Rifle Green on the 1st of June (Tuesday), and ordered to assemble at 12 noon at the Echelon Barracks, Fort. I was ordered to go to the southern division of the city at 5 p.m. so as to prevent people getting in from beyond the Wellewatta Bridge. I and my men were on duty at that post from 5 a.m. on the 1st to the forenoon of the 2nd.

"On the evening and night of the 1st there were no disturbances.

"But on the 2nd, at 9 a.m., the Wellewatta Spinning Mills were threatened, and Mr. Marsden, in charge of it, shot and wounded a rowdy. Then the crowd became fierce, and grew larger and larger. I 'phoned for help, and a band of the Ceylon Planters' Rifle Corps arrived quickly just as the crowd was preparing to set fire to the mills, tins of kerosine oil being requisitioned. *The Rifle Corps fired, and the crowd quickly dispersed.*

"When I went to the Law Courts, Hultsdorf, at noon (on the 2nd), looting was going on on the high road, just opposite the Court of Requests."

Another gentleman says :—

"The looting at Hultsdorf was witnessed by a large number of lawyers right in front of the Court of Requests, Colombo, in the presence of the police, Town Guards, and Panjábis, who numbered about one-hundred strong. They were looking on, while one Sinhalese man was standing with a drawn knife among some ruffians, who were pulling out the goods from the boutiques and hurling them out. Even women removed the articles thus thrown.

"*Captain E. W. Jayawardene asked the Officer-in-charge of the Panjábis and the Officer-in-charge of the police to disperse the crowd, and arrest the looters. But their reply was 'No orders.'*"

It appears that, when a party of the Ceylon Mounted Rifles and of the Town Guard went on duty on the 1st of June at Layard's Broadway, Grandpass, and Urugodawatta, the former had guns and bayonets but no ammunition, and the latter had only riding whips and canes. When they went to Layard's Broadway, the Moors and the Sinhalese were pelting stones at each other, and many a Sinhalese, bleeding from the wounds caused by the stones, was breaking open Moor boutiques. The largest crowd was at the junction of Layard's Broadway and Grandpass Road, about three-hundred men. They were pushing on to the mosque. The military units spoke to them and tried to calm them, but as the Moors at the mosque threw stones at the Sinhalese, the latter attacked the mosque.

The closing of all shops and stores on account of the "mesmerized" condition of the Police, and the difficulty of obtaining food supplies.

I shall now narrate some of my own experiences. I arrived from India on the morning of the 2nd of June (Wednesday), and heard of the disturbances which had begun at Kandy and rolled along to Colombo, with the result that all the stores and shops in the city had to be closed, tramways ceased to run, and the streets considerably thinned of foot and wheel traffic. Soon after I reached my house in the Cinnamon Gardens, I was informed that it was difficult to buy provisions, and, if things continued in the present state for two or three days, the people in the city would have little to eat. I drove through many parts of Colombo after breakfast, to judge for myself the actual condition of affairs. Patient suffering was depicted in all faces. At their respective doors people stood looking concernedly at each other, and the few passers-by in the streets did not know what to do, and what would happen next. At the time I passed Main Street all the shops were closed, and I saw very few policemen on duty all the way to Kotahena Road *via* Sea Street. I stayed for some time in the Hindu Temple premises (facing the harbour), where more than a hundred stone sculptors, masons and coolies were working. They said they were in fear of their lives owing to the brutal conduct of the Sinhalese ruffians on the roads, and to the police doing nothing to arrest them, and they begged to be allowed to return to their homes in India. I had already heard that rickshaw coolies and drivers of carriage horses, who are mostly Tamils, had already fled to India without giving notice to their masters, and both the European and Ceylonese gentry could not go about for want of rickshawmen and drivers of horses; and as for the Hambayas and other Indian Muhammadans, they were leaving Ceylon as fast as possible both by rail and ship. My workmen said that the Tamil traders and their assistants and clerks were also preparing to go, as they considered that the police were not doing their duty, and they themselves did not know how to protect themselves. Having been in Colombo for only a few hours, I did not see the exact situation in proper perspective, and did not know what the authorities, from His Excellency the Governor downwards, were doing. I was inclined to think that my workmen were in a needless panic, and I told them so.

In the meantime I had to send an urgent telegram to my architect, and I wrote it out and asked one of the temple servants at 5 p.m. to take it quickly to the Chief Telegraph Office at the Fort. He returned in ten minutes, breathless with running and shaking with fear, and told me that, as he was hastening with the telegram, he saw a Muhammadan, walking on the middle of the road near St. Anthony's Church, brought down violently on his face by a Sinhalese man, who stooped suddenly behind him and pulled him down by the ankles; that the man fell prostrate and never rose; that two constables and two Town Guards, seeing the man bleed profusely from his mouth and nostrils, carried the body to the drain side and left it there; and that no one seized the Sinhalese man, when he was running away by Jampettah Street. Some of the workmen at the temple, who heard this narrative, told me other stories of violence, which they had witnessed in the streets of Colombo, and how passive the police remained in the presence of the rowdies.

Quickly finishing my business at the temple works, I resolved to drive straight to the Telegraph Office, and on the way to ascertain the fate of the man described by my servant. I passed St. Anthony's Church at 5.45 p.m., and was told that the man had been sent in a cart to the hospital. Going through Sea Street to Kayman's Gate, I saw a great deal of police and military activity at the junction opposite the Town Hall. I turned towards Main Street and was challenged by the armed men. I was told that Main Street was closed to carriage and passenger traffic. Here again was a difficulty for the transmission of my telegram. I enquired the reason of this strange order. Captain Rockwood, who was in his uniform, came to me and said that martial law had been proclaimed, and the military units were simply carrying out orders. He handed me a *Government Gazette* notice of the proclamation of martial law.

Proclamation of Martial Law.

Avoiding Main Street, I drove to Maradana, and was challenged again when I came to the junction beyond the Technical Institute at 6.15 p.m. I saw the trunk road from San Sebastian to the railway bridge quite empty, except for the military units dotting the road at intervals. Some Volunteers walking on the pavement were bidding the inhabitants of the houses to close the doors and remain in. " What is all this for? " I said to myself. " Why should the good and peaceful citizens of Colombo be imprisoned in their houses? Why don't the authorities deal with the wrongdoers themselves? What is the situation they are trying to grapple with? "

Closing of main thoroughfares to carriage and passenger traffic.

Compulsory confinement of good and peaceful citizens in their houses between sunset and sunrise.

Being challenged at the junction and at the railway bridge, I replied I was going home. " All right, sir," they said, " but you can't return this way."

Longing for information, I entered the Headquarters of the police, next to the railway bridge. I enquired for the Inspector-General of Police. He was not in, neither the Second, nor the Third Officer. There was only a Sub-Inspector of Police, who did not know anything of the situation. " We never expected anything like this, sir; we have lost our heads. There is no one here to guide us," he exclaimed in sore distress.

" We have lost our heads "—

"But who are these people in uniform?" I asked, not being able to see clearly in the dark.

"They are Volunteers, sir," he said.

—and no one knows the situation.

I went amongst them and met Captain E. W. Jayawardene. I asked him whether he could explain the situation. He said he could not. Just then Major Cockerell arrived, and he, too, did not understand the situation. He was simply carrying out the orders of the Brigadier-General. He was narrating some of his experiences with the roughs who sought to enter Colombo over the Victoria Bridge, when he was summoned to the Military Headquarters. On his hastening away, I moved about the Police Station for a few minutes and found no one there ready or willing to accept responsibility. The Sub-Inspector was appealed to, in my presence, by several applicants for help in regard to looting alleged to be going on not far from the station, but the poor man seemed too frightened and confused to issue any orders.

There is no doubt that disorganisation reigned at the Headquarters of the Police in Colombo at the time I visited the place.

Measures taken by the leaders of the people to restore confidence and revive trade.

I next turned my attention to some of the Sinhalese and Muhammadan leaders resident in Colombo, and invited them to see me the following morning (3rd June) to consider the situation. They called, and were most anxious to continue their work of going to different parts of the city, and out of it, too, in order to allay the false rumours current among the people and bring about a better understanding between the lower strata of the Sinhalese and the Muhammadans. They were all agreed that the mob beyond the gravets of Colombo verily believed the maddening stories of those who professed to come from town and bazaar centres, illustrative of the ferocity and future machinations of the Moors; that the mob in Colombo who resorted to violence consisted mostly of the very scum of the people, whose main idea was loot; and that these rascals, at the head of a mixed rabble of loafers and mischief-makers, would not have dared to play havoc with the city if the police had been armed in time and put under proper guidance.

Many were the experiences cited in proof of these statements. For instance, Mr. S. L. Naina Marikar, one of the wealthiest of the Muhammadans in Colombo, told me that, on the 1st of June, finding that there appeared to be a dead set made against the Muhammadans, and the police quite useless, he gave orders to shut the garden gates of his residence opposite the Victoria Park, and took measures to protect himself and his family by requisitioning some guns and pistols, and that when it grew dark his gardener came running and said that there were about 50 Sinhalese men at the gate demanding payment of 50 rupees at once, on pain of the gates being forced and the house looted. Mr. Naina Marikar sent word to say that if they came within the garden they would be shot, whereupon they quietly departed. His son-in-law, Mr. O. L. M. Macan Marikar, the Turkish Consul, told me similar stories of intimidation and actual violence by the roughs of the town.

As regards the proposal of the gentlemen whom I met—that we should divide ourselves into parties and go in different directions outside Colombo to decry false alarms and turn back the crowds of people who were coming into the city to defend their Sinhalese brethren—I said that, in view of the proclamation of martial law, which placed in the hands of the Brigadier-General the entire responsibilty of protecting the lives and properties of the inhabitants of most of the provinces of the island by such measures as he might devise and order, our first duty was to correlate ourselves to the military authorities and act with their sanction, lest our efforts be misunderstood and bring us into conflict with them. In the absence of His Excellency the Governor, who was said to be at Nuwara Eliya or Kandy, I proposed to call on the Colonial Secretary with one Sinhalese and one Muhammadan gentleman of acknowledged weight, to have the benefit of his advice generally on the subject.

The Turkish Consul, Mr. D. S. Senanayake, and I motored to the Secretariat at about 12 noon (3rd of June), not without being challenged on the way, and explained to Mr. Stubbs the desirability of leading Ceylonese being brought into relation with the military authorities in the work of quelling the excited state of the people by peaceful methods. I said that, though Brigadier-General Malcolm was my colleague in the Legislative Council, I did not know him personally well enough to ask him to let me and my friends move about the country freely and speak to the people, especially after he had been made the sole arbiter of the destinies of the people under the martial law.

Impossibility of Civil Authorities taking part in the peaceful restoration of order, because all power had been vested in the hands of the Military Officer Commanding the Troops.

The Colonial Secretary said that he could not now interfere; that the Officer Commanding the Troops was in touch with the Mayor of Colombo (Mr. Byrde) as regards Colombo, and with the Government Agent, Western Province (Mr. Fraser), as regards the Western Province; that if I desired to be useful in Colombo, I should speak to the Mayor and get through him whatever could be obtained; and that all he could do for me was to request the authorities that were in charge of the road from the Secretariat to the Town Hall to permit me to proceed to the Town Hall to see the Mayor!

"Is this all you can do for us?" I asked.

"Yes; I can't do more," he replied. "My open letter may save your motor-cars from being commandeëred on the way."

"If I and my friends go to the Town Hall with your open letter, and fail to meet the Mayor, what are we to do? What will become of our cars and ourselves?"

"That I do not know," he said, with a shrug of his shoulders.

Then the Turkish Consul related the difficulties he experienced in defending his house from the attacks of the rowdies, and begged for a letter to the police to respond to his call for help, and an authority to a European shopkeeper to sell him a gun and a revolver; for, he explained, firearms could not be bought now after the introduction of martial law.

Mr. Stubbs was sorry that he could not give Mr. Macan Marikar either of the documents.

The open letter given to me was as follows:—

> "Mr. Rámanáthan is, at my request, about to confer with Mr. Byrde.
>
> "I shall be obliged if he may be allowed to pass freely with the two cars which he has with him.
>
> "R. E. STUBBS,
>
> "3rd June, 1915. "Colonial Secretary."

With this document our motor-cars sped on to

the Town Hall. On the way, near the Racquet Court, the Turkish Consul mentioned to me that, as the fez-cap he was then wearing might attract a stone to his head, he had borrowed an English hat, and asked me whether he might wear it instead of the fez-cap. Just then a Sinhalese man, going along the road with another Sinhalese, exclaimed, "Anna Hambaya" ("There goes a Hambaya"). The Consul lost no time in doffing the fez and donning the foreign hat! He was not a "Hambaya" at all, but a genuine "Moor." To the Sinhalese man in the street, however, this was a distinction without a difference, in the present state of affairs.

On reaching the Town Hall I explained to the Mayor the object of our visit.

"How can I interfere?" he said. "It is not for me to offer any suggestions or advice to the General."

"But," I said, "in the official relation which has been created between him and you, he ought to be glad to hear from you. He does not know local conditions, and how is he to fulfil his duty of protecting the lives and properties of the people of this city in a satisfactory way unless you tell him in time the needs of the occasion?"

He did not seem to agree with me. He asked me to put my proposal to the General myself.

The dread of the General entertained by even high civil authorities.

It was quite clear to me that the Officer Commanding the Troops was either too dreadful a personage to speak to except when spoken, or had laid down the law for all his subordinates much too incisively for anyone to interpose anywhere.

I said I would see him, and wished now to know whether some effort should not be made to persuade the rice merchants to open their stores so as to enable traders to supply themselves with rice throughout the city.

"How can the rice merchants be made to open their stores?" he asked.

I told him that if, instead of motor-cars full of armed soldiers flitting about the town in different directions, he could get one or two soldiers stationed at either ends of certain streets in which the large stores were, I would induce their owners to open them. He preferred me to speak to the General Officer Commanding the Troops on this point also.

"Then what about getting the meat and vegetable stalls of the Municipal markets in different parts opened at once under proper protection, and getting the tramcars to run as usual?" I inquired.

The Mayor said that he would take measures to effect these two ends.

In conclusion, I asked him whether he could give me and my friends a pass to go about Colombo to assure and pacify the people, and he readily gave me the following open letter :—

> "To all officers in charge of military parties. Please extend your help and assistance to the Honourable Mr. Rámanáthan, C.M.G., who is engaged in quieting and assuring the people.
>
> "R. W. BYRDE,
>
> "3-6-1915. "Mayor of Colombo."

I then went with several Sinhalese gentlemen to the streets in the Pettah where the larger rice stores were. The streets were almost empty, being patrolled occasionally by a few armed Town Guardsmen. In the outer verandahs, however, there were many men to be seen. As soon as they saw me and my Sinhalese friends, they hastened towards me and were glad to know that I had come to confer with the leading merchants of that quarter, who were mostly Muhammadans from Bombay (known as Borahs and Memnons), and Tamils from the Madras Presidency. The doors that were shut were half opened, and many men of standing in the rice and other grain marts came out, carefully closing again the doors, to greet us.

The street we were in was now swarming with people, and we were invited to a large house belonging to Mr. Adamally, and offered chairs. At this conference many men spoke, some in favour of, and others against the opening of the stores. I explained the position of affairs, pointed to the Sinhalese gentlemen present, whom they all knew to be most reliable men, as willing to help in the preservation of peace and good order, and I promised to see the Brigadier-General and do my best to obtain from him some soldiers to guard both ends of their streets, if they would consent to open their stores and do business from the following day. At last they agreed to do so.

I then proceeded to Moor Street, where many of the owners of the shops in Main Street live, and obtained from their leaders also a promise to open their shops from the following day.

Passing on to other streets, I was met by groups of men, who came down from their houses to my car with anxious questions, which I answered, much to their relief. They were so glad that business would begin again on the following day.

On the morrow the city was astir, tramcars running, and shops opened, until an order came from the General about noon, bidding tramcars to withdraw and telephones to close, and immediately thereafter a cordon of troops was placed round the Pettah, and a house-to-house search made for arms! "The occupants of the houses were taken by surprise," says the *Times of Ceylon* in its issue of the 5th June, "but no resistance was shown anywhere. Not more than a couple of guns were found, but the collection of pieces of iron, clubs, knives, etc., amounted to a few cart-loads."

House-to-house search, ordered by the General, for seizure of dangerous weapons in Colombo, and how it ended.

This house-to-house search created much bitterness in the hearts of the citizens of the Pettah, owing to the want of faith of the authorities. Only a couple of guns found! The rest of the things carried away were implements of household use, mostly kitchen knives, choppers, axes and axe handles.

On the next morning (5th June), I called on Brigadier Malcolm. He allowed some more pickets for the streets named by me. He asked me to become a Special Constable, "following the good example of Chief Justice Wood Renton," he said; but I told him I was wanted for work independently of the military. He had not heard of the city being threatened with famine until I explained the matter to him

I must now say a few words on the course of the riots along the seaboard southwards and northwards, from Colombo to Matara and to Chilaw.

The course of the riots from Colombo southwards along the seaboard served by the railway.

Twelve miles south of Colombo is Moratuwa, with a population of 30,000 souls, under the protection of a Local Board. In a memorial presented by many wealthy and influential inhabitants of that town to H.E. the Governor, the causes of the riots in that town were stated to be (1) the sudden arrival by train of a gang of ruffians, (2) the example of loot set by them to the vagabonds of Moratuwa, and (3) the negligence of the police authorities to give the Local Board the help it was entitled to for the checking of the disorder and damages caused by the miscreants.

How the town of Moratuwa suffered, owing to the paralysis of the police.

"Shortly after eleven in the morning of the 1st of June," the memorialists said, "a gang of ruffianly people got down at the railway station at Angulana, at the north of the town, and began all of a sudden to break into the Moorish boutiques there. They were joined by some of the vagrants and vagabonds of the place, and the poorer people carried away what these miscreants had plundered in the boutiques and thrown into the streets. The work of outrage soon spread further down. About noon some boutiques at Rawatawatte, belonging to Coast Moors, were attacked by the mob. About half an hour later, a boutique at the Digaralla Junction, three miles from Angulana, though kept by a Sinhalese trader, was broken into . . . . The boutiques at Koralawella, at the southern extremity of Maratuwa, were attacked in the afternoon . . . . and on the morning of the 2nd began the sacking of the two principal shops in the heart of the town.

"At great risk to their lives, the people in various parts of the town took under their care the goods and money and even the persons of many of their fellow-townsmen Moors. But it was plain that they could not hope of themselves to quell a disturbance which had come to such a point.

"*It was in vain they sought the aid of the duly*

*constituted guardians of peace and order.* On the afternoon of the 1st June, *the Mudaliyar of the Korale and the Chief Police Officer of the Station,* powerless like themselves, *joined some of the chief residents in telegraphing to Colombo for help. The reply was,* the memorialists learned, *that no help was available.* Later they understood a telegram was received by the local Unofficial Police Magistrate, giving him authority to open fire on the rioters. But not a shot was fired.

"*Their first head of complaint is that the inhabitants did not receive the help they were entitled to expect from the police and other authorities towards the checking of the riot.*

"Had such help been available, the damage suffered might have been much less. But they were left unprotected, though for years they have been paying a police tax of 1½ per cent. on the income of their properties."

Similar causes ushered in the disturbances at the towns of Panadure, Kalutara, Ambalangoda, Galle, and Matara. The wave of loot northwards along the seaboard.

The wave of loot moved simultaneously northwards, along the seaboard, injuring some boutiques in Negombo, Kochikadde, Natandiya and Madampe, and in the direction of Minuangoda and Divulupitiya, through want of Police protection.

From Natandiya looters moved eastwards to Kuliyapitiya and, joining hands with other looters from Kurunegale, began to attack the boutiques near the Giru Ela bridge, but their attempts were frustrated by the timely arrival of the Volunteers, who fired on the rioters and dispersed them quickly.

The true dimensions of the disturbances.

It is needless to describe further the course of the riots. Their beginnings and ends were all similar. They did not prevail throughout the island. A study of the course of the riots in connection with a map of Ceylon and the returns which have not yet been published by the Government of Ceylon as regards the damages caused by the rioters, will show that the dimensions of the disturbances are not so great as represented by careless observers and loose thinkers.

At the last census, taken in 1911, the nine provinces of Ceylon were found to contain 4,107,000 people, of whom only 503,000 lived in towns, and 3,604,000 in villages. The Metropolitan province, which is the Western, though smallest in area, contains more than one-fourth of the entire population in Ceylon, and the Buddhists inhabiting the Western Province represent 6,700, and the Muhammadans 680, out of every 10,000 persons. Hence, the disturbances were mostly in the Western Province, within which is Colombo.

It is misleading to think of five Provinces as "the disturbed areas." The five Provinces in question cover 10,780 square miles, but the areas of those towns and villages where riots took place may amount to about one-fortieth of that square mileage, or say 300 square miles out of the 25,330 square miles covered by Ceylon.

To understand still better the true dimensions of the riots, we have to remember that the present population of Ceylon is 4,220,000, and that, if as many as 20,000 rioters be said to have roused fear in 200,000 persons, the remaining four millions were passive spectators from a safe distance. It should also be borne in mind, in order to realise the intentions of the rioters, that even the very wicked among them did not raise a finger against Government Officers or other Europeans, or their property, and that they were not bent on killing anyone. Disloyalty and treason were not in their hearts. The rioters had no guns or ammunition to fight the forces of the Government, as the house-to-house search made by the military in towns and villages proved; and they had neither the means nor the sympathy of the respectable and well-to-do people to molest the Moors beyond a few minutes in each of the disturbed places.

The damages estimated by Government officers highly overdrawn, and afterwards considerably reduced.

The Commissioners appointed by the Government to estimate the damages caused by the rioters reported such damages in the Western Province to be Rs. 4,000,000; in the Central Province and the Province of Sabaragamuwa, Rs. 500,000 each; and in the Southern and North-Western, Rs. 250,000 each: making a total of Rs. 5,250,000. But the Attorney-General, in reply to an observation I made in the Legislative Council, explained that the amount of the estimate was considerably reduced in many cases by the final assessment. He did not state what was the amount of reduction. In some memorials presented by me to the Council, the petitioners, who had been called upon to pay compensations, alleged that the reduction was as much as 70 per cent. The Government has not yet furnished to the Legislative Council any return showing the assessment of damages in each of the towns and villages. It remains to be seen at what amount the Government will finally assess the damages at every town and village where property was destroyed or looted.

It is probable that the sum of $5\frac{1}{4}$ million rupees originally estimated as the damages suffered by the Moors will be reduced by about 50 per cent., in which case the damages to property will represent in sterling money about £175,000 for all the disturbed areas.

The true causes of the riots.

The idea entertained by the Government during the week that the riots lasted, that they were all signs of a revolt, was entirely wrong. The true causes of the riots are those set forth in the preceding pages.

Summary of the causes of the riots.

The first cause was the intolerant and aggressive conduct of the Hambaya Muhammadans towards the Buddhists in Gampola in August, 1912, and their attack on those Buddhists who formed part of the religious processions in Kurunegala in January, 1915, and in Kandy on the 29th May following.

Then came the cold-blooded murder of an innocent Sinhalese youth by a Hambaya in the presence of a well-behaved crowd of Sinhalese on the night of the 30th May, and the utter indifference displayed by the Police in regard to their duty of arresting then and there the murderer, who was sheltered under the roof of another Hambaya. The cries of the excited crowd to the Police to arrest the offender being of no avail, some of the more indignant and active spirits entered the shop to seize him. The inmates escaped, and the goods stored were hurled into the street and burnt.

The angry crowd then moved on to some other Muhammadan boutiques and continued destroying the goods, until the Police Magistrate arrived with a larger body of constables, when it melted away. The murder of the Sinhalese youth and the failure of the Police to arrest the murderer were the causes of the riot on the 30th of May.

On the following day, the people of the neighbouring villages poured into Kandy to see that no harm befell the sacred Temple of the Tooth, which the Hambayas had openly threatened to demolish, and for which purpose they actually brought a number of ruffians by train from Colombo. The Government Agent, not being in touch with the people, did not know the afflictions of their heart; and, when he was told by independent and responsible men in the town that he should meet the crowd personally and assure them that they and their Temple would be protected, and that the conduct of the Police who neglected to do their duty would be enquired into, he refused to meet the people in the street, or their leaders in the adjoining Town Hall. Even after this communication of the requirements of the people, he did not inform them of the arrival of the Panjábi soldiers at Kandy from Colombo, or of his readiness to protect their Temple. Nor did he post a few soldiers near the Temple. His want of sympathy with the cares of the people, and his studied reserve and reticence at a time when he should have courted them with words of assurance and willing help, were felt by them bitterly, and paralysed the efforts of their leaders to calm and guide them.

In this state of high tension, while the crowd was still standing in the street craving for a conference with the Government Agent, someone kicked at the door of a Muhammadan tailor, who madly rushed out with a club into the street and whirled it about among the people, until he was felled to the ground. Then his two nephews jumped out of the house and stabbed some Sinhalese men and were arrested. It was after the subsidence of this street fight that the

Inspector-General of Police led the Panjábi soldiers to the scene, and they had no difficulty in sending the crowd away, without firing a single shot or using the bayonet.

Had the Government Agent met the people in the street and given them the assurance they needed, they would have retired and gone about their business, and the street fight between the Muhammadan tailor and his two nephews on the one side and a few Sinhalese on the other would not have occurred.

It is needless here to recapitulate how the riotous spirit roused in Kandy spread to other places. It is sufficient to remember that the religious animosities between the Hambaya Muhammadans and the Buddhists enabled the criminal classes to creep in for purposes of loot, and intensify the seriousness of the situation, only because the Police appeared to be "mesmerized" in the presence of an angry crowd.

This passivity or supineness of the Police, and the neglect of the Magistrates and other public officers to disperse the crowd in proper time, by adopting the methods prescribed by law, have operated as two additional and powerful causes for the spread of the riots in five of the Provinces of Ceylon.

## CHAPTER II.

### THE ACTION OF THE GOVERNMENT OF CEYLON IN CONNECTION WITH THE RIOTS.

THE several oppressive measures taken by the Government of Ceylon in connection with the recent riots may be ranged as follows :—

1. The proclamation of Martial Law on 2nd June and its continuance till 30th August, 1915. (pp. 69—90.)

2. The appointment of Military Commissioners to assess the damages suffered by the Muhammadans only, and to force the principal men of the Sinhalese community to sign debt-bonds for the amount allotted to each town and village. (pp. 90—96.)

3. The passing of an Ordinance to legalise such bonds, though obtained by intimidation and compulsion, and to establish a drastic procedure for assessing, apportioning and levying compensation from innocent inhabitants for damages caused hereafter by riots. (pp. 96—98.)

4. The arrest and incarceration of influential and loyal Sinhalese gentlemen, without an iota of evidence against them. (pp. 99—100.)

5. The trial of civilian citizens by Courts Martial

after the cessation of the riots, and while the ordinary Courts of Justice were uninterruptedly sitting. (pp. 100—106.)

6. The disarming of the people. (pp. 106—107.)

7. The unjust dismissal and dishonour of loyal public servants. (pp. 108—113.)

8. The abuse of the censorship of the press and private letters and telegrams. (pp. 114—117.)

9. The refusal of grants in aid to those managers of schools who, or whose teachers, have criticised the Government regarding their actions. (pp. 117—119.)

10. The obtaining of an Order of Indemnity from the Privy Council, avoiding public discussion, in the Legislative Council, of the acts done, and proceedings held, under Martial Law. (pp. 119—125.)

Reasons for the Government not knowing the causes of the riots.

Before dealing with these measures, it is necessary to show why the Government failed to discern the true causes of the riots, and to apply less drastic and more suitable remedies for the quelling of them and the quieting of the people. The failure of the Government was due to its complacent belief that Government Agents, Assistant Agents, and the officers of the Police know exactly all that is going on in the country, even more so than its native gentry, and would report affairs in due time.

Want of social intercourse between the rulers and the people.

This knowledge, however, is impossible, owing to the gulf of social separation which exists between the rulers and the people. The British official no doubt comes in contact with many Ceylonese daily in the exercise of his public duties in and out of his office, but in this sphere confidential interchange of views is not practicable, even if the official really cares for it. No native will unbosom the truth until he is quite sure that the official does not belong to that class of men who love to have proofs of the correctness of their own surmises or convictions, and hate to hear things to the contrary. From want of intimate social intercourse, true estimates of character cannot be formed, and thus, when the official meets the non-official, there is mutual caution and distrust, with the result that the truth, and nothing but the truth, is not expressed. The official of average ability, living in his own world of ideas, which is a compound of imperfect generalizations made by himself, his English colleagues in office and friends at the club, is too sure of his ground. He seldom suspects the possibility of his being mistaken, especially since the time the Government expressed the view that he ought to know, and does know, the real state of affairs in the country, and should therefore be considered to be qualified to speak on behalf of that vast class of Ceylonese who have not been educated in English on European lines. It was Governor MacCullum who maintained this opinion and insisted—in his Despatch to the Secretary of State, dated 21st May, 1909—that those of the Ceylonese "who have acquired a training and an education of a purely European type" have dissociated themselves from their fellow-countrymen to such an extent that they cannot represent them, and so have "forfeited the right of speaking on their behalf."

The self-sufficiency of Government officers.

The fallacy of their belief that the English educated Ceylonese know nothing of, and have no right to speak on behalf of, those who have not been so educated.

It is not true that well-educated Ceylonese who have profited by English methods of thought stand aloof from those of their countrymen who have not had a similar education. There is not a single educated Ceylonese who, having relatives amongst the agricultural and trading classes, does not associate with them on terms of equality and mutual friendship, or, having no relatives, does not take an interest in the welfare of his less fortunate countrymen, or is not appreciated for any work which he may be doing to uplift them. Most of our lawyers, doctors, merchants and other professional men, who have been trained on English lines, are landowners also, and have much to do with the labouring classes as employers or otherwise; and therefore they know their wants much better than the Europeans, who as a rule never cross their thresholds, and do not speak the language of the country.

Acknowledgment by Indian officials of the liability of Government officers being too easily misled.

It is unfortunate that our present Governor (Sir Robert Chalmers) acquiesced in the false theory of his predecessor, little knowing what some eminent officials in India have published in their biographies, written many years after their retirement from office and the widening of their experience by living among the people of the country, without the distance created by vain notions of superiority and inferiority. Their discovery, made too late, was that, during their official life, they had often been deceived by appearances, owing not only to the disinclination of the gentry and peasantry to state to the official anything that is likely to displease him, but also to the ingratiation of clever but unprincipled men who are ready to urge him, in what seems to him to be right, by assurances of such policies being acceptable to the people, or necessary in the circumstances of the case.

The Government saw in the course of the riots

from Kandy to Colombo, during the first four days (29th May to 1st June), that the rioters were keen on destroying the boutiques and mosques of the Muhammadans, and rightly concluded that religious and racial animosity was a cause of the riots; but there was no reason whatever for supposing that the rioters, who were obviously drawn from the lower orders of the Sinhalese, were being urged and financed by the upper classes, or that they were disloyal to the Government.

Riots not due to conspiracy between the upper and lower classes of the Sinhalese against the Government.

The ideas of conspiracy and disaffection were instilled into the minds of the authorities by a few rash and narrow-minded gentlemen who were at variance with the popular movements of Temperance and Racial Unity (free from the trammels of caste and religious sectarianism), started some years ago by a band of earnest, enthusiastic and hard-working Sinhalese gentlemen and ladies. The believers in caste and creed were jealous of the rapid growth of the two organizations, as well as of the social importance to which many of the young men of education and wealth who supported them had risen. The former set up the story that "the nobodies who had become somebodies" by means of the Temperance and Racial Unity Associations were responsible for the riots; and the Government, who were disappointed by the impossibility of selling toddy-taverns in the districts affected by the Temperance movement, readily believed the accusation. For, after the proclamation of the Martial Law, the Government arrested all these public-spirited men and kept them in prison for six weeks or more, in the hope that those who were preparing cases for prosecution before Courts Martial would procure evidence sufficient to

By whom this false story was started.

place them on their trial. But not a scintilla of testimony was forthcoming against them, and they had to be released.

Councils of hysteric and panic, mistake and jealousy.

What happened at the recent crisis had also happened before on similar occasions, when the authorities yielded to " counsels of hysteric and panic," or those born of mistake and jealousy. An extract from Major Skinner's Memorandum on the "Past and Present Social Condition of Ceylon, from 1820 to 1849," dated 9th June, which was submitted to the Parliamentary Committee of that year (Vol. I., p. 525) may be usefully quoted here :—

Major Skinner's experience of the false information, and wilfully exaggerated reports, of those who try to ingratiate themselves with the Government.

" The first supposed interruption to the contentment and loyalty of the Kandyan population occurred in 1834, towards the close of which reports of disaffection in some of the districts were made to Government, with such precision and minuteness of detail as regarded the time and mode, and such exaggeration as regarded the means of an intended attack, that on the night on which it was said the preparations were completed by the rebels in Kandy, and on the eve of the supposed insurrection, the troops were turned out in silence, and at a given signal before daylight, certain officers, of whom I was one, were told off for the apprehension of the most influential chiefs and priests. The Government supposing, from the information it had received, that the temples and houses of the chiefs were prepared for resistance, each officer was provided with a military party. My own inglorious office was the seizure of the first Adigar, Molligodde, in whose Walawa (or palace) there was such an entire absence of preparation, either offensive or defensive, that the martial array by which we were supported (suggested by the false and exaggerated information on which Government had acted) gave to the whole affair, when daylight dawned upon it, a character of extreme burlesque.

"My own impressions have been, that the reports of this intended insurrection were wilfully exaggerated by informers, who hoped by their zeal, and the importance of their information, to ingratiate themselves with Government. The result of the State trials, at the beginning of 1835, was seriously to impair the influence and authority of Government in the minds and affections of the people."

The delusion of the Government that there is no public opinion in Ceylon, and the danger of such delusion.

Another delusion of the Government is that there is no public opinion in Ceylon. If this were true, the local Government would be the only body capable of informing and guiding the Secretary of State for the Colonies, and it would not be possible for the local Government to realize its mistake on matters of fact.

What is called public opinion in England is called "the talk of the country" in India and Ceylon. "What will people say?" is the great concern of those who would be "respectable" both in the East and in the West; and respect for what the world says is so strong a spring of human action everywhere, for the ruled and the rulers as well, that no country which claims to be civilized can be without public opinion. There is no doubt that it is better organized in Western lands by free education among the masses and by efficient newspapers and clubs. But in Ceylon, too, education is fairly widespread, though not free or so high, and its many daily newspapers and active associations are constantly expressing themselves. The Government, however, wedded to its own narrow views, makes light of public opinion, and will not stay its hand of execution even to consider the evidence upon which it is based. It is the official majority which it commands in the Legislative Council that precipitates it into many a financial and legislative blunder. It feels so powerful, with its official majority and its right to nominate the greater part of the non-official members just as it pleases, that it often despises and defies public opinion, and beguiles the Secretary of State too. Until this defect is remedied by a better constitution of the Council, serious mistakes will continue to be committed by even well-meaning Governors.

The action of the Governor.

H.E. Sir Robert Chalmers was in Nuwara Eliya during the first three days of the riots. Having heard of its ramifications in the Central Province and of its extension to the Western Province and the Province of Sabaragamuwa, he came down to Kandy on 2nd June, and, without conferring with men who enjoy the confidence of all classes of people, and who by daily intercourse with them possess a thorough knowledge of their ways, wants and wishes,—and without carefully considering the law that regulates the suppression of riots and rebellions,—ordered Martial Law to be proclaimed on 2nd June, and was even willing to request the Government of India to forward reinforcements to co-operate with the troops in Ceylon.

The Governor evidently took a most serious view of the situation. He must have thought that the rioters were fully armed with guns, bayonets and bombs, and had ample resources to keep up the disturbances, and probably intended to subvert the administration of the country.

But we have evidence that, after the proclamation of Martial Law and the complete cessation of the riots, that is, between the 2nd and the 6th of June, his fears of the rioters' design against the Government were also abated, for there was an announcement in the London newspapers made by the Colonial Office on the 7th of June, as follows: "The Governor reports that the disorder is due to a sudden outbreak of racial and commercial animosity, and is not directed against the European community or Government."

Nevertheless, Martial Law was not abrogated. The panic-stricken officials believed that, though the overt rioting was over, the conspiracy still existed, and required the rough-and-ready methods of that law to stamp it out.

The Governor's unjustifiable suspicions of the native gentry.

There are good reasons for believing that, at this crisis, the Governor suspected the native gentry, and held himself aloof from even the best of them.

I endeavoured in vain for several days after his arrival in Colombo on 3rd June to see him, and was much astonished to receive the following letter on the 10th June, when the riots had wholly subsided, and His Excellency was well known to be engaged with General Malcolm and the Attorney-General (Mr. Anton Bertram) upon various measures which needlessly wrung the souls of "the innocent and irreproachable Sinhalese" (to quote the words of the Attorney-General uttered in the Legislative Council) throughout five provinces in Ceylon.

The letter ran as follows:

" Queen's House,
" 10th June, 1915.

" Dear Mr. Rámanáthan,

" I hastened to mention to His Excellency this afternoon the desire you expressed to me for an interview on the subject of the disturbances. His Excellency, who is much pressed for time, directs me to say how much he would value it, if you would kindly set out in writing, for his information, the representations you desire to make.

" If, however, you do not wish to put them in writing, His Excellency desires me to ask you to seek an interview with the Hon. the Brigadier-General, in whose charge matters have now been placed under the Martial Law Proclamations.

" Yours truly,

" W. T. Southorn,
" P.S. to H.E."

This was a most unusual communication to me from the Governor, because our official intercourse had ripened into personal regard for each other, and His Excellency was always glad to receive me whenever I called at Queen's House, without making a previous appointment. The subject about which he desired me to write, being most complicated, could not be explained in writing in a few words, especially as the wrong convictions, formed already by the authorities, had to be eradicated first. Obviously useless, also, was my trying to persuade General Malcolm, who was working vigorously at the task which the Governor himself had sanctioned, to arrest its further prosecution. It was plain that the

Governor did not want my advice. The fearful machinery of the Martial Law was moving in every direction with such rapidity that it could not be held up without exposing the Government to ridicule for all the needless display of force which was being made, as if the Germans had come and taken possession of Ceylon, for Colombo and other places were like camps full of soldiers fussing about with rifles, bayonets, and Maxim guns!

It was also observed that the Governor, on leaving Nuwara Eliya on the 2nd June for Kandy, left his Sinhalese A.D.C., Sir Solomon Dias Bandáranáyaka, who was the head of all the Sinhalese Mudaliyárs (Chiefs), behind at Nuwara Eliya, at a time when he should have gone among the people to assure and quiet them. The Mahá Mudaliyár (great chief, as he was officially known) might have done effective work had he gone in time to Veyangoda and other disturbed areas, instead of idling at Nuwara Eliya. The people missed his presence greatly, and credited him with being one of the authors of their calamitous treatment by the Government officials, for his duty was to wait on the Governor, and he might have saved the people, they thought, by speaking to the Governor. But H.E. does not appear to have taken him into his confidence.

It was afterwards ascertained that the moment the Mahá Mudaliyár was free to leave Nuwara Eliya a week after all the riots were over, he came straight to his residence at Veyangoda about the 15th June, called up his estate officers and labourers, inquired into the doings of each man during the days of the riots, recorded evidence, found out the names, residences and acts of the rioters, and reported them all to the Government Agent, Western Province, and expressed his readiness to help him in every way to bring the offenders to justice. Mr. Fraser, however, did not accept the proferred aid, nor did he prosecute the men named by the Mahá Mudaliyár, much to the amusement of those offenders who were left to stand out and see other men, innocent, loyal and influential, prosecuted, upon complaints preferred by designing Muhammadans, whose object was to implicate well-to-do Sinhalese men for the purpose of either having their property confiscated and utilised for the payment of compensation to themselves, or extorting money from them on threats of false accusation.*

I was not able to interview the Governor till the 6th July—more than a month after the first outbreak of the riots—when he told me, as he did to others,

* See *King v. Ismail*, decided by Mr. Felix Dias, District Judge of Kandy, on 8th June, 1915, in which the accused Muhammadan was convicted and sentenced to four years' rigorous imprisonment for extorting twenty rupees (equal to £1 6*s.* 8*d.*) from Mr. A. Ratwatte, a Kandyan chief, by stating to him that a petition had been presented against him charging him with having taken part in the Wesak (May-June) riots; that the accused had been asked to give evidence against him; and that if he would give the accused Rs. 20, he would keep quiet. The accused received the money and was charged.

At the close of the trial, the District Judge said that the wickedness of the accused might have subjected Mr. Ratwatte to the gallows or life-long imprisonment, if he had been tried by Court Martial; and considering that so many cases had ended in convictions resting solely upon the testimony of Muhammadan witnesses, he added, "Until the day of resurrection we will not know how many people have been falsely sent to the gallows."

that a revolt had been put down with rose-water. I pointed out to him that it was not a revolt at all, but an affair between the Buddhists and the Muhammadans, arising out of the intolerance and aggression of the latter, and that this feud was taken advantage of by the criminal classes in towns and villages to spread the riots for their profit. His Excellency was impressed by what I stated, and granted other interviews to other gentlemen on the 9th and 11th July, and had a long conference with me again on the 25th July.

The Governor's explanation to the Legislative Council.

On the 6th of August, more than two months after the outbreak and cessation of the riots, and while Martial Law was continuing to operate, the Governor convened a meeting of the Legislative Council and explained his conduct as follows, in his address delivered on that occasion :—

"Had the outbreak been confined to up-country I would have dealt with it without proclaiming Martial Law. . . . . But when, gentlemen, the outbreak reached the low-country, and when the criminal classes of Colombo and elsewhere joined in a movement which had simply become predatory and anarchic, then the time had clearly come for the sternest measures; it was necessary to display and to exert the force which was at Government's command.

"I proclaimed Martial Law accordingly, empowering the Officer Commanding the Troops in Ceylon to take, throughout the five provinces affected, all steps he might deem necessary for the maintenance of order and the defence of life and property.

"These steps General Malcolm took with a

promptitude which quickly succeeded in suppressing the overt disturbance. I may here add that, as soon as I reached Colombo from Kandy on June 3rd, I asked the General whether he needed reinforcements from India or elsewhere. He said no, and events have justified my confidence in his cool judgment."

This passage in the Governor's Address contains his specious justification for proclaiming Martial Law in Ceylon. He says he would not have proclaimed it had the disturbances been confined to up-country, meaning the Central Province and the Province of Sabaragamuwa, but that, as the outbreak reached the low-country and the criminal classes joined in it, the movement became "predatory and anarchic," and it was necessary to display and exert the force which was at Government's command.

Reasons why his proclamation of Martial Law cannot be justified.

The premises may be conceded, but the conclusion does not follow. There are five kinds of forces available to the Government for the protection of itself and the innocent people, viz. :—

1. The civil force, known as the police, the magistracy and the prison.

2. The force of special constables, or the arming of the well-disposed people against the ill-disposed in order to help the civil force to maintain order.

3. The volunteer force organised for the defence of the country against internal and external attack.

4. The military force of the regular army, acting in concert with the civil or volunteer force, and

5. The military force acting according to the sole will of the General Officer Commanding the Troops.

The question is, why did the Governor fail to utilize the second, third and fourth forms of force, and why did he spring upon the vast majority of the inhabitants of the five provinces, who were peaceful and well-disposed towards each other and the Government, the horrors of Martial Law?

As observed by Dicey, in his *Law of the Constitution*, "officers, magistrates, soldiers, policemen, ordinary citizens, all occupy in the eye of law the same position. They are each and all of them bound to withstand and put down breaches of the peace, such as riots and other disturbances. They are all and each of them authorized to employ so much force, even to the taking of life, as may be necessary for that purpose, and they are none of them entitled to use more."

The Criminal Procedure Code of Ceylon specially authorizes the Magistrates, Government Agents and the Inspector-General of Police to call out the Military to aid the Police in dispersing riotous crowds; and actual experience has proved that the rioters disappeared the moment the Military intervened with their rifles and bayonets.

The Governor's explanation that Martial Law appeared to be necessary because the union of the criminal classes with the anti-Muhammadan Sinhalese made the movement predatory and anarchic, means only that there was looting and lawlessness in certain parts of the Western, Southern and North-Western Provinces. What national emergency was there for suspending the constitutional safeguards of life and property, and exposing the innocent people to the dangers of military despotism? Would not the united force of constables and soldiers, arrayed under the civil power, have sufficed for the quelling of the disturbance? It was well known to the Governor that the conduct of public business in the various offices of the Government, Municipalities and Local Boards was not in the least interrupted by the rioters; that Courts of Justice of every kind never ceased to sit at the usual places and hours; that no Government building or officer in the revenue, judicial, legal, medical or other public departments was molested; and that the rioters were mostly unarmed with guns and bombs. What was the dangerous pressure of the moment which could not have been overcome by measures other than the proclamation of Martial Law?*

In his Address to the Legislative Council, the Governor did not refer to the disturbances as a revolt or rebellion, nor did he explain why he did not take advantage of the ordinary law of the land, and order the military to help the civil authorities to put down the riots. He does not state on what points he sought the advice of the Law Officers of the Crown, and what their opinion was as to the choice between the introduction of the Martial Law and the calling out of the Military for the restoration of that order which the police failed to keep. Nor

* See the Circular Despatch of Lord Carnarvon to Colonial Governors, dated 30th January, 1867, on the undesirability of introducing Martial Law except on the pressure of grave national emergencies. The Governor "cannot be relieved from the obligation of deciding for himself, under that pressure, whether the responsibility of proclaiming Martial Law is or is not greater than that of refraining from doing so." Printed in Vol. 2, p. 667, of Clode's *Administration of Justice under Military and Martial Law.*

does he state what necessity there was for continuing the Martial Law and the Courts Martial after the suppression of the riots.

The further explanation offered by the Governor to the Legislative Council regarding the establishment of Courts Martial in Ceylon shows that they were all based upon an Order of H.M. Queen Victoria made by and with the advice of her Privy Council on 26th October, 1896, nearly nineteen years before the outbreak of the religious riots.

Does H.M.'s Order in Council of 26th October, 1896, justify the establishment of Courts Martial in Ceylon, when there is no enemy at war with the King, in Ceylon?

Does this Order really afford a good foundation for the Courts Martial held in the island? It was made expressly in the interests of eight Colonies, including Ceylon, in order to safeguard them against the attack and machinations of a foreign enemy. Ceylon was not attacked openly from without, or secretly within, by an enemy. It was no doubt advisable, after the outbreak of the present war with Germany, to proclaim in Ceylon the Order of the Queen in Council, in order that its provisions might be utilised in connection with the defence of the Colony against a possible attack from outside, or against insidious conspiracies between the enemy and residents inclined to help him. But as there was no such foreign attack, nor any conspiracy of the enemy with the people in Ceylon, the British subjects there could not be subjected to trial by Court Martial, professing to be created under the Army Act.

If, then, the authority of the Queen's Order in Council of 1896 cannot be legitimately invoked in support of the establishment of the Court Martial that condemned the 385 persons out of the 452 who were dragged before them, what should be done with the prisoners now undergoing the illegal sentences? What redress is there on account of those who have been shot or hanged? What punishment is to be meted out to those who misused the law and tormented the people?

The necessity of administering Martial Law according to the principles of justice, honour and humanity.

The introduction of Martial Law, which put to flight the rioters, did not conduce to the confidence and safety of the good citizens of Ceylon. It glorified the power of Government officials, adding one cubit to their stature in their own estimation, terrorised both the wicked and the innocent, and engendered in the hearts of the latter the wish that they had not been born to see the glorious reputation of the British Government for justice and mercy combined desecrated by men who knew not the truth that Martial Law must be administered "strictly according to the principles of justice, honour and humanity —virtues adorning a soldier even more than other men, for the very reason that he possesses the power of his arms against the unarmed."*

Otherwise Martial Law becomes military oppression.

Martial Law became military oppression in the hands of the Troops to whom certain orders were issued by the General on the 3rd of June.

Many of these orders were loosely drawn, and capable of licentious interpretation by persons who think of Martial Law as no law at all. The General's own conception of it, according to his farewell address, is that it is "absolute power" (or power absolved from all limitations) to do as he liked. But

* Extract from the instructions issued in April, 1863, by the Government of the United States of America for the guidance of their armies during the Civil War, quoted with approval in Clode's *Administration of Justice under Martial and Military Law.*

the truth is that likes and dislikes have no place in Martial Law, because the will of the General and the minds of his soldiers must be strictly guided by the principles of justice, honour and humanity. One has no right to treat another under Martial Law differently from how he would himself claim to be treated in the same circumstance. Therefore, the orders given "to the troops," consisting mostly of men noted for their worship of physical power, love of excitement and dash, were exceedingly liable to be misapplied at every turn.

The orders issued by the General were capable of being misinterpreted and mis-applied.

They were grossly misapplied by even Police Magistrates and Superintendents of Police, as will appear presently; and when the subject of compensation is unfolded later on, the oppressive conduct of the Government Agents, who were made Military Commissioners, will also be seen.

Order III (1) clearly states the number of soldiers required for towns and villages: "The Regulars and Volunteers will be disposed in groups of twelve or six. Twelve men are enough for a village or small town; an additional post of six to be established in larger towns."

Order III (2) declares: "Each post of twelve will be posted in a central roomy place, where it cannot be rushed. It should have two sentries watching different directions from which attacks are possible. It will have a motor patrol of four armed men and two motor patrols with two men each."

Instances of military oppression.

Order III (3) gives the power to Police Officers to commandeer private motor cars on pain of imprisoning the owners in case they refused to let them take away their cars. Injustice, and breach of faith and of express agreement, characterized the execution of this order.

Misuse of commandeered motor-cars.

The cars, thus seized, were to be used by parties of four soldiers or less to scour the country, not only where disorder existed, but also where disorder was likely to occur. The cars were often used for amusement and holiday journeys of even 200 miles, and were returned months afterwards to the owners in a ruined condition without any compensation.

It was ordered that information should be obtained locally of persons who instigate the riots. This gave exceptional opportunities for an unscrupulous person to report falsely against those who were hostile to him in business or social life. Hundreds of such cases are known.

Authority to shoot persons reported as instigators of riots;

Having received such a report, the military unit might be shown the same person at some place where a disturbance is going on. Whether he is taking part in the disturbance or not is of no consequence. It is enough if he was there, only seeing the row, and the order empowers the military unit to pick him off. The words are : "If these persons are seen where any disturbance is taking place, they should be picked off," that is, shot dead or disabled. Hundreds of these cases are also known.

to shoot persons assaulting each other;

The military units were each given forty rounds of ball per man, and the orders for firing are that, if one man assaulted another, he might be shot, if there is no other way of stopping him. Assaults unconnected with riots and loots have drawn forth bullets from the troops.

to shoot persons resenting unfair treatment;

Ringleaders in the act of looting and burning must be shot. But need a person who has been unjustly treated by a soldier, and who resents such treatment, be shot also? There are many such cases. Mere remonstrance has met with maiming and death.

All places of business, including shops, were to be shut at 4 p.m., and the men must get back to their homes, however distant, before six; and should they be found in the public streets between 6 p.m. and 6 a.m., they could be arrested and imprisoned, if not shot. There were scores of cases of respectable men shot and killed in the streets of Colombo and other towns, who ran (after six) on being challenged; some of them being passengers who were trying to go home direct from the railway station from a belated train.

to imprison or shoot persons found in the streets between 6 p.m. and 6 a.m.;

And the serious dislocation of business, caused by closing work at 4 p.m., and by confining all the inhabitants of the towns and villages to their houses between 6 p.m. and 6 a.m., may be imagined. No settlement of accounts, no recoveries of money, no arrangements for the following day's business, no purchases of provisions for the house, no social calls, no communications with relatives and friends regarding sudden illness and the like, no bringing in of doctors or priests in cases of emergency, none of these things could be done.

to compel the closing of shops and places of business at 4 p.m.;

Why were the good and innocent people of five provinces thus tormented, when it was possible to control and keep in order the rioters themselves by efficiently supervising and directing the police and a body of soldiers to disperse the crowd and restore peace, under the rules of the ordinary law of the country?

Some more orders to be "strictly enforced by both Military and Civil Authorities in all towns and villages in the five Provinces under Martial Law" were published on the 9th June, making life still to prevent use of musical instruments in places of worship and on festive occasions;

more miserable. No drums or other instruments of music could be played without a special permit. No meetings could be held in private houses. No foot passengers could walk on the roads, where there was a pavement or footpath, and if there was no pavement or footpath, they were to walk on the side of the road.

to flog wayfarers if they did not walk on the pavement, etc.

The consequence was that constables prowled round to see that no drums or other instruments were used at Temples during worship, or in marriage and other festive houses; and they seized those who failed to walk on the pavement or footpath, and flogged them then and there, to the dismay of everybody about. Clerks serving in mercantile offices were also flogged, first by the station officer, then by a constable, as each passed out of the station in dread of being taken before the Court Martial. Police constables and officers who behaved a few days before like whipped curs in the presence of an ordinary rabble, now became audacious under the ægis of the General, and delighted to beat wayfarers in public.

They flogged even the coachman of Chief Justice Wood Renton, leaving painful marks on the body, with which he went before the Police Magistrate of Colombo, only to be told that the constable was acting under the Martial Law! The Chief Justice sent for the record of the case, but somehow the matter mysteriously slided, and no decision was given.

The Panjábi soldiers and the Volunteers flitted about the country in every direction, moving day and night in pursuance of the order that "motor patrols will scour the whole locality thoroughly, especially places where disorder is likely." Each military unit sent out could exercise his discretion as to the place that required to be scoured. He was free to enter any house or hut, and remain for any length of time, ordering the men and women in it to stay in or stand out, or provide him with food or bed, or to seize an inmate and carry him off to Colombo on a charge trumped up by a Muhammadan. It was death to the person who ran at the sight of the motor-car, for many are the cases I have heard of men, women and girls shot down for this offence, and others of like nature. The people had no sleep, night after night, through fear of the motor patrols coming into the village.

Case of Leo Fernando, who was shot without trial by order of a Police Magistrate.

Now, let me come to the case of the Police Magistrate who, by misapplying Martial Law, has made himself liable to a charge of murder. He is still safely sheltered in the ranks of the Civil Service.

On the 7th of June two motor-cars arrived at Divulapitiya with four Panjábis and one Police Sergeant under the command of a "Captain," and entered the house of one Leo Fernando, a respectable and well-to-do Sinhalese young man of 22 years of age. They searched his residence and found five muzzle-loaders there, which he had borrowed for defending himself and his many houses against the attacks of the rioters. In another house belonging to him they found some calico, which had been entrusted to him by some Moslem tenants of his when their boutiques were looted on the 1st of June. They arrested Leo Fernando and took him with the piece goods and the five guns in the motor-car.

The mother, a widow, alarmed about the safety of her only son, started for Negombo, and reached her lawyer's house there early in the morning of the 8th, and was informed that her son was seen a few minutes earlier in a motor-car in the company of Panjábis apparently going back to Divulapitiya. Her counsel told her that, as Leo Fernando would be brought back to Colombo for his trial, she should stay there. Finding, however, that Leo Fernando was not brought back even though Wednesday, the 9th, had dawned, her counsel bade her return to Divulapitiya.

On her return home at noon, she found the dead body of her son with four wounds, one through his forehead and three through the heart.

She ascertained that, on Tuesday, the 8th, her son was brought back to Divulapitiya by the Police Magistrate attended by the Mudaliyár of Minuangode, two police officers and four Panjábis, taken to an open yard opposite to Leo Fernando's house, and made to stand against the wall of one of his boutiques, blindfolded and manacled. Then the Police Magistrate asked the Mudaliyár to invite the people to come forward and hear him. He said, through the Mudaliyár, "This man appears to be the captain of the rioters in this place. He has a bad heart, and I order that he be shot through the heart."

Thereupon, in the absence of the mother, Leo Fernando's aunt came and fell at the feet of the Mudaliyár and prayed that he be not shot until a full inquiry was made, but she was ordered off, and Leo Fernando himself then said: "Before God I declare that the piece goods found in one of my houses belong to one of my Moor tenants, who entrusted them to me for safe custody before their boutiques were looted. Before shooting me, summon the Moors and ask them whether what I have said is true or false." But the Police Magistrate was deaf. The order to fire being given, the Panjábis fired at his heart, and the youth fell on his face. On lifting up his head, he received another shot on his forehead and died.

Leo Fernando was never tried at Divulapitiya or at Negombo. The Panjábis, who removed the manacles and bandage over the eyes, removed also the silver chain from the body, worth about Rs. 100, and appropriated it, as if it was their due!

About a week afterwards certain lawyers, who had heard of this awful tragedy, arrived at Divulapitiya, inspected the place of execution, and returned to Negombo. These lawyers were summoned before the Magistrate and ordered to give security for good behaviour!

The cases of Simon Perera and Jeris Appu, who were shot by order of a Superintendent of Police professing to act under Martial Law.

I shall give another instance of military oppression brought to my notice by another widow, a young woman of about twenty-five years of age. The hero of the former story was a Police Magistrate. The hero in this story is a Superintendent of Police.

Podi Nona, of the village of Kaleliya, stated:—"I am the widow of Simon Perera, who was shot and killed by some Panjábis on the order of Mr. A——, a Superintendent of Police, on the 5th June. At this time, I was in my house in Kaleliya. My husband, with one Jeris Appu and the watcher of Kakalle Estate (belonging to Mr. H. Dias Bandaranayeke of Kanuwana), was seated on a bedstead which was in the outer verandah. Jeris Appu was seated on an easy chair, and the watcher was seated on the same bedstead with my husband.

"It was about 9 in the morning when Mr. A——, two Panjábis and a Town Guard, accompanied by Segu Mohamadu, of Kaleliya, arrived walking at our compound, having left their motor-car on the high road, which was about two furlongs from my house. When they arrived and faced us, the Moorman said, 'Here are the people.' Thereupon Mr. A—— said, 'Come forward.' Then my husband, Jeris Appu and the watcher, who had jumped up from their seats, continued to stand where they were. Mr. A—— walked into the outer verandah and beat my husband with a stick, and pushed him out, and the two others also, and went into the house, followed by the Moorman. In the hall were two bags of rice, which my husband had removed from his own boutique on the roadside for safety's sake, and brought into our residence, which is about two furlongs from our boutique. The Moorman pointed out to Mr. A—— the two bags, and claimed them as his own, though he was not a boutique-keeper. My brother-in-law, Sarnelis Appu, arrived just then, and said, 'How can you claim these bags of rice as yours, when you are not a boutique-keeper?' Mr. A—— gave him a cut with his stick, and asked him to go and sit where the three others were squatting. Finding nothing else in the house, Mr. A—— and the Moorman came out Mr. A—— said, 'Simon Perera will be shot in five minutes.' The Moorman said he had no complaint against the watcher, and he was sent away.

"Turning to Jeris Appu, Mr. A—— asked him why he was there. Jeris Appu said, 'I came here to get someone from my kinsman to accompany me to the *vederála* (physician). Mr. A—— asked the Moorman to bring up his witnesses. He went up and brought his brother Abbaas, who is the headman of the village, and another brother named Yesu and one Junoos Lebbe and Ismail Lebbe. Ismail Lebbe said, pointing to my husband, 'This is the first guilty man (waradak-karaya)'; and pointing to Jeris Appu, 'This is the second guilty man.'

"Then Mr. A—— caught hold of the heads of my husband and Jeris Appu and knocked their heads together, and made them stand up, and asked Sarnelis to go away.

"When they were making preparations to shoot my husband and Jeris Appu, I came forward and worshipped Mr. A——, and said, 'Sir, my husband is innocent, he is not a thief, he has his own boutique; the two bags of rice were brought from his boutique for safety to our house.'

"Mr. A—— then said, 'If you do not clear out, I will shoot you also.' I did not move from the spot.

"My husband then said, 'Before you shoot me, please make a proper inquiry.' He asked me to produce his books and prove to Mr. A—— his innocence by the entries of the sales and purchases. I produced them, but he threw them away, saying, 'I have not come here to look at your books.'

"My husband then cried out, 'Don't shoot me till I am tried and convicted.'

"My husband has had continuous transactions for several years with a number of traders in Colombo. I now produce a heap of bills, in proof of the statement that he is a trader in rice and other provisions, and has had cash and credit transactions with other traders in Colombo. These documents will show that he has traded with M. N. Nagoor Meera Saibo, of No. 110, Fourth Cross Street, Pettah, Colombo; with Ana Ravana, of No. 61, Bankshall Street, Colombo; with A. C. V. Sockalingam Pillai, of No. 107, Fourth Cross Street, Pettah; with W. J. Peris, of No. 148, Dam Street, Colombo; with K. D. Carolis Appuhamy, of Nos. 10 and 11, Gas Works Street, Colombo; with Cha Ana, of Bankshall Street, Colombo; with T. U. K. Thomai Anthony Villavarayar, of No. 7, Gas Works Street, Pettah, and with many others. These are all cash transactions shown in these bills, signed by the respective traders named, from Rs. 800 downwards. The many promissory notes I now produce were made by my husband in favour of several storekeepers and moneylenders, and duly retired by him on the due dates. Amongst the file of promissory notes will be found several for Rs. 1,000 each. My husband's life was also insured for Rs. 2,000, and the policy of insurance is with me. His estate matters are in the hands of Mr. Proctor Arthur Silva, of Negombo, and I have not yet obtained Letters of Administration from the Court.

"Mr. A—— did not look into these papers at all, nor did he make any investigation. He accepted the false statement of the Moorman, and ordered that my husband be shot. He was neither manacled nor blindfolded. He was ordered to stand near a wall and one Panjábi shot at his right leg, just above the knee, which brought him down immediately. Amidst his cries and groans, Jeris Appu, who was gazing on this awful scene, was shot by the same Panjábi on the shin bone of his left leg. He too fell with piercing shrieks. I produce a bullet, and another piece of metal, which my brother-in-law Sarnelis found near a heap of tiles behind where he had been shot. It appeared to have passed through the leg, hit the cemented basement of my house, and fell near the tile heap. My house has a tiled roof and the outer verandah floor is cemented.

"Mr. A—— and the Town Guard ordered a cart to be brought up, and immediately walked away.

"We raised the wounded men and put them into two carts, and took them to Wallipitawella Hospital (three miles from the Veyangoda Railway Station). When we arrived at the hospital at about 1 p.m. my husband and Jeris Appu were carried in. My husband died about 4 p.m., and the doctor wanted to amputate Jeris Appu's leg the next morning, but Jeris Appu would not give his consent, and he was therefore carried back to the cart early the following morning. He died about two hours after he reached home.

"The looting of the boutiques at Kaleliya took place on the 3rd June. My nusband had no hand in it at all. For two or three days previous to the 3rd June and afterwards also, he had been ill, and he told Mr. A—— that he was incapable of rioting or looting because of his feeble condition, and pulled off his shirt and showed him the state of his body. Why should he rob people? He was a well-to-do man. Mr. D. L. Wijewardane, proprietor and manager of the Desiccating and Oil Mills near Mirigama Railway Station, knows the worth and character of my husband, as he had dealings with him for many years. My husband has often bought whole crops of cocoanuts from the estates of Sir Christofel Obeyesekara and the Mahá Mudaliyár and sold them to different mill-owners."

The attitude of the authorities towards the officers and soldiers who perpetrated such atrocities.

If Police Magistrates and Superintendents of Police could perpetrate such atrocities under the name of Martial Law, which is based on justice, honour and humanity as surely as Military Law and Civil Law are based on the same principles, need we hesitate to accept the numberless stories of the people regarding the brutality of the inferior military units who were sent forth to restore order and peace? Without recounting them here, let me state the following incident, to show the attitude of the military and civil authorities towards such cases.

One day, at a gathering of officials and non-officials, the General, who was proud of his soldiers, desired to know what they thought of "my Panjábis." The answer was,—"The latest story we have heard is that the unpaid headmen of a certain group of villages were ordered to provide, each in his turn, free of cost to the military, fowls, eggs, grain, milk and other provisions to the soldiers quartered there. The headman of Gangodawilla duly executed his part, and went the following day to see how things were getting on, when it was the turn of another headman to offer the supplies. The Panjábis, being annoyed with the delay of this headman in sending provisions, seized the headman of Gangodawilla, in the presence of thousands of people who had assembled at the Village Court (*Gaṇsabáwa*), manacled him and severely lashed him, though he protested that he was not the man that was responsible for the delay. The General, much chagrined at this narrative, said, 'What could the poor fellows do, if no food was brought to them in time?'"

The incident reported to him was as true as other atrocious deeds done by them elsewhere. But the high Military and Civil officers of Government did not mind such things. They seemed to have dropped their sense of justice and human sympathy. They found excuses for lawless deeds done by themselves and their men, and hushed them up, though they were lynx-eyed, loud-tongued and vindictive in regard to lesser offences committed by the Sinhalese.

The degeneration of Military Law in Ceylon into a grinding oppression was due to the wrong conviction of most of those entrusted with power that the Sinhalese were going to massacre the British in Ceylon.

But, bad as all this violent partizanship was, what poisoned the whole system of Military Law in Ceylon and reduced it to a grinding oppression was the common belief of the authorities that there was a widespread conspiracy among the Sinhalese to kill not only the Muhammadans but also the British. It blinded the officers of the Ceylon Government. The idea of being massacred made them gnash their teeth. A Scotchman of good family and calm observant habits, Mr. Francis D. Stuart, whose mercantile avocations brought him in close and constant touch with all classes of people in Ceylon, being known to be a nephew of the late Hon. Mr. R. W. Moir, Government Agent of the Central Province, who was noted for his righteousness and sympathy with the Ceylonese, writes as follows in his letter, appearing *in extenso* in the last chapter of this book :—

" An incident occurred during my journey that I think worth while to relate, as it gives a fair idea of the sentiment prevalent among most of the Europeans at the period of which I write. I made the acquaintance in the train of an English officer who, upon hearing that I was going to Galle as a witness for the defence of a Sinhalese, expressed much astonishment, adding, ' Leave the rascals alone! The more they are got rid of the better!' He subsequently told me that he had assisted at a Court Martial in the Ratnapura District, and that it had been clearly proved that there was a conspiracy of the Sinhalese to massacre first of all the Moors, and then the Burghers, and then the Europeans; that it had been discovered just in time, and that sacks full of treasonable correspondence with a certain foreign State had been found secreted among the rafters of the bungalows occupied by the Sinhalese who had been arrested."

This was all pure fiction. No such correspondence was found in possession of the Sinhalese gentlemen arrested in Colombo or elsewhere. And yet groundless rumours and irresponsible chatter of this kind were accepted as gospel truth by the Military and Civil Officers. When they set to work with the assumption that sedition and treason were rife everywhere, and that they would be massacred if they did not look sharp and strike home, their efforts ended in oppression and gross injustice.

The Governor's remedial measures.

In his Address to the Legislative Council, the Governor further explained his policy as follows :—

" With the suppression of violence it now becomes possible to go forward with methodical and thorough measures for punishing the guilty, and for ascertaining the scope of the havoc wrought on the Muslim community.

" The special measures taken by the Officer Commanding the Troops, with my previous cognizance and full approval, were, first and foremost, to appoint Special Commissioners, whose instructions were to travel speedily through the affected localities, assessing on the spot the damage done, dealing summarily with minor offenders, and reserving the principal offenders for trial by Court Martial under the Order in Council of 1896, which the foresight of the Home Government had provided in advance for emergencies of this nature in time of war."

The Governor credits General Malcolm with the scheme that Special Commissioners were needed to assess the damages caused to the Muhammadans, to investigate the complaints brought against persons for offences, to deal summarily with minor offenders, and to reserve for trial by Court Martial the cases of the principal offenders. We are not told what the Attorney-General thought of the legality of these proposals. The Governor, having sanctioned them, was obliged to continue the Martial Law to enable the General to carry out his scheme.

The object of the Government in continuing Martial Law after the cessation of the riots.

At the first opportunity I had, I said in Council, on the 11th August, that the continuance of the terrors of Martial Law was not necessary after the cessation of the riots, and that it was not difficult to see that Martial Law was kept up for the purpose of effecting four illegal objects, namely :—

(1) To arrest alleged offenders more easily than under the formalities of the Civil Law;

(2) To try alleged offenders too summarily and punish them, without allowing such cases to go before the regular Courts of the Island, which were sitting uninterruptedly;

(3) To assess speedily the damages suffered by the Muhammadans without having to observe the safeguards of the Civil Law; and

(4) To recover compensation from the Sinhalese by methods which the ordinary laws of the Colony would not permit.

Neither the Attorney-General, nor anyone else on the official side, disowned this charge, or offered any explanation in justification of the continuance of the Martial Law after the 6th of June.

Mr. Fraser's methods of assessment and allotment followed by the other Special Commissioners in the Western Province.

Upon the General appointing the Special Commissioners, the chief of them, Mr. Fraser (the Government Agent for the Western Province), and his colleagues, Messrs. Brayne, Izat, Moore, Willet, Archibald, etc., arrived at Dompe, on the 9th of June, 1915, with a caravan of twenty motor-cars full of armed soldiers and civil officers, and informed the headmen and the people assembled there (according to the evidence before me), that he came first to Dompe because he had been told at the *kachcheri* (his office in Colombo) that the villagers at Dompe did all the damage at Walgama (which is a Moorish village situated about five miles from Dompe, near the Kaleni Ganga); that he would estimate the damages caused there, and afterwards deal with the people concerned in the disturbances. Then he caused the damages to be estimated in his own superficial way; and when the estimate was ready, he summoned before him about ten leading men from Dompe and informed them that the estimated damages amounted to Rs. 25,000; and that, if they did not pay this amount down in twenty-four hours, they would be shot. Many leading inhabitants of other villages appear also to have been similarly dealt with.

I have before me an affidavit, showing that in the case of Rassapane, *alias* Malwana, a house to house

A typical case of intimidation, ending in a fabricated charge of rioting.

search was made for looted property; that none was found in the houses of the Sinhalese; that, nevertheless, one Mr. Pedrick Perera, of Pahale Mapitigama, a very successful physician, much respected for his helpfulness to the poor, and some other leading men, were ordered to pay Rs. 15,000 at once for damages done in Malwana; that on their declining to pay that amount, they were ordered to bring and deposit title-deeds as security for that amount till payment; that they protested against this order; that, at the request of the Commissioner, his interpreter asked the Moors present whether Pedrick Perera and others standing by him were not among those who damaged and looted the boutiques, and the Moor said, "Not these men; no respectable people came there to damage or loot our property"; that the interpreter, again pointing to Pedrick Perera and the others, asked the Moors, "Were not these men along with the rioters who came to your village?"; that on the Moors saying, "Yes," Pedrick Perera was immediately arrested and not allowed on bail; that, at the preliminary investigation that followed, he was not allowed to have any communication whatever with any of his friends, so as to prove his innocence; that he was in such fear and shame that he was seized with a fit upon a Panjábi soldier dragging him by the hand; that he fainted again during the trial before the Court Martial held at Weke; that the counsel was not permitted to do his duty as in a Court of Justice; that the man was convicted and sentenced to rigorous imprisonment for life; and that that sentence was afterwards reduced to twelve years.

Mr. Pedrick Perera did not go to see the riot at all, but because some Moormen said he was "along with the rioters," he was put upon his trial before the Court Martial and condemned. If he had yielded to Mr. Fraser's order to pay the compensation he would not have been charged.

Rejection of complaints against the Muhammadans.

In the course of the inquiry at Dompe there was a serious complaint made against several Muhammadans for combining together to loot a Sinhalese village near Dompe, and one of the Special Commissioners, Mr. Archibald, who went to that village, reported to Mr. Fraser upon the damages done to the Sinhalese and to their property. This was evidently distasteful to Mr. Fraser, for Mr. Archibald was sent away from Dompe to another Province, for speaking the truth as regards the mischiefs done by the Muhammadans.

All the Special Commissioners of the Western Province learnt their lessons under their chief, Mr. Fraser, who, being in touch with the Governor, must be pleased in his own way.

How the General's desire to arrest and punish "the leaders who directed the efforts of the mob" ended in the arrest and punishment of innocent Sinhalese 'gentlemen who were possessed of money and property.

On the 11th of June, General Malcolm issued a circular inviting the attention of Special Commissioners to the importance of securing the arrest of the " ringleaders " at the recent disturbances. He said he did not desire that persons who might be proved to be present at the disturbances or to have joined generally in the looting should be arrested unless actual deeds of violence were proved against them; and he further explained that the objects to be secured were :—

(1) The arrest of the persons responsible for inflaming the passions of the mob by false reports;

(2) The arrest of the leaders who directed their efforts;

(3) The return of such of the loot as can be recovered; and

(4) The disarming of the villagers;

and he advised the Commissioners to make all this clear to the people among whom the Commissioners were working.

A gentleman, who was a passive observer of the course of proceedings at this period, says that, whatever the General meant, his executive officers certainly misinterpreted these instructions, for the Moors were made to understand that they were not to bring up the poorer class of offenders, but the moneyed men and the men with property; and the headmen were ordered to make out a list of such men, because every leading man in the village was assumed to have used his influence to attack the Moors. This was a gross misconception, which later on was freely recognised by most of the officials, from the Governor downwards, but during the period of panic the Special Commissioners understood the " leaders who directed the efforts of the mob " to be men of money and property. The Moors, who heard this interpretation, thought it their duty not to bring to justice the disreputable men who did all the looting mischief; and they turned their attention to men of money and property whom the authorities suspected of having directed the actual offenders. They had no evidence against the leading men of such complicity, but, like Ismail who was convicted by the District Judge of Kandy for extortion, they made the best of their opportunities by trying to levy blackmail upon the innocent but well-to-do Sinhalese, who, of course, laughed at their folly and audacity. The Muhammadans persisted, and went about openly from one gentleman to another because the Special Commissioners had refused to entertain any complaints against the Moors from any Sinhalese man. The river of blind partiality was running so high that the officials, steeped in it, did not see the consequences. Failing in extortion, the Muhammadans trumped up false charges, with the result that vast numbers of irreproachable Sinhalese men are now undergoing rigorous imprisonment, while others have been deprived of their lives.

The desire of some of the authorities "to level up" the men who were rising into the ranks of the middle class.

During the last five-and-twenty years the steady rise of prices for cocoanuts and copra have enabled many a Sinhalese man to rise from impecuniosity to positions of comfort and commanding influence in the villages. As the Special Commissioners thought that these men were responsible for the riots, the talk among themselves was that it was necessary to "level up the fellows." Before the expansion of trade in modern times every country had its princes and peasants only, and between the two rose the great middle class in England and other countries of the West during the last one-hundred years, forming their very backbone in regard to sound common sense, love of learning and thrift, and ambitious of office and honour. The Special Commissioners of Ceylon, in desiring to "level up the fellows" who were swelling the great middle class of Ceylon, which stood next to the highest class, consisting of those who belong to old families and have the means of keeping up their dignity, were simply endeavouring to ruin its backbone.

The carrying out of the programme without regard to principles.

In the estimate of the damages caused by the rioters, the Special Commissioners were carrying out the programme ordered without regard to principle.

It has been well said that in these strenuous days parties, caucuses, machines and wire-pullers do not much concern themselves with principles, as their business is with programmes; that principles more and more tend to receive the go-by; and that vain is the boast of being practical without being principled, for to neglect principles in any field of action is to plunge us in due course into difficulties and public miseries. This is what has come to pass in Ceylon at the hands of the Special Commissioners.

Issue of printed notices by Special Commissioners that persons not obeying the orders of the Civil and Military authorities will be shot at sight.

On the 10th of June, 1915, Mr. Fraser issued a printed notice throughout the Western Province in which he stated that, as he had been appointed by the General a Special Commissioner of the Western Province for the purpose of inquiring into the recent riots, assessing damage, and levying compensation for such damage, all persons in the said province should give every assistance to him and the other Military and Civil authorities, and that *persons not obeying orders will be shot at sight.* In my speech in the Legislative Council, which will be found in Chapter III., the full text of this notification is given. If any order of any kind given by any Military or Civil officer is disobeyed, the penalty is death.

Notification that Special Commissioners were vested with the powers of District Judges and Police Magistrates.

Following this tyrannical notice came an announcement in the *Government Gazette* by the General that all the Special Commissioners appointed by him were entrusted with the duties specified in Mr. Fraser's notification, and that they were also vested with the powers of District Judges and Police Magistrates.

These two official publications deprived the people, in five of the Provinces of Ceylon, of all their constitutional rights of freedom of thought and action, and reduced them to abject slavery. A District Judge or

Police Magistrate, if approached according to the procedure prescribed in the Civil and Criminal Procedure Codes, has power to send a man to jail for not answering questions or being contumacious in regard to their orders, or to issue warrants to search their houses or seize their persons; but as these powers were vested in the Military Commissioners appointed under the Martial Law, such powers were exercisable arbitrarily, without the safeguards of the Codes, and Mr. Fraser and many of the other Commissioners gave notice to the people that the penalty for not obeying their orders was shooting at sight.

Such officers compel the people to sign debt bonds to pay and discharge the damages caused by the rioters.

The trembling villagers were ordered to produce their title-deeds and to sign debt-bonds in favour of His Majesty the King, the debt being the amount estimated by the Commissioners, without any opportunity to the villagers to check the estimate. Most of them were the leading gentry in their respective villages, and had nothing to do with the wretched rioters, and they were asked in the presence of armed soldiers, who were known to have shot and bayoneted innocent men in many of the villages and towns, to hypothecate all their property and to deposit their title-deeds with the Commissioners in order to secure the alleged debt.

Debt bonds cover five and a-half millions of rupees.

The total amount thus secured in the five Provinces was five-and-a-half millions of rupees.

The oppressed people petition to the Legislative Council for redress.

Upon the Commissioners departing from the villages, the people petitioned the Legislative Council for the redress of their grievances. About 350 petitions from various districts were received for presentation by me and my unofficial colleagues in Council. In the meanwhile the Government had drawn up an Ordinance to confirm all the bonds which the Commissioners had extorted from the villagers, and to authorize the assessment of other villages and towns, and to recover compensation from them, upon the lines followed by the Commissioners.

The Government decline to inquire into the complaints of the people, and pass an Ordinance to confirm the bonds.

I moved in Council for the appointment of a Select Committee to consider and report upon the complaints made in the petitions, namely, that the estimate of damages made by the Commissioners was far in excess of the actual damage suffered; that the apportionment and allotment of the damage among the residents and landowners in each village was grievously unjust; that though the disturbances did not take place in the villages of many of the petitioners, and though the inhabitants thereof did not take part in the riots, yet compensation was imposed on them all; that the compensation imposed was utterly beyond their power to pay, and would ruin them altogether if attempted to be levied; that the Special Commissioners, attended each by a number of armed soldiers, intimidated the villagers, and so compelled them, while in terror of Martial Law, to produce their muniments of title to lands and to sign mortgage bonds, securing to His Majesty the King the payment of the oppressive compensation imposed on them; that the bonds signed by them in favour of their Gracious King were not voluntary; and that while the Special Commissioners called for claims for damages from the Muhammadans, and readily awarded compensation to them, no notice whatever was taken of the damages suffered by the Sinhalese (whether Buddhists or Christians) at the hands of the rioters and looters, even though such claims were pressed on them.

And I moved that until the Report of the Select

Committee upon the foregoing complaints was made, the consideration of the Compensation Bill be postponed.

The Government were wholly deaf to the array of facts and reasons which I presented to the Council in my speech delivered on 14th October, 1915, and fully reported and printed in the next chapter.

The passing of the Riot Damages Ordinance most vexatious.

The Government, having used the official majority against me and my unofficial colleagues and thrown out my Motion, proceeded to carry through the Compensation Bill. I opposed that also at its second reading in my speech which appears in full in Chapter III. Nothing would make the Government desist from the unholy course they had set their hearts upon of grinding down the people on the theory, long since abandoned by them, that the Sinhalese were disloyal and traitorous, and deserved all the horrible treatment they had been subjected to, and the equally vexatious measures of the Compensation Ordinance. The Government appeared to be dead to the declaration of Her Majesty Queen Victoria,—" It is our earnest desire to administer the Government for the benefit of all our subjects. In the prosperity of our subjects is our strength, *in their contentment is our security*, and in their gratitude is our reward;" and to the exhortation of our present Sovereign that " the task of governing will be made the easier, if we on our part infuse into it a wider element of sympathy, and to such sympathy there will be an ever abundant and genuine response."

I must now refer to the most unjustifiable arrest and incarceration of certain influential and loyal Sinhalese gentlemen without an iota of evidence against them. The statements of several of these gentlemen will be found in Chapter IV., detailing the efforts they made to send away the crowds who were coming to Colombo from distant villages and restore peace and order, and how in return for the labour of love towards the King, the Government, and the well-disposed people, they were awakened from their beds one morning and forced into the cells of convicts, and kept there for several weeks, and harassed by police officers and commissioners, and at last released without any evidence whatever being offered against them by anybody. Some of them are barristers-at-law, one a doctor of medicine, one a member of the Municipal Council of Colombo, and several wealthy estate owners and merchants: all occupying distinguished positions in Sinhalese society, and noted for public spirit, philanthropic work and unswerving loyalty to the King.

Arrest and imprisonment of influential and loyal Sinhalese gentlemen without any charge or evidence against them.

Among the many gentlemen who were thus arrested on the 21st June without any reason whatever, and kept in jail for several weeks, without any evidence forthcoming against them, was Mr. W. A. de Silva, J.P., whose friends sought the interference of Members of Parliament in England, and obtained his discharge. Upon being released, Mr. de Silva asked His Excellency the Governor whether his recent incarceration might be said in any way to reflect discredit on his conduct or reputation. He was favoured with the reply, from the Governor's Private Secretary, dated 11th September, 1915, that His Excellency gave him the assurance that his incarceration under Martial Law in no way reflected on his conduct or reputation, and further gave him permission to make this assurance public.

Such high-handed proceedings have wrung the affections of the people towards the British Government, and it is earnestly hoped that the Order of Indemnity obtained by the Governor from His Majesty's Privy Council will not be in the way of enquiring into the seizure and imprisonment of these gentlemen, and giving them the redress they are entitled to.

Trial of civilian citizens by Court Martial after the cessation of the riots.

I have already commented, at pp. 73 and 87, upon the Courts Martial, professed to be established under Queen Victoria's Order in Council of 1896, and the spirit of violent prejudice which, according to the evidence of Mr. Stuart, pervaded the hearts of many of its members during the trial of civilian citizens.

For the defence of some gentlemen charged in five cases pending before the Court Martial Mr. Eardley Norton, a distinguished barrister of the Calcutta Bar, appeared as counsel in Colombo and other places, and he has expressed himself as follows upon the proceedings held by the Court Martial. I give a few extracts only, to show how he, as a cultured Englishman of vast experience, felt during the conduct of his cases. He says:

Mr. Norton's opinion of the proceedings of Court Martial in Ceylon.

"When the Viceroy of India, Lord Hardinge, was bombed and nearly killed at Delhi, no police officer in India was heard to suggest that the wrongdoer had been guilty of treason against the representative of the King. How can the offence of rioting and injuring a person in Ceylon be elevated to the dignity of treason? Riots as turbulent are dealt with in India by the ordinary Civil jurisdiction, and nothing has occurred in Ceylon to justify the ouster of that jurisdiction and its transfer to Courts Martial which have neither the education, nor apparently the inclination, to sift, criticize and appraise complicated evidence.

" That there were serious riots in the Island is a fact. That firing by the troops and the police was necessary may be admitted *argumenti causa.* But once the disturbances were quelled and quiet restored, civic life should have been permitted to re-assert itself, and the rioters handed over for trial to men whose lives have been devoted to the administration of the Criminal Law. What happened in fact was, Martial Law was proclaimed, the Order in Council of 1896 was made applicable to the Island, and though none of the Civil Courts were closed or suspended, case after case,—involving the appreciation of conflicting testimony, the applicability of the rules of evidence, and some knowledge, and deference to, case-law and opinions of expert judges,—was withdrawn from the control of Courts competent to deal with them and transferred to Courts Martial, which neither by temperament nor training were qualified to sift and appreciate the matters laid before them.

" The Order in Council invests the Governor with the power of selecting to what tribunal, Civil or Military, each case shall be submitted. The Governor is therefore himself responsible for having sent the cases to a Court Martial. No reason has been assigned for the selection. The ordinary tribunals were and are open. Educated judges were and are sitting to try rioters. There is nothing in the evidence to discriminate these cases from the ordinary cases of riot of every day occurrence. Why then have the accused been deprived of the right to be tried by the Civil tribunals of the country and assigned to a special forum ignorant of law, uneducated in appraising and discriminating between a conflict of evidence, and impatient to rush through a hearing to the inevitable verdict of 'guilty'?

"As one instance of the mental attitude of the Court Martial, I would mention an incident which occurred at Kalutara while Mr. Elliot was replying for the second accused. Counsel was commenting on the inordinate delay that had occurred before any action had been taken against his client, and rightly quoting the view of learned judges of the evidentiary value of first information speedily laid. The President of the Court Martial delivered himself thus: 'Counsel after counsel gets up and tells us what other judges think. We don't care twopence what other judges say.'

"Remembering the question was a point of law, the disinclination to learn what the President must have been wholly innocent of affords a pregnant illustration of the danger to which the accused persons were subjected and from which they have not emerged.

"A committal to a Court Martial means a suspension of a citizen's right. There is no appeal from the verdict. Courts Martial, General or District, are accompanied by at least the forms of civil justice. A Judge Advocate is usually present to advise the Court on all points of law. The proceedings are ostensibly judicial. In the Court which tried these cases no senior lawyer supervised it's proceedings. The shorthand reporter was by special permission allowed to take down evidence for the convenience of counsel only, and one day the President annexed the notes on the ground that the reporter was exceeding his license by recording the speech of the Crown Counsel. At the first Court Martial counsel was forbidden to take a note himself. With the exception of Edmund Hewavitarane's case, there has been no record, or a very imperfect record, of what was truly said and done. Under such circumstances the careful consideration of the evidence by any supervising authority becomes an empty farce.

"It would take more than one Governor to undo the benefits resulting from the British administration of many patient years, but one Governor has it in his power—and the present Governor has exercised it—to bring British administration temporarily to horror and contempt.

"Better than any local remedy for the injury done to these persons is the one I suggested about a month ago, that some duly qualified agent should place the true facts before Parliament and the Secretary of State for the Colonies. A very long experience of India has taught me the uselessness of looking to local authority for redress against injuries caused by the local powers. They are rich in words, but poor in deeds. Their own prestige is the object nearest their hearts. Judging the Governor by what he has done in the past, I should expect little from his prescience or his courage. Both were put to the test by the recent riots, and both have broken down. I do not wish to base my views on any but the five cases in which I have been personally concerned. Judged by these, His Excellency and his advisers have been suffering from so acute an attack of treasonitis that nothing short of a complete change of venue from Ceylon to England can in any measure atone for misdeeds which it shames me as an Englishman to recall."

The "*treasonitis*" mentioned by Mr. Norton manifested itself in the charge-sheets of the Court Martial, as follows:

"The above-named accused, being persons subject to Military Law, are charged with treason, in that they did at —— and neighbouring villages on or about the —— day of June, 1915, *levy war against our Sovereign Lord the King*, contrary to Section 41 of the Army Act, 1881."

Nature of the evidence led in many of the cases tried by Court Martial.

In most of these cases the evidence led by the prosecution showed only that a crowd had gathered opposite certain private boutiques, and that the accused were there looking on, and speaking to the crowd in words of double meaning. Even if they were construed to be words of encouragement to the law-breakers, who had no guns, bayonets, or bombs, and who were avenging themselves on the community which was intolerant and aggressive to the religious procession of the Buddhists, the offence could not be said to be waging war against the King, or treason.

Vindictive sentences.

The sentences awarded in many cases were death or life-long imprisonment. Some of the gentlemen who were sentenced for life were allowed by His Excellency the Governor the option of paying a fine of *five thousand pounds sterling*, or to suffer rigorous imprisonment for twenty years.

Mr. Charles Dias and his two nephews, Messrs. Arthur and Harry Dias, each paid the commuted fine of five thousand pounds sterling, and obtained their release.

Mr. Don Cornelius Lewis, an old gentleman of over seventy years, resident at Welikade, was charged with rioting by the Inspector of the Kotte Police, but the Police Magistrate of Colombo acquitted him. Then he was re-arrested and charged before another Police Magistrate, who committed him before a District Court, which also acquitted him. When returning home after his acquittal, he was arrested on the order of Special Commissioner Brayne, taken to the Commissioner's camp at Wellampitiya, forced to enter into a bond for Rs. 5,000, and then allowed to go to his house to fetch the money. He was given the following document: Case of D. C. Lewis.

"Don Cornelius Lewis, of Welikade, is to-day giving a bond for the payment of Rs. 5,000 to the Riot Fund in five instalments of Rs. 1,000 each.

"Upon the faithful performance of the terms of this bond, and full payment of the money, Don Cornelius Lewis *hereby purchases amnesty from all further or pending criminal charges* in connection with the recent riots.

"Given this 10th day of August, 1915, at Wellampitiya.

"C. V. BRAYNE,
"Special Commissioner."

Mr. Brayne arrogates to himself the Royal prerogative of pardon, and even sells it for the sum of Rs. 5,000! The pardon is to cover all existing and future charges that may be brought against Mr. Don Cornelius Lewis!

Another Special Commissioner, Mr. J. G. Forrest, was complained against by Mr. M. Aron Fernando in his petition to Governor Chalmers as follows: Case of Aron Fernando.

"That during the late riots he was ill in bed and did not in anywise take any part in them; that after the riots, a strong rumour was current that the petitioner was going to be shot without even a trial, and as, to his own knowledge, there were several men shot without trial, he was in great fear of being shot himself; that on the 25th of June last he was ordered to come to the camp at Ruanwella, and, when he went there, he was ordered to pay Rs. 10,000. On his protesting, he was ordered to 'shut up'; that as the Special Commissioner had warned him that he had power to send the petitioner to jail, and even to shoot him, he took time and borrowed the money, and paid it on the 17th July last. A copy of the receipt obtained by the petitioner is hereto annexed for Your Excellency's information."

"Received from Aron Fernando the sum of Rupees Ten thousand in full payment of Riot damages account.

"L. BAYLEY, Major C.M.R.,
"30th July, 1915. O.C. Ruanwella."

The chief endeavour of the Special Commissioners seems to have been to collect as much money as possible from well-to-do Sinhalese gentlemen to swell the Riot Damages Fund, and if the money were not paid, the police would accuse them before the Court Martial, with the certainty of a conviction in 80 per cent. of the cases.

The petitioner addressed me on the 14th October "on the subject of the extortion of Rs.10,000 by the Commissioner J. G. Forrest from me," and said,—"I have not received any answer from the Governor regarding the refund of this amount. May I beg that you will be good enough to lay before His Majesty the King and the Secretary of State for the Colonies the circumstances of my case, so that justice may be done."

The disarming of the people, and the impossibility of protecting their produce.

I now come to the disarming of the people. On the 22nd of June, 1915, Mr. H. O. Fox, signing as "Additional Government Agent, Western Province," printed and published a "Proclamation" notifying that, in accordance with the instructions issued by the General regarding the surrender of firearms or dangerous weapons, etc., all persons other than those who belong to the European community or are entitled to bear arms as a member of a duly enrolled corps, should produce their guns, together with the licenses, to the Special Commissioners on circuit, or to the Government Agent or his assistant, or to any police officer not below the rank of Assistant Superintendent of Police; that, after the licenses have been checked, the guns might be restored, *except in the case of the Sinhalese;* and that no gun was to be restored to a Sinhalese except on the authority of the Government Agent, on his being satisfied that such person might be allowed to keep firearms."

The guns belonging to the Sinhalese, on being collected, were broken to pieces, and thrown into the deep sea far from the harbour of Colombo.

Most of the Sinhalese own and cultivate lands, and for the purpose of protecting their produce in the rural districts, they require guns to keep off birds and beasts, as well as thieves. The deprivation of the Sinhalese of their guns has caused them no end of trouble in the protection of their property.

The levies of compensation and other charges made on them have stood in the way of their buying new guns which, though muzzle-loaders, cost about Rs. 25 each. The Government ought to restore to each owner his gun, or the value of the same.

Unjust dishonour of loyal public servants.

The unjust dishonour of the public servants of the Sinhalese community has been the subject of much comment and dissatisfaction in Ceylon. I would refer to one or two typical cases.

The case of Hulugalle Adigár.

Mr. S. N. W. Hulugalle is a most respected member of the Kandyan Sinhalese community. He began service in 1868, was appointed Ratemahatmaya in 1875, was chosen to represent the Kandyan Sinhalese in the Legislative Council in 1900, and retired from that seat in 1907. In 1903 the rank of Dissáwe was conferred on him, and the still higher rank of Adigár in 1906, while holding the office of Ratemahatmaya, from which he retired in 1913, owing to ill-health and old age. Having served the Government for forty-seven years loyally and efficiently, he was held in the highest esteem by his countrymen.

Soon after the riots ceased, the Government Agent for the North-Western Province requested Adigár Hulugalle to immediately explain why he left the district on or about the 2nd June, and made no attempt to assist the present Ratemahatmaya in keeping order, or to communicate with him (the Government Agent) as to the offer of his services.

The Adigár explained that, when he left Hulugalla on the 30th of May there was not the slightest indication of any disturbance there; that as he had retired from the Government service, and was suffering from the infirmities of old age, no one had requested his aid; that having received an invitation to a wedding at Balapitiya in the Southern Province, he visited, on the way, Mr. Charles de Soysa, at Moratuwa, and attended the wedding on the 1st June; that he signed the marriage register as a witness, returned with Mr. Charles de Soysa to Moratuwa on the 2nd, and proceeded on the 3rd to his daughter's residence at Vanduragala; that he remained with his daughter till the 13th instant, met the Government Agent on that day, and, in response to his wishes, remained at Maho to help the Ratemahatmaya in preparing returns connected with the riots; and that after that work was over, he went to his daughter at Vanduragala on the 17th June, as her time of parturition required his presence there.

The Government Agent, by his letter of 4th September, 1915, informed him that, as he was absent from the scene of the riots in the Kurnegalle District between the 1st and 13th June, and had failed to assist in suppressing the disturbances, His Excellency the Governor had decided to deprive him of the rank of Adigár. A notification to that effect appeared in the *Government Gazette.*

Mr. Hulugalle fell a victim to the utterly groundless theory that he was a conspirator with the rioters. Did he leave the district for a fortnight for the purpose of denying to the rioters the pleasure of his presence at the scene of the riots? The Government and its Agent had no eyes to see the absurdity of the suggestion nor the completeness of the reason assigned by Mr. Hulugalle for his absence. He left the district upon an invitation to a marriage fixed months before, was present at it, and signed the marriage register, and stayed at his daughter's house during her confinement, and readily responded to the call of the Government Agent to go and help the Ratemahatmaya in making up the papers connected with the riots. In the face of this complete explanation, and of the fact that a man close upon seventy years of age, and made more infirm by illness, could not go amongst a band of ruffians and take an active part in the quelling of their disturbances, he was deprived of the great rank which he had earned as a just reward for his life-long devotion to the King and the Government. What confidence can the people have in Government Agents or Governors who are prepared to depart from justice and righteous judgment without the least concern for truth?

The case of Magistrate Herat.

The case of Mr. P. B. Herat, of the Ceylon Civil Service, is also worth mentioning. He was the Police Magistrate of Avisawella, and as such had much to do with the rioters and the Police.

One Mr. Gunawardane, who was the *Vidáne Áráchchi* (rural police officer) of Kaluaggala, being charged before a Court Martial with treason and riotously damaging a mosque, some Muhammadan witnesses for the prosecution swore that he came in a motor-car, and gave to the second accused a parcel wrapped in a paper, and went away, and that the second accused distributed the contents of it to some persons in the crowd, who bored holes, and that thereupon some explosions were heard and a mosque was injured. The suggestion was that the first accused handed a packet of dynamite. He denied this *in toto*, and narrated how he was occupied throughout that day in the work of suppressing the riots. He cited Magistrate Herat and other witnesses to prove his innocence.

The Court Martial rejected the evidence for the defence and found all the four accused guilty, and sentenced them to death. Subsequently, the Governor, upon further enquiry, commuted the death sentences on the second, third and fourth accused to rigorous imprisonment, *released the first accused*, and directed the prosecution of the four Muhammadans who gave evidence against them for perjury.

But before this remarkable reversal of the case for the prosecution happened, the Government Agent for the Western Province reported to the Governor, on 7th of July, 1915, that all the damage done by the rioters at Puwakpitiya, Avisawella, Talduwa and Nápagama, amounting to Rs. 50,000, was, in his opinion, due to Mr. Herat not dispersing by a timely use of force by the Volunteers and Police, the crowd who caused the damage. Mr. Fraser added, "His constant associations on these days with Proctor de Mel, who is proved to have attended meetings held by Jayatilaka, and such like people, is suspicious."

But Mr. de Mel is the leading lawyer in the district, commanding a great influence over the people by reason of his high character, independence and proficiency in Sinhalese. Mr. Herat explained that there was no other gentleman in the district so powerful for good as he to confer with, and to help him, who was a stranger in Avisawella and carried no weight with the people except that of a Magistrate; and Mr. Jayatilaka is a distinguished Barrister practising in Colombo, whom the Mayor of Colombo had chosen to go and address the people who were coming from Avisawella to Colombo, *via* Hanwella, for the purpose of helping their fellow-religionists, who were reported to be in fear of massacre by the Muhammadans.

Mr. Herat explained to the Government how he did his very best to pacify the rioters, and how impossible it was with only five armed constables to oppose a crowd of over a thousand persons, whose passions were aroused against the Muhammadans on account of their intolerance and aggression. He said that, if he had ordered the five men to fire on the crowd, they would have clubbed them to death before they could reload their guns. He explained that, to avoid useless provocation and irritation he asked them to put away their guns, and did not think it advisable to let the European planters, who had enlisted as Volunteers, to use their guns; that in doing so, he followed the example of the Police Officers in Colombo; and that Mr. Jackson, the officer in command of the European Volunteers at Avisawella, agreed with him, that, as there was no disturbances at Avisawella that night, and no crowd present, it was not necessary to make a display of armed force.

He further explained that he ordered the release of certain men, who had been arrested as rioters, because he found that the Police could not possibly keep the rioters in confinement without drawing upon themselves the danger of being attacked and done to death by the crowd, and without the police station itself being wrecked. In this order of release, too, he was following the example of the Colombo

Police, as reported in that very morning's newspapers which he had read.

On the 9th of October, 1915, the Colonial Secretary wrote to Mr. Herat as follows :—

" I am directed to state that the Governor in Executive Council has carefully considered the evidence and charges against you, your reply thereto, and the report of the Committee of the Executive Council before which you were examined.

" His Excellency regrets that he has been compelled to come to the conclusion that you have shown yourself to be unfitted for Government appointment, and that it is, therefore, impossible to retain you in the public service.

" In these circumstances he is prepared to accept your resignation, if tendered within seven days. In the event of your not taking advantage of the opportunity now offered to you, it would be necessary to take other steps to terminate your employment under Government."

Mr. Herat tendered his resignation without prejudice to his cause, and begged for a copy of the report of the Committee of Inquiry of the Executive Council, which the Government however refused to give.

If the conduct of Mr. Herat deserved the forfeit of his office on the ground that he could have prevented, by the timely use of force by the Volunteers and Police, the damage done by the rioters in the Avisawella District, why has not the Government meted out the same punishment to Mr. Fraser and his Assistant Agents, and to other Police Magistrates, and the Inspector-General of Police, for not dispersing the crowds in other places by timely using the methods prescribed in the eighth chapter of the Criminal Procedure Code?

Abuse of the Censorship of the press and private letters and telegrams which do not relate to the war.

A few words are necessary regarding the abuse of the Censorship of the press and private letters and telegrams, which came into operation after the declaration of war with Germany and Austria in August, 1914.

Ten months after the outbreak of war, the riots in Kandy and other places happened during one week. The Censor appointed by the Government took care to keep out of the press every statement of the reporters containing descriptions of events that showed the inefficiency of the Police or the bungling of the Government Officers; so much so that the editors of newspapers and other journals in England complained of the unnatural excision of many important and relevant parts of the story of the riots.

How many private letters were opened and how many telephone messages were "tapped" by order of the Censor in various post and telephone offices, one cannot tell; nor, if told, could they be remedied. But what shall we say of the refusal of the Government to forward telegrams to the Secretary of State, complaining bitterly of the doings of the Ceylon Government against the people?

On the 25th of September last, nearly a month after the termination of Martial Law, the leaders of the people held a great public meeting to memorialize the Secretary of State in regard to their grievances suffered at the hands of the Government Officers appointed under the Martial Law. The Chairman of the meeting, Mr. James Peiris, M.A., Barrister-at-law, desiring to forward a telegram to the Secretary of State, apprising him of the resolution passed at the meeting, and begging him to defer action until the memorial of the public meeting reached his hands, forwarded to the Colonial Secretary at Colombo, under cover of a letter dated 1st October, a telegram with a sum of Rs. 100, and requested him to have it forwarded to the Secretary of State. The Colonial Secretary, by his letter dated 6th October, replied as follows :—

The Governor's refusal to forward a telegram from the people to the Secretary of State.

" I am directed by His Excellency the Governor to state that the telegram forwarded with your letter cannot be transmitted to the Secretary of State for the Colonies.

" The sum of Rs. 100 sent by you to meet the cost of the telegram is herewith returned."

By what authority did the Governor keep back from the Secretary of State the telegram of the Chairman of the public meeting, which complained bitterly of the acts of Government officers and begged for immediate redress? Is it right on the part of the Government to harass and oppress the people and then to gag their mouths which cried to the King and his Minister for help? Any power that a Governor may have under the Postal and Telegraph Ordinance to stop a letter or telegram, cannot surely be used for the selfish purpose of screening the Government from its own iniquity.

Hearing of this high-handed proceeding, and feeling that the time had come for my going to England and personally representing to the Secretary of State the case of my electorate and the people of Ceylon in general, I handed in at the chief telegraph office in Colombo the following telegram on the 27th of October, at one p.m.

"From P. Rámanáthan to Rt. Hon. Bonar Law, London.

"Referring ordinance providing compensation for losses by rioters which validates bonds signed before Military Commissioners, I moved fourteenth instant for appointment of Select Committee to consider complaints contained in three hundred petitions presented to Council, and for postponement of second reading until report is tabled. Complaints are Commissioners' assessments and apportionments violate your statements in Parliament, and bonds taken were forced, by threats to shoot and imprison, in presence of armed soldiers. My motion strongly supported was defeated, and ordinance hurriedly passed same night, to dismay of people. Pray defer action, until I personally submit people's awful grievances with documents. I am starting immediately French mail steamer *Paul Lecat*. Arriving London eighteenth."

I also paid the cost of this telegram. The Censor seemed to be very much upset by the contents, and would not let me know even at six p.m.—five hours after it was handed in—whether he had despatched it or not. Speaking through the telephone, he said, in reply to my questions, that he was not at liberty to say "yes" or "no" to my questions, nor under what law he assumed this attitude of withholding the information which I, as the sender, ought to have; nor, in the absence of any law, whether or not he had any orders from the Governor to delay, or not to despatch, the telegram.

The Governor in Executive Council has power under Ordinance No. 35 of 1908, Section 5, when a public emergency arises, to order a telegraphic message to be intercepted, detained, or not be transmitted. I felt that there was nothing but selfish emergency to support the possibility of the Censor not transmitting the telegram, and my electorate was put to the trouble and expense of sending a gentleman to Madras (in India) to forward a similar telegram to a friend in London to apprise the Secretary of State that I was coming to see him, and that he should defer action till then.

The temper of many of the Government Officers is to give trouble to the people, when it is possible to do so. They seem to think that the power vested in their hands by the King may be used, not to protect, and produce contentment in, the people, but to vex them and to show off their own greatness.

Government circular regarding grants-in-aid to registered schools.

Another source of annoyance and heart-burning has come to the people by the recent order of the Government, conveyed through a circular issued by the Director of Education, as regards grants-in-aid to registered schools.

The circular states that no school, of which the proprietor, manager or teacher has taken part in any social or political movement directed against the Government, or tending to create any animosity between different sections of the community, shall receive any grant-in-aid.

The revenue of Ceylon has been appropriated by Government to not only useful undertakings, but also to works that are not immediately necessary or useful; and the pressure upon the revenue recently has been so great that various proposals of taxation have been made and carried out. Retrenchment has already been practised in almost every department of the State, and further retrenchment being necessary to make both ends meet, an excuse seems to have now been found in the affair between the Buddhists and the Muhammadans, to withhold the payment of the votes sanctioned by the Legislative Council for the payment of the usual grants-in-aid. The Director of Education is requested, when he comes to the payment of grants-in-aid, to see whether the proprietor, manager or teacher of any school which has earned the grant, has taken part in any social or political movement directed against the Government, or done something to create animosity between different sections of the community. It has been already shown that there never was in Ceylon any social or political movement against the Government. Everyone is entitled to criticise Government measures, and those who formed themselves into Associations may also do so. What, then, is the meaning of the words that any school of which the proprietor, etc., has taken part in any social or political movement directed against the Government, shall not receive a Government grant? Both Buddhists and Christians as proprietors, managers and teachers, have found it necessary to speak and write against the Government constitutionally. Surely it cannot be intended in such cases to deprive a school, in which they have an interest, of its lawfully-earned grant? Why should the Director of Education be charged with the duty of deciding upon this subtle question, which even trained judges may not find it easy to adjudicate upon; and why should he break the peace which now reigns in the educational world by going into the circumstances necessary for the creation of animosity between the sections of the people? It is not desirable to keep the pot of trouble boiling continuously.

If discontent is forcibly produced in the hearts of teachers, the work of governing the country will certainly become more difficult than it is. I hope the circular will be withdrawn. The denial of the grant is an infliction on innocent schoolboys, because by withholding it many a school will have to be closed.

I have only one other matter left to touch upon, and that is the Order of Indemnity obtained by the Governor from His Majesty.

The Order of Indemnity obtained by the Governor from the King in His Privy Council, without going to the Legislative Council of Ceylon first.

Without informing the Legislative Council of his intention to beg the King for an Indemnity Order, and showing no reason whatever for not introducing in the Legislative Council a bill to indemnify the acts, matters and things done while Martial Law was in force, the Governor, preparatory to withdrawing Martial Law in Ceylon, as he did on the 30th of August, obtained through the Secretary of State His Majesty's Order of Indemnity on the 12th of August, 1915.

Had the Governor submitted a bill of indemnity to the consideration of the Legislative Council, a discussion would have followed on the propriety of the Governor proclaiming Martial Law in Ceylon, and on the other measures he devised for the protection of life and property in the Island, during the three months ended 30th August last; but he avoided the possibility of such a useful discussion in the interest of good government, by quietly moving the Colonial Office authorities.

In the preamble of His Majesty's Order, His Majesty the King casts the responsibility of the proclamation of Martial Law upon the Governor himself, and states that it is desirable to withdraw it, and to indemnify the acts ordered and done in good faith while Martial Law was in force. The scrutiny of the Legislative Council established by the King for its sound administration has been avoided by the Governor in a way that is not to be commended. But his responsibility is not over. The beguiled Secretary of State has yet to see that justice is done to the Sinhalese.

The remedies needed are :

1. An enquiry into the affairs of Ceylon consequent upon the riots of 1915.

2. The repeal of the Compensation Ordinance, and the refunding of the moneys extorted from the people.

3. The release of the prisoners convicted upon perjured testimony.

4. The withdrawal of the Government Circular regarding grants-in-aid to schools whose proprietors, managers, or teachers have criticised the acts of the Government; and

5. The punishment of Government Officers who have oppressed the people.

---

*Governor's Proclamation terminating Martial Law.*

In the Name of His Majesty George the Fifth, of the United Kingdom of Great Britain and Ireland and of the British Dominions beyond the Seas, King, Defender of the Faith.

PROCLAMATION.

By His Excellency Sir Robert Chalmers, Knight Commander of the Most Honourable Order of the

Bath, Governor and Commander-in-Chief in and over the Island of Ceylon, with the Dependencies thereof.

ROBERT CHALMERS.

Know Ye that We, the Governor of Ceylon, do proclaim as follows :—

Martial Law is hereby terminated in the Colony from and after 12 o'clock midnight of the Thirtieth day of August, 1915.

Given at Colombo, in the said Island of Ceylon, this Thirtieth day of August, in the year of our Lord one thousand nine hundred and fifteen.

By His Excellency's command,

R. E. STUBBS,
Colonial Secretary.

*Governor's Proclamation publishing the Order of Indemnity of H.M. the King in Council.*

IN the Name of His Majesty George the Fifth, of the United Kingdom of Great Britain and Ireland and of the British Dominions beyond the Seas, King, Defender of the Faith.

PROCLAMATION.

By His Excellency Sir Robert Chalmers, Knight Commander of the Most Honourable Order of the Bath, Governor and Commander-in-Chief in and over the Island of Ceylon, with the Dependencies thereof.

ROBERT CHALMERS.

Know Ye that We, the Governor of Ceylon, do hereby proclaim and publish the Order of His Majesty the King in Council, of the 12th day of August, 1915, set out in the schedule to this Proclamation.

And We do hereby notify that the same is in force in the Colony from and after 12 o'clock midnight of the Thirtieth day of August, 1915, and do call upon His Majesty's loyal subjects and all other persons being in the said Colony to govern themselves accordingly.

Given at Colombo, in the said Island of Ceylon, this Thirtieth day of August, in the year of our Lord one thousand nine hundred and fifteen.

By His Excellency's command,

R. E. STUBBS,
Colonial Secretary.

GOD SAVE THE KING.

*The Order of Indemnity of His Majesty the King made by and with the advice of His Privy Council.*

## SCHEDULE TO THE PROCLAMATION.

AT THE COURT OF BUCKINGHAM PALACE, THE 12TH DAY OF AUGUST, 1915.

*Present,*

THE KING'S MOST EXCELLENT MAJESTY,
Lord President, Lord Stamfordham, Sir G. Fleetwood Wilson.

WHEREAS His Majesty has power to make laws for the peace, order and good government of the Colony of Ceylon (in this Order referred to as "the Colony"):

And whereas it has been found necessary by the

Governor of Ceylon to proclaim that certain Provinces of the Colony shall be subject to martial law for the time being :

And whereas it is desirable to withdraw martial law from the Provinces in which it has been proclaimed and to indemnify acts, matters, and things in good faith advised, commanded, ordered, directed or done while martial law was in force :

Now, therefore, His Majesty, by virtue of all powers vested in Him in that behalf, is pleased, by and with the advice of His Privy Council, to order, and it is hereby ordered, as follows :—

1. No action, prosecution or legal proceeding whatsoever shall be brought, instituted, or maintained against the Governor of Ceylon, or the person for the time being or at any time commanding the troops in the Colony, or against any person or persons acting under them or any of them respectively in any command or capacity civil or military, or in pursuance of any orders general or special given by them or any of them in that behalf, for or on account of or in respect of any acts, matters, or things whatsoever in good faith advised, commanded, ordered, directed or done for the maintenance of good order and government or for the public safety of the Colony between the date of the commencement of martial law and the date of the taking effect of this Order.

2. Every such person aforesaid by whom any such act, matter, or thing shall have been advised, commanded, ordered, directed or done for the purposes aforesaid shall be freed, acquitted, discharged, released and indemnified against all and every person and persons whomsoever in respect thereof.

3. Every such act, matter, or thing referred to in the preceding articles shall be presumed to have been advised, commanded, ordered, directed or done as the case may be in good faith until the contrary shall have been proved by the party complaining.

4. The several sentences and orders pronounced by military courts held in the Colony during the continuance of martial law are hereby confirmed, and all persons tried by such courts and confined in any prisons or other legal places of confinement in the Colony under or by virtue of such sentences shall continue liable to be confined there or elsewhere as the Governor may direct until the expiration of the sentences respectively passed upon them or until their discharge by lawful authority; and such sentences shall be deemed to be sentences passed by duly and legally constituted Courts of the Colony and shall be carried out or otherwise dealt with in the same manner as the sentences of duly constituted Courts of Law of the Colony and shall be carried out or otherwise dealt with in the same manner as the sentences of duly constituted Courts of Law of the Colony.

5. All persons who have been in good faith under proper military or police authority arrested or detained during the existence of martial law shall be deemed to have been lawfully arrested or detained.

6. Every bond taken during the existence of martial law upon which any person so arrested or detained has been admitted to bail shall be and is hereby declared to be of full force and effect.

7. Every bond executed during the existence of martial law for the payment of any contribution in respect of damages caused by mobs or any expenses

incidental to or consequent upon such damages shall be and is hereby declared to be of full force and effect.

8. This Order may be cited for all purposes as "The Ceylon Indemnity Order in Council, 1915," and shall come into operation and take effect upon the date on which martial law shall be terminated in the Colony by Proclamation of the Governor of Ceylon.

ALMERIC FITZ ROY.

# CHAPTER III.

## SPEECHES DELIVERED BY MR. RAMANATHAN IN THE LEGISLATIVE COUNCIL OF CEYLON ON THE ILL-CONSIDERED MEASURES OF THE GOVERNMENT OF CEYLON, AND THE OPPRESSIVE CONDUCT OF ITS OFFICERS.

## (1) *Mr. Rámanáthan's Speech on the Failure of the Police to control the Riots. Delivered in the Legislative Council of Ceylon on August* 11, 1915.

The present strength of the Police in the City of Colombo, insufficient.

The Hon. Mr. Rámanáthan (the Ceylonese Member) :—At the Finance Committee meeting, Sir, we had the assistance of the Inspector-General of Police in regard to the administration of his Department, and the information that we were able to gather from him showed that that Department requires a good deal of strengthening at Your Excellency's hands as early as possible. I find, Sir, that as regards Colombo, there are, or ought to be, three Assistant Superintendents of Police. One of them is told off to the Northern Division of Colombo, the centre of which is the Fort, and then there are the Harbour Station and the Pettah Station. The Harbour Station is in charge of an Inspector with 30 constables; the Fort Station is in charge of an Inspector with 60 constables; and the Pettah Station is in charge of an Inspector with 90 constables. Thus the Northern Division of Colombo is in charge of an Assistant Superintendent of Police, with 3 Inspectors and 230 constables.

Then the Central Division is worked from Maradana Headquarters, and in Maradana there is an Inspector and 80 constables. Kotahena has an Inspector with 50 constables; Grandpass has an Inspector with 45 constables; and Modera has an

Inspector with 50 constables. So that the Central Division, under one Assistant Superintendent, has 4 Inspectors with 225 constables.

Then in the Southern Division there is the Cinnamon Gardens Station with an Inspector and 40 constables; Colpetty with an Inspector and 40 constables; Wellawatta with an Inspector and 60 constables; Borella with an Inspector and 25 constables; Dematagoda with an Inspector and 40 constables; and Slave Island with an Inspector and 40 constables. The Southern Division has thus 6 Inspectors and 290 constables.

The total number of constables for the city of Colombo is thus 674.

Neither officers nor constables sufficient.

The Inspector-General of Police says that the number of police is insufficient for protecting the city from troubles like the one that arose recently, and he does not think that there are sufficient officers to direct the force in Ceylon. He thinks that there ought to be three more Assistant Superintendents. However that may be, Sir, I find that three out of the existing fifteen Assistant Superintendents were drafted into the Army for service at the front in the months of March, April, and May, and I understood the Inspector-General of Police to say that he informed Government at the time that he could spare the three Assistant Superintendents, but when the disturbances arose he found that he could not possibly get on without them, and so he wrote to Government, after the occurrence of the disturbances, about the desirability of furnishing the Department with the full staff of officers.

Now, out of a total of fifteen Assistant Superintendents in the whole Department, the war took away three, and therefore twelve were left. Of these, three were in Colombo. One of them had to be sent to Kandy, one to Ragama in connection with the deported prisoners, and a third was sick; so that, at the time of the rioting, only one Superintendent was in Colombo, and that was Mr. Daniel. Furthermore, Sir, in addition to the depletion of the staff of Assistant Superintendents in this manner, we find that 180 constables, out of the 674 that ought to have remained in Colombo, were sent to Kandy; and the Inspector-General of Police himself, owing to a message received from Kandy on the night of May 29—that is to say, the day following Wesak Day—was obliged to proceed with some soldiers to Kandy by a special train at 11 o'clock at night, reaching there on the 30th at 3 in the morning. I suppose he was quite busy there, notwithstanding that there was a superior officer with a number of constables. Colombo was thus left to take care of itself. I feel certain, Sir, that, if the Inspector-General of Police had been in Colombo on May 31 and June 1, instead of going away to Kandy, and if the three Assistant Superintendents were all in their places in Colombo, the trouble that arose in the city would have been easily quelled, and all the subsequent painful events would not have taken place.

At the time of the disturbances in Colombo there was only one Superintendent of Police, and no Assistant - Superintendents at all; though there ought to have been three;

and the Inspector-General of Police was absent in Kandy.

Owing to absence of supervising officers and to 180 constables being sent away to Kandy out of the 674, the disturbances in Colombo could not be controlled by the Police.

Now, Sir, there is no reason whatever for supposing that the riots were due to a conspiracy between the upper and lower classes of the Buddhists against the Muhammadans or the Government. It is admitted that the police, though drawn from all classes of people, viz., Sinhalese, Tamils, Malays, Muhammadans, Burghers, and others, never expected a rising on the part of the Buddhists, and never heard at any

No evidence whatever that riots were due to a conspiracy between the upper and lower classes of the Buddhists against the Muhammadans or the Government.

time that there was going to be a disturbance either in Colombo or anywhere else; and it is equally certain that, when a collision took place between the Sinhalese and the Muhammadans, the police officers in Colombo lost their heads, as did the constables on the several beats, and that this failure of the police gave an opportunity to the criminal classes and to the hungry poor to rise in different places and do just what they liked with the city. If the commanding officers of the police had remained in the city, and properly marshalled the police force against the rioters and looters, the disturbance would have been nipped in the bud, and the after consequences would not have been so serious. There would have been no necessity for compensation and no necessity for the introduction of martial law, or the establishment of Courts Martial, or the appointment of Commissioners, and so on.

The failure of the Police enabled the criminal classes and the hungry poor to loot.

I wish to know, Sir, whether the Government have taken this subject into their consideration, with a view to placing the protection of the city on a more satisfactory basis. The disturbances which we all deplore are due undoubtedly to the failure of the police, both in Kandy and Colombo, at the critical moment, and the failure of the Police Magistrates and other authorities to call out the military to disperse the rioters and looters under the provisions of the Criminal Procedure Code. I have much to say on the subject, but for the present I shall dwell on the duty of the Government to see that no such failure will occur ever hereafter.

The neglect of the Police Magistrates and other Authorities to disperse the crowd by the methods prescribed in the Criminal Procedure Code, also caused the disturbances to spread quickly.

I remember, Sir, some thirty-five years ago, speaking to Sir Arthur Gordon, when there was an alarming collision between the Roman Catholics and the Buddhists. The city of Colombo was fearfu' to behold.

The streets were deserted and there was no traffic whatever, not by any order of the police or of the military, but for reasons of personal protection all passenger and carriage traffic suspended itself as a matter of course. Many gentlemen of importance, both British and Ceylonese, asked me to see the Governor as to the desirability of calling out the military. I went to him at Queen's House, and he told me that as things stood then he could not possibly direct the military to deal with the situation. He said the Inspector-General of Police had never reported to him that the police was insufficient for protecting the city, and that if the Inspector-General of Police had made any such report it would have been his duty, even in those days of retrenchment, when the Government was trying to make both ends meet, to find funds for the rehabilitation of the police. He said that no report regarding the strength of the police had reached his hands, and that even at that crisis the Inspector-General of Police had not represented the inadequacy of the police. His Excellency further said that if the Inspector-General had made any such representation, he would have asked him why he did not make the report earlier, and would have held him personally responsible for the disturbances and the consequences arising from them. He said that the question of interposing military force rested on principle. The calling out of the military depended upon a demand on the part of the Inspector-General of Police for military assistance. If such assistance was not demanded, it was not his duty as Governor of the Island to ask the military to go forth and suppress the rioters by gun and bayonet.

The duty of the Inspector-General of Police to represent to the Government in due time the inadequacy of the Police.

Governor Gordon's opinion as to the conditions under which the military may be called out to suppress riots.

The present Inspector-General of Police says that

674 constables in the city are sufficient for all purposes, but we know, as a matter of fact, that when disturbances take place both inside and outside the city that number will not do. I desire to know whether Your Excellency's attention has been called to the present inadequate and inefficient state of the police, and what measures are being taken to prevent occurrences of this kind by putting the Police Force on a better basis.

His Excellency the Governor (noticing the Hon. the European Urban Member about to rise) :—Mr. Harry Creasy.

The Hon. the European Urban Member :—I will speak after the Hon. the Colonial Secretary, Sir.

His Excellency the Governor :—If it is on this item, I think it would be convenient if you spoke now.

Mr. Creasy's opinion of the inefficiency and supineness of the Police.

The Hon. Mr. H. Creasy (the European Urban Member) :—Before passing this vote of a million odd rupees, I wish to endorse in a very great measure all that has fallen from the Hon. the Ceylonese Member. This town of Colombo in the early days of June was exposed to the violence of the mob and the lowest class of persons in Colombo and round about. The lives and property of the inhabitants were at the mercy of this mob, and had it not been for the local Volunteer Force, I believe that the damage would have been serious, and possibly great loss of life would have occurred. At the meeting of the Finance Committee the Inspector-General was present, and he told us that he had a sufficient force of police in Colombo for ordinary purposes to maintain order, but that if people come in from outside the force at his disposal is insufficient. Sir, if Colombo was fortified all round, or was situated several miles out at sea, that might have been a sufficient protection for us and satisfied public opinion, but as Colombo is surrounded by the other parts of the Island where all these persons live who are likely to create disturbances, I do not think that it is a sufficient protection to the inhabitants of this city to limit the force to a number sufficient to put down a riot or disturbance among the inhabitants of the town itself.

Constables not armed, but allowed to go about with truncheons only, while looting and rioting were taking place all around them.

We further learnt from the Inspector-General, as already stated by the Hon. the Ceylonese Member, that the police were left under the command of three junior officers. On June 1 the police constables were parading the town with only truncheons, whilst looting and rioting and murder were taking place all around them. Now, Sir, had a senior officer been present, I feel no doubt in my own mind that he would have directed the constables to be armed with ball cartridges and to have acted energetically against the mob, using their rifles if necessary. I attribute the riots and the loss of life and property to the fact that the constables on duty were armed simply with truncheons. I happened to be on guard myself at one of the streets, and I asked the constables why they did not disperse the people who were loafing about the streets—perfect strangers—and they said they had no instructions, and could do nothing. I think, Sir, that such a state of things ought not to have been allowed. It is a reflection on the Government and on those concerned in the maintenance of order, and before this vote is passed I wish to impress upon the Government the necessity of maintaining a sufficient force to preserve order in a similar emergency. As I mentioned to the

Constables not armed for want of a Senior Officer in Colombo to give the order.

Supineness of the Police encouraged disorder.

Inspector-General of Police, after the riots referred to by the Hon. the Ceylonese Member, a special force of Malays was formed—a body of specially trained men—for the purpose of putting down any sudden riot or disturbance which might be too much for the ordinary police, and that force was to my certain knowledge maintained for a considerable time, but was finally disbanded. I was glad to hear from the Inspector-General of Police that it is in contemplation to constitute again some such force for special emergencies.

## (2) Mr. *Rámanáthan's Speech at the Second Reading of the Criminal Procedure Code Amendment Ordinance, providing for the Establishment of a Special Tribunal to try certain classes of cases. Delivered in the Legislative Council of Ceylon on August* 11, 1915.

Memorialists prayed for a Special Tribunal in the hope that Courts Martial would be closed.

The Hon. Mr. Rámanáthan (the Ceylonese Member) :—In introducing this Bill the Hon. the Attorney-General said that a desire had been expressed in many quarters that a special tribunal should be constituted for dealing with the cases that are now being tried by Courts Martial, and that the Government had come to the conclusion that the time had arrived to give effect to that desire. Certain leading gentlemen in Colombo, I know, petitioned Your Excellency for a special tribunal only because, a week earlier—on June 28—the Attorney-General had declared in the hall of the Supreme Court that the Government was then not willing to put an end to the operation of the martial law proclaimed on June 2. Terrified by the abnormal procedure peculiar to Courts Martial, the memorialists prayed for a special tribunal to dispose of all the cases remaining untried by such courts.

The memorialists, Sir, are deeply thankful to Your Excellency for considering their suggestion and taking measures to give effect to their wishes; but unfortunately the present Bill goes far beyond their wishes, for they did not intend the continuance of Courts Martial, or their working concurrently with the Supreme Court and a special tribunal. Nor did they intend that the jurisdiction of the special tribunal should be confined to cases of sedition, and to such cases as it may please Your Excellency to place before the special tribunal. Nor did they intend the continuance of the special tribunal beyond, perhaps, a period of two or three months. Nor did they pray for enhanced punishment.

I was glad to hear the Attorney-General say, Sir, that he would simplify the procedure of the Bill by taking the Ceylon law as it stands.

The Hon. the Attorney-General :—I said with regard to offences committed before the passing of the Ordinance. I was not referring to the general principle.

The Hon. the Ceylonese Member :—It is a small modification, but certainly the memorialists did not ask for enhanced punishment or for the introduction of the English law on the subject. The continuance, Sir, of the terrors of martial law was not necessary after June 10, but I believe it was kept up by the Government, firstly, for the purpose of arresting alleged offenders more easily on the complaint of the unfortunate Moslems than under the formalities and safeguards of the civil law; secondly, for trying alleged offenders summarily and punishing them heavily, notwithstanding the regular and unimpeded sitting of the ordinary courts of the Island; thirdly, for assessing speedily the damages suffered by the Moslems; and fourthly, for recovering compensation from the Sinhalese by methods which the ordinary law of the Colony would not permit.

Why the Government kept up Martial Law after the suppression of the riots.

To effect four illegal objects.

The Attorney-General said that one of the causes of the recent disturbances was the outbreak of sedition in this country. He meant, of course, amongst the Sinhalese. I know the Sinhalese intimately; I have known them all my life, and I have no hesitation in saying that they are remarkably free from seditious libels, seditious conspiracies, and seditious meetings.

The Attorney-General's error in supposing that the disturbances were due to sedition.

By sedition is meant an attempt to disturb the peace of the State by stirring up ill-feeling among the King's subjects, and according to English law, which the Bill seeks to introduce here, the term "sedition" includes, not only seditious libels, seditious conspiracies, seditious meetings, but also seditious attempts to urge others to the crime of treason, which is an attack on the sovereign State, or the King, Queen, or their heir, or the levying of war against the King in his realm, or the killing of his Chancellor, Treasurer, or Justices, or the forging of the Great Seal or Privy Seal. Accordingly, great writers on English criminal law have said that sedition is a far-reaching term in England, and includes offences ranging from libel to treason.

Meaning of sedition.

It is noteworthy, Sir, that in England sedition does not carry rigorous imprisonment. In Ceylon it is punishable with simple imprisonment with or without a fine. Now, why is that? A great deal has been spoken of sedition here as if it was a most dreadful offence, but is it really so? We can determine its real dimension or size by reference to the punishment which the Legislature not only of this country but also of England, India, and other places imposes for this offence. It is simple imprisonment with or without a fine. Why did they not provide rigorous imprisonment? For this obvious reason, Sir, that

The reason why sedition is punished with simple imprisonment.

words are really of no consequence until their effect is accepted and espoused by those for whom they were uttered. It is only then that sedition, or the attempt to stir up ill-feeling among the King's subjects, becomes dangerous. A man may urge the people of the country, but if nobody accepts his words, and only laughs at him, where is the sting in sedition? For reasons of public expediency the Government of the country says: "Sedition may work harm, but it will not if one who has attempted by seditious words or libels, or seditious conspiracies, or seditious meetings, to stir up ill-feeling among the people, be restrained by simple imprisonment for a year or two, according to the circumstances of each case." Such being the true dimensions of sedition, we must take care not to magnify its importance. We have no reason whatever for believing that the Sinhalese people have been tainted with disaffection against their Government or their King, or are really bent upon compassing evil for the country.

The Sinhalese are not seditious.

Now I know, Sir, of only one man in Ceylon who has been so blind to the greatness and goodness of the British Government as to speak and write seditiously; but to the credit of the Sinhalese be it said that he was disowned and tabooed the moment he opened his mouth to stir up ill-feeling. They refused to hear him; they have something like detestation for him; and finding himself to be an unrecognized prophet, he was obliged long ago to depart from these shores and to waste his sweetness in a foreign land.

They refuse to hear seditious speeches.

I also know, Sir, that there are still in the country four or five persons who ventilate their fancied wisdom by writing frothy articles in Sinhalese newspapers; but that is merely foam. The real water of the ocean is unmoved. We are not afraid of the foam and froth of the ocean, nor are we afraid that frothy articles produced in the newspapers by a handful of men will shake to the bottom the British Government or jeopardize the safety of the people of this country.

How growlers in Western Countries are treated.

It is too much to expect perfection in every nook and corner of society. We must make allowances for a few misguided men here and there, whose happiness is to create trouble in the minds of others. In England, as we know, there are lots of growlers. Go where you will, you will find many people, both men and women, grumbling at the Government and saying, "Whatever it does, I am agin the Government." What happens in England? What happens in the United States of America? What happens in Germany, Australia, and other places?

Nobody takes notice of these urgings. They give a ludicrous turn to life, and create mirth and laughter for the time being. The grumbler there is left to go on grumbling as much as he likes. Why don't we treat these handful of men in Ceylon in the same manner? Why do we magnify the state of things which must necessarily exist wherever human nature is imperfect? Why don't we take them less seriously, like the other enlightened nations of the world? Why do we proclaim that, owing to the discontent of a few men, the whole body of the Sinhalese people are a nasty, dirty lot, disloyal to the King, scheming against the British Government here, and trying to create dissension there and everywhere, and that they require a special tribunal and Courts Martial to make short work of them? I, who know the Sinhalese people through and through, say that this exhibition of feeling in the case of an offence so small as sedition is neither just

Neither Special Tribunals nor Courts Martial are required in Ceylon.

to the Sinhalese nor creditable to ourselves as members of the Government of Ceylon.

It is defamatory to say of the Sinhalese that they are seditious.

Now, the Attorney-General said the recent disturbances had revealed the existence of a deadly disease in our midst to an extent to which he or we had not suspected, and which required to be carefully watched. Sir, I cannot support him in that statement. The Sinhalese community as a whole repudiates this defamatory statement; but I feel that the Attorney-General did not mean to be defamatory at all. He has simply taken up the cry which was common some seventy days ago, when British residents here saw most unexpectedly the spread of riots in different places, and yet did not know the reasons which actuated the rioters. They said to themselves: "What is the meaning of this?" British residents could not answer that question. Nobody among them could say why the rioters were behaving in this manner, because they were not in close touch with the people of the country. They had not studied local history on the spot day by day, nor entered into the feelings of the people. They therefore took up the first suggestion that was made by a fool, who said: "Oh! there is the Temperance Association, and there is the celebration of racial unity on National Day. Can't you see that these associations and meetings on National Day have been hatching a conspiracy to do away with the British Government and assume the administration of the country in their own hands?" Some other man who is by nature jealous, and is a fool to boot, goes to a high official and says, "I give you my assurance that this is the beginning of a great scheme. First the Moors are to be expelled, then the Burghers, then the British—neck and crop." What are the British

Why Britsh residents believed in a conspiracy against them and the Government.

The work of fools and knaves.

residents, who are not on terms of intimate friendship with the natives, to do, when they find such positive statements made by persons who, they are under the impression, are entitled to speak on the subject? They say, "Is that so? It must be so. It is so."

Well, Sir, Your Excellency made the rioters feel the terrorism of martial law. The moment the rioters came in contact with bullets and bayonets everything subsided, and a dead calm reigned. Then Your Excellency sent your trusty officers throughout the length and breadth of seven of the Provinces of the Island, and they have been practically making a house to house search for signs of seditious libels, seditious conspiracies, and seditious meetings. Could any of these officers honestly say that they have found any such evidence whatever in Ceylon? I think not, Sir. I have good reasons to say so. And to-day, after seventy days of torture, particularly to the Sinhalese and generally to us all, we must concede that the surmises which were created in the minds of both officials and unofficials have all proved to be wrong, and that the Sinhalese nation continues to be as loyal at heart as any other nation in the British realm. I say, Sir, most unhesitatingly, that a great and grievous injustice has been done to the Sinhalese, who keenly appreciate and are most thankful for all the countless blessings which they have enjoyed under British rule during the last 100 years. They fully recognize these blessings, and have to our knowledge vied with each other in expressing their thankfulness from time to time, and showing that love and reverence are in their hearts for the great and glorious Throne which stands unmatched in the world. They feel that it is indeed a great privilege to be members

The house to house search made by the Military Commissioners did not reveal any sign of seditious conspiracies and seditious meetings.

The gratitude of the Sinhalese for the blessings of British rule.

of an empire so vast and powerful as the British Empire, which is undoubtedly the greatest and best in the world. I am perfectly certain, Sir, that these sentiments are the sentiments that prevail in the hearts of the Sinhalese. And when I saw error on the rampant and defamation on the lips of men whom I thought had better sense than that, it became my duty to go about here, there, and everywhere and remove the false impression. It has taken me a good many days to bring about a change of opinion and make the officials and unofficials think kindly of the loyal Sinhalese, our brethren and fellow-subjects in the British Empire.

A change of opinion among the British in Ceylon has been brought about by removal of false impressions.

Sir, such being the case, I want to know why we want a special tribunal now, in the new circumstances in which we find ourselves. We were all trembling with fear at the display which Your Excellency said it was necessary to make when the police proved themselves to be a failure in regard to the protection of the city. Your Excellency did a wise thing in calling out the military to deal with a situation so fearful in its consequences. The terrible situation lasted only for about one week—from May 28 to perhaps June the 7th. Your Excellency is new to the country; the public feel that you can only do your best, relying upon those who surround you for such information as will guide you aright. Your Excellency determined that the military despotism should continue for some days more. As soon as Your Excellency was convinced that this military display was not necessary in the North-Central Province and the Province of Uva, you at once withdrew the operation of martial law. It came into force on June 2 and was withdrawn on June 29. Why, Sir,

Military force not required beyond one week.

has it not been withdrawn in the case of the remaining five Provinces? Your Excellency is actuated by feelings of something like affection for the people, I know, and Your Excellency is one of the strongest Governors we have had in the Island, both great and wise. If such a Governor does not withdraw the martial law from the remaining five Provinces, it is because there is some remnant of thought in your mind which makes you think that it is necessary to continue it for some time longer. I wish I could get at that remnant of thought, Sir, because a little discussion will dissipate it and lead to the withdrawal of the martial law in the Provinces I have mentioned.

The Sinhalese are loyal and may be depended upon.

I assure you, Sir, with all the emphasis that I am capable of, that you can rely upon the Sinhalese people. Whatever other people may say, you can rely upon their loyalty and be certain that there will be no disturbance of the peace hereafter. I, who feel all this, am bound in duty to you and in justice to the Sinhalese to say that no special measures are necessary in future; that the time is now come for the withdrawal of martial law and for the cessation of the operation of military courts in the Island, and for entrusting offenders or alleged offenders to the ordinary courts of justice, to be dealt with by the normal law of the country.

Martial Law must be withdrawn.

Special Tribunal not necessary to try a few newspaper editors.

Sir, circumstances have greatly changed since the memorialists asked for the special tribunal. I desire to know what is the necessity for the special tribunal now. Who are the persons that are going to be tried? Mainly a few newspaper writers, I understand. Is it really necessary that we should place on our Statute Book a measure so defamatory of the Sinhalese people as this Bill? No, Sir; I do not think so. I hope my honourable friend the Attorney-General and Your Excellency and all your advisers will come to think as I do.

These are my sentiments, Sir. I shall be so pleased to hear that the Government will consider this Bill by the light of what I have stated and make such orders with regard to it as may seem necessary and just in its wisdom.

### (3) *Mr. Rámanáthan's Summaries of* 120 *Petitions presented in the Legislative Council of Ceylon, complaining that divers acts of injustice and oppression were done by the Government Officers appointed to assess and apportion the Damages caused by the Rioters, and that the signatures of the petitioners to the mortgage bonds in favour of His Majesty the King in respect of such damages were obtained by threats held out in the presence of armed soldiers (October* 14, 1915).

The Hon. Mr. P. Rámanáthan (the Ceylonese Member) :—Laying aside, Sir, the petitions addressed to Your Excellency, which I was asked to hand over to you, I shall proceed with only those petitions which are addressed to you as President and to the Members of the Legislative Council. This bundle of petitions, Sir, that I have in my hands is all from Hapitigam korale. The first of these is from a number of petitioners of Wattemulla and Pahala Kaluaggala in Yatigaha pattu. They say that they have been called upon by the Special Commissioner to pay a sum of Rs. 7,000 as compensation and to deposit deeds to the value of double the amount, and that through fear they gave their deeds as security and signed the papers put before them. They say they are very poor people possessing very few lands, not sufficient to keep their families going. They are ordinary coolies, and their earnings are not sufficient for their expenses. The burden is impossible to bear.

Through fear the petitioners gave their title-deeds and signed the bonds.

The second is a petition from some villagers in the Yatigaha pattu of Hapitigam korale. They say that on the 14th instant the villagers were ordered by the Police Headman to meet the Special Commissioner, as he had received orders from that official through the Mudaliyar to that effect In obedience to this order, the petitioners proceeded to meet the Commissioner, and they were told that, as compensation for the losses sustained by the Moors, they must pay Rs. 10,000, and as security for this sum of money the title deeds in their possession were taken. They were further told that, if further deeds were not brought in a couple of days or so, armed Panjabis would be sent after them, and that they would be eventually dealt with according to martial law. In obedience to the order of the Commissioner, and through fear of martial law, the petitioners took their deeds and delivered them over to the Commissioner, upon which they were asked to sign four papers, which they did, but up to date they are ignorant of the contents thereof. They all eke out a living by doing cooly work, and since the commencement of the titanic struggle in Europe there is hardly any cooly work to be done in the village, with the result that they are at present in very distressed circumstances. There are only about 150 people who pay poll tax in the village, and of these a good many go to jail for default of paying it. They pray for relief, Sir.

Threat of armed Panjábis being sent after the petitioners.

Through fear of martial law they signed the bonds.

Unable to pay even poll-tax.

This is a petition from the inhabitants of Bokalagama in the Yatigaha pattu of Hapitigam korale. They say, Sir, that they have been called upon to contribute a sum of Rs. 23,000 from the village towards the Riot Fund. The Special Commissioner came to the village and called upon them to hypothecate their title deeds and sign a bond to secure the payment of the said sum. Through fear of the Special Commissioner, and out of respect to Your Excellency's Government, they signed the bond and deposited their title deeds. They earn their livelihood as labourers on estates, and about a third of their village is owned by outside capitalists. The contribution is Rs. 23,000, and the petitioners would be reduced to poverty for generations to come if they are compelled to pay the said sum. They pray for relief, Sir.

Title-deeds deposited and bonds signed through fear.

Will be reduced to poverty if compensation is recovered.

This petition is from several persons living at Udulla and Kitulwala, Pahalagama and Henapola in the Yatigaha pattu of Hapitigam korale. They were asked by the Special Commissioner to pay a sum of Rs. 6,500 as compensation, and to deposit deeds to the value of Rs. 13,000 as security for the payment. Through fear of military guards they deposited their deeds and signed the papers put before them. They are very poor people, hardly able to maintain their poor families. In the villages mentioned by the petitioners there was no Muhammadan boutique, nor did any villagers take part in the riots, and yet they are asked to pay compensation. They pray for Your Excellency's clemency.

Title-deeds deposited and bonds signed through fear of the military.

Did not participate in riots.

This is from a body of villagers in Kuligedara in Yatigaha pattu of Hapitigam korale. The petitioners lead a hand-to-mouth existence, and their earnings are not sufficient for the maintenance of their families. No one in their village was implicated in the recent disturbances, nor was there any Muhammadan boutique looted or any stolen goods traced to their village. They have been ordered—

No Muhammadan boutique looted, nor looted goods traced to their village.

rather compelled—through the instrumentality of armed Panjabis, not only to set their signatures to certain documents placed before them, but also to pay a certain sum in cash for the expenses of the Punjabis and the stamp fees. They pray that Your Excellency may be pleased to grant them relief.

Through armed soldiers petitioners made to sign bonds and pay cash.

This is from the inhabitants of Kudagammana and a portion of the village of Balagalla in Yatigaha pattu of Hapitigam korale. The Special Commissioner ordered the villagers to pay a sum of Rs. 8,000 as a contribution towards the loss and damage suffered by the Moorish people in the recent disturbances, and they had to deposit their title deeds too. The presence of the Punjabi soldiers armed with sword and rifle caused such terror among the poor petitioners that they were obliged to submit to the order of the Special Commissioner, although they were unable to pay such a large sum of money. Their village is about 150 acres in extent, nearly half of which belongs to outsiders, and there are about 40 families who have no landed property. There are about 90 families in all, and the total adult male population who are liable for the poll tax is about 125, whose chief employment is manual labour and petty agricultural work. They say that a Moorish boutique situated near the boundary of their village was broken into by the mob which came from the adjoining villages. They are quite unable to pay the amount of compensation demanded.

Orders of Special Commissioner obeyed through fear of armed soldiers.

This is from the inhabitants of Muddaragama in the Yatigaha pattu South of Hapitigam korale. On August 17 last the petitioners and the inhabitants of four adjoining villages appeared before the Special

Orders of Special Commissioner peremptory. He would not accept any excuse or explanation.

Commissioner in obedience to orders. The Special Commissioner announced that the sum which it had been decided to levy upon the five villages jointly was Rs. 117,000, and that the petitioners would have to pay that amount and hypothecate title deeds for double the amount. They were further ordered to put their signatures to certain bonds, by which they professed to undertake to make the payments and to mortgage their lands. The petitioners made an attempt to explain to the Commissioner the hardships of their position, but he would accept no excuse or explanation. His orders were peremptory, hence the petitioners could not help but do exactly as they were ordered, though they knew that they would be unable to pay what they had been made to undertake to pay. The tax-paying population of the village is exactly 199. The rest of the inhabitants consist of 35 men who, by reason of their age, have been exempted from the payment of poll tax, 205 boys and girls, and 385 women. They are nearly all daily labourers, very few of them being cultivators. The latter class get from their paddy fields little more than is sufficient for their maintenance. The rates of pay have been reduced to 40 cents, and in some cases to 30 cents, a day; in addition to which their chances of finding work have become much smaller, since owners of property and employers of labour have during the last ten or twelve months found it necessary to curtail their expenses and to exercise the most rigid economy. They are quite unable to pay this levy in addition to the poll tax and the Gansabahawa tax. They entreat Your Excellency to save them from destitution, which the exaction of the levy is certain to bring upon them. There were no riots

No riots in their village; nor attack on Moor dwellings, nor plunder of Moor boutiques.

in their village, no plunder of Moorish shops, no attacks on Moorish dwellings, no outrages on the persons or property of any Moor. A Gansabahawa road runs through the village, which is used by Moorish people in coming from and going to places beyond. Even at the time of the riots this road was used by them, and none of them suffered the slightest molestation or insult. The villagers have not broken the law, and they earnestly entreat that it may please Your Excellency and this Honourable Council to grant them relief.

If levy made they will suffer from destitution.

Commissioner announced compensation was a fine.

This petition is from the inhabitants of the village of Gaspe in the same korale. On their appearing before the Special Commissioner on August 17 last, in obedience to orders, he announced to them that the Government had decided to impose upon the areas concerned in the riots of June last a fine which would go towards the fund out of which Moorish sufferers in these disturbances were to be paid compensation for losses. It was further announced that Gaspe should pay Rs. 9,800. After these announcements they were ordered to give up the title deeds of their properties, and when they were given up the petitioners were ordered to sign certain documents, whereby they bound themselves to pay the sum named, and mortgaged to the Crown their lands and title deeds as security for due payment. They were further ordered to pay down the sum of Rs. 26 as stamp duty on the bonds. They could not help feeling the extreme hardship imposed upon them, but any attempt at explanation was of no avail, and seemed likely to prove dangerous. The only resource left to them is to appeal to Your Excellency and this Honourable Council. This is the prayer they now

He ordered delivery of title-deeds and the signing of bonds and payment of cash.

Any explanation seemed dangerous.

bring before you. Gaspe has a total population of 720, of which only 185 men are of tax-paying ability, and they are unable to pay so large a sum in addition to the poll tax and the Gansabahawa rate. In any case of need, such as sickness, purchase of clothing, and payment of taxes, &c., or for defraying the expenses attendant upon the giving in marriage of their children, they have to raise money upon the mortgage of their little properties, hence even the temporary parting with their title deeds has created for them a serious disability. In their village there were no riots nor any disturbance of the peace. They pray for relief.

The hardships of taking away their title-deeds.

No riots in Gaspe.

This is from village No. 48, Rassapana, in the same korale. The petitioners are poor Buddhist villagers. They were asked to appear before the Special Commissioner, and were ordered to contribute Rs. 3,600. There are 71 adults who pay the commutation tax with the greatest difficulty. There are no Moorish boutiques in this village, nor has any one been charged or convicted for having participated in the recent riots.

No participation in riots at Rassapana.

This memorial is from the villages of Pannalpitiya, Henepola, Pamunuwatta, and Hidiyawala, also situated in Udugaha pattu of Hapitigam korale. The four villages are occupied by about 136 persons who are liable to pay the poll tax, and the number of houses in the villages is 70. The Special Commissioner ordered the memorialists, through the headmen, to produce the title deeds of their properties at the Pasyala Court on August 9, 1915, and required them to pay a sum of Rs. 8,000 by way of compensation to the Moors. They were also directed that the deeds should cover Rs. 16,000. On August 11, 1915, the

Petitioners sign bonds, not of their free will, but through fear of punishment and maltreatment by armed soldiers.

memorialists signed the documents without having understood their nature or contents, and such a course was adopted, not as a result of their free wish, act, or deed, but through fear of punishment, bodily danger, and maltreatment by the armed Punjabis, of whom there were a large number in the Pasyala Court when the Commissioner directed them to sign. No property of the Moors was attacked by them. No Moors resided in the villages or within a three-mile radius of the limits thereof. The memorialists are all manual labourers earning amounts ranging from 36 cents to 50 cents a day, and it is utterly impossible for them to pay the sum of Rs. 8,000. The demand is unjust, because they did not participate in any offence.

No Moors reside within a radius of three miles.

Utterly impossible to pay compensation.

This is from the villagers of Kukulnape and Pelapitigama in the Yatigaha pattu of Hapitigam korale. They have been called upon to pay a sum of Rs. 7,700 as a contribution to the Moors. There were no houses or boutiques belonging to any Moor or Muhammadan in either of these villages. The nearest house or boutique belonging to any Moorman is five miles away from these two villages. Not one of the villagers has been charged or convicted of any offence in connection with the recent riots. They work in plumbago pits and cocoanut estates, and earn barely enough for the maintenance of themselves and their families. Since the outbreak of the war work in the plumbago pits has practically ceased, and the work on estates has also been reduced on account of the fall in the price of cocoanuts. They pray for relief.

Nearest house or boutique of Moormen is five miles away.

Did not participate in riots.

This is from the inhabitants of Hangawatta and Naranapitiya in the same korale. They have been called upon to pay Rs. 3,900. They say they have

Did nothing whatever to incur the penalty.

done nothing whatsoever to incur such a penalty. There are no boutiques or other buildings in these villages belonging to Moors, and no disturbances of any kind occurred within their limits. None of the inhabitants took part in the riots elsewhere.

Villagers quite unable to pay compensation.

I now come to petitions from Alutkuru Korale South. This is from the residents of Peliyagoda Pattiya of Ragam pattu. The Commissioners have asked them to pay a lump sum of Rs. 12,000 to compensate the Moors. The whole village is about 210 acres in extent, of which only 33 acres are owned by the petitioners, while the remaining portion belongs to outsiders and to Tamil residents, who are exempt from payment of any compensation for the simple reason that they belong to a different race. This village has 197 male inhabitants, of whom 123 are Roman Catholics and 74 are Buddhists. Of these, 15 are clerks, 16 boutique-keepers and petty traders, 92 labourers and artisans, such as carpenters, fitters, etc., and 74 ordinary labourers, who form the poorest class in the village. The effects of the floods of 1913 are still to be seen as one of the features of the country. The villagers are quite unable to pay the compensation, and can only pray for relief at Your Excellency's hands.

Delivered title-deeds and signed bonds because they were terrified.

This is from certain petitioners of Pedipola and Watumulla in Dasiya pattu of Alutkuru Korale North. They have been called upon to pay Rs. 17,000. They were obliged to deliver their title deeds and to sign bonds, much against their will, because they were terrified. Some of the petitioners who had no deeds were made to sign a paper before the headman. The petitioners did not dare to say a word objecting to the payment of the said amount. The majority of

Petitioners are too poor to have more than one meal a day.

the petitioners are a beggarly lot, who eke out a living by doing cooly work, and their present circumstances are such that almost all of them can afford only one meal a day, while there are others who cannot afford even that, and semi-starvation is their lot. They cannot understand why they should pay this compensation.

Called upon to pay compensation on pain of being court-martialled.

This is a memorial from the inhabitants of Udugampola and Goigama in Dasiya pattu of Alutkuru Korale North in the Negombo District. They have been called upon to pay Rs. 40,000 on pain of being court-martialled and punished.

Petitioners, extremely poor, were ordered to bring title-deeds and sign bonds.

This is from the villagers of Welangana, Wekada, Kunumada, Mallawagedara, and Dalupatgedara in the Dunagaha pattu of Alutkuru korale. The villages adjoin each other and are under one headman. They consist of a male population of about 200 villagers paying poll tax. Of these, the majority are extremely poor, hardly able to earn a living sufficient for their daily sustenance. About 2,000 acres of land in their villages belong to gentlemen of property and wealth, who live elsewhere, such as Mr. L. W. A. de Soysa, Mr. W. A. de Soysa, Mr. L. S. J. Karunatilleke, Mr. L. A. C. Fernando, Mr. J. E. de Soysa, Mr. B. Rajapakse, and others. The Special Commissioner has ordered the villagers to pay a compensation of Rs. 17,000, and as security their title deeds were taken from them and their signatures were alsc obtained. Owing to their extreme poverty they pray for a discharge.

Commissioner said that if petitioners failed to pay compensation, double the amount would be recovered by force of arms.

This is from the village of Dombawala in Alutkuru Korale South. The residents were ordered by the police headman to assemble at the Government school at Udugampola to meet the Special Commissioner there. On going there they were ordered to pay a sum of Rs. 6,000, and they were told, if they failed to do so, they would be compelled to pay double that amount by force of arms. After this they were ordered to bring their title deeds to cover an amount equivalent to double the above sum. They took their title deeds and handed them to the Special Commissioner, and they were asked to sign four papers, which they did, but up to date they do not know their contents. More than a third of the properties in the village belong to outsiders. The majority of the villagers live by doing cooly work. Wherefore the petitioners pray that in the name of His Gracious Majesty the King Emperor Your Excellency will be graciously pleased to look into their case and exempt them from contributing the sum demanded, and thus grant them redress.

Petitioners signed through fear.

This is from the residents of Pathanduwana in the Dasiya pattu of Alutkuru korale, in the Negombo District. They have been asked to pay Rs. 6,000. Through fear they promised to pay the amount and deposited their title deeds.

Petitioners claim to be exempted on ground of non-participation.

This is from Tammita in the Dunugaha pattu of Alutkuru korale. The village consists of about 100 houses. Of these, about 28 families are dhobies, 6 families are beaters of tom-tom, 20 families are dependent on their breadwinners, who are cooly labourers, and the rest are cultivators of the soil. Over 300 acres of land are owned by persons living outside the village. The memorialists beg to draw Your Excellency's attention to their petition dated July 27, where they laid down their grievances for your kind consideration. After the petitions had been sent in, the memorialists were called upon to

They obeyed the order of the Commissioner through fear of the armed soldiers, who threatened to bayonet them.

bring the title deeds of the small properties they possessed and produce them at Diwulepitiya before the Special Commissioner, on July 28, and they were further ordered by the Special Commissioner to sign some documents and to pay the sum of Rs. 6,000 as compensation to the Moors, although there was not a single boutique or dwelling house in the village belonging to Moormen, and none of the villagers were convicted or arrested in connection with the recent deplorable disturbances. The presence of the Panjabis instilled such fear into the memorialists that they did not even step out of their houses, as they threatened to bayonet any one whom they came across, and this fact greatly induced the memorialists to sign the documents put before them. They ask for exemption on the ground of non-participation.

Petitioners obeyed the orders of the Commissioner to give up their title-deeds, and signed the bonds, through devotion to the British Throne, and the fear of armed soldiers.

This is from the residents of Widiyawatta in the Dasiya pattu of Alutkuru Korale North. They were asked to assemble at Minuwangoda bringing their title deeds to the value of Rs. 20,000, and they were ordered to pay the sum of Rs. 10,000 and to sign certain bonds. The memorialists openly demonstrated their obedience and devotion to the British Throne by readily appearing before the Special Commissioner on the first day in the presence of the Punjabis, who were a source of great fear and alarm to the villagers. Owing to their loyalty and devotion to the British rule, for which the Sinhalese are conspicuous, they signed the documents and gave up their deeds, although in doing so they were aware that they were not in a position to pay the amount demanded. The villagers are very poor and quite unable to pay. There is not a single boutique in the village belonging to a Moor. They pray for exemption.

This is from the village of Kehelbaddara in the Dasiya pattu of Alutkuru korale. The damages to the Moors are put down at Rs. 25,000, to be paid within a year in four instalments. The petitioners were informed that as security for the due payment of the amount they should deposit with the Commissioner their title deeds to cover an amount equivalent to double the compensation, together with Rs. 63.50 as stamp fees for the bonds. They were further informed that, if they failed to comply with this order, they would be hauled up by the Punjabis before the Special Commissioner and severely punished by Court Martial. Through fear the petitioners took their deeds and the amount required for the stamp fees and handed the same to the Commissioner, who asked them to sign certain papers, which they did, but up to date they are absolutely ignorant of the contents thereof. The majority of the villagers do cooly work and sell fish. The people who own any property are few and far between. The majority are so poor that they lead a hand-to-mouth existence, and they find it extremely difficult even to pay the poll tax. They pray for relief.

Petitioners being told that, if the orders of the Commissioner were not complied with, they would be hauled up by armed soldiers and severely punished by Court Martial, gave up their title-deeds and signed the bonds.

This petition is from Nedagomuwa in the Dasiya pattu of Alutkuru korale. The villagers have been asked to pay Rs. 20,000 within a year in four instalments. They were informed that they would have to bring their title deeds to cover an amount equal to double the above amount and to deposit them with the Commissioner, and also to pay Rs. 51 as fees for the deeds. They were further informed that, if they neglected to comply with this order, they would be taken up by the Punjabis and punished according to Court Martial. They are very poor. There is not a

Petitioners did not take part in looting. They delivered their title-deeds and signed bonds because they were threatened with arrest by armed soldiers and punishment by Court Martial.

single Moorish house or boutique in the village, and not one of the petitioners participated in the looting of Moorish boutiques. They are coolies, and quite unable to maintain themselves.

Petitioners did not take part in looting. They delivered their title-deeds and signed bonds because they were threatened with arrest by armed soldiers and punishment by Court Martial.

This is from Polwatta in the Dasiya pattu of Alutkuru korale. The amount demanded of them was Rs. 14,000. They were told, if they did not sign the bonds and pay the fees (Rs. 36), that they would be taken by the Punjabis before a Court Martial and tried for disobedience. In this village there is no boutique or house belonging to the Moors. None of the petitioners participated in the recent disturbances.

Ditto.

This is from the inhabitants of Watinapaha and Wankepumulla in the Dasiya pattu of Alutkuru Korale South. They were called upon to pay Rs. 18,000 as the sum fixed by the Government in four instalments. They were asked to sign deeds and to pay Rs. 46 in cash as fees. They were threatened that, if they failed to do so, they would be punished according to martial law. The residents in these villages are extremely poor, and their poverty can be gauged by the fact that most of them find it difficult to pay even the Rs. 2 poll tax due for a year.

Petitioners did not participate in riots. No Muhammadan boutique within five miles.

This is from Galagedara, Makalandana, and Welikada in the Dasiya pattu of Alutkuru korale. The amount demanded as compensation from these villages is Rs. 7,000. They submit that there was no Muhammadan boutique within a distance of five miles from their villages, and that none of them participated in the riots.

Commissioner made the petitioners sign bonds and give up title-deeds.

This is from the inhabitants of Wewagedara, Diwulepitiya, Horagasmulla, and Bombugammana in the Dasiya pattu of Alutkuru korale. These villages are under one headman, and consist of a male population of about 300 people paying poll tax. Of these, 200 are extremely poor. The remaining 100, including about 50 who are exempted from paying poll tax, are people whose individual capital ranges from Rs. 500 to Rs. 2,000. The Special Commissioner has ordered them to pay a compensation of Rs. 31,000, and as security for such payment he has made them sign bonds and surrender their title deeds.

Petitioners did not participate in the riots.

This petition is from the residents of Matammana in the Dasiya pattu of Alutkuru Korale North. They are all Buddhists of the Wellala community, and no charge of participation in the riots has been preferred against any of them. No looted articles have been discovered in the village. The headmen are all satisfied that not a single resident of Matammana was responsible for the smallest fraction of damage caused in the neighbouring districts. Your Excellency's Commissioner, Mr. H. M-M. Moore, however, declared that this village must pay by way of compensation for damage it had in no way caused, a sum of Rs. 10,000. The petitioners and two others were required to sign a bond, the contents of which were not explained to them. The presence of the Commissioner attended by armed soldiers caused trepidation among the people. The petitioners were told by the Special Commissioner that they must pay Rs. 10,000, and their signatures were taken to a document. It is utterly impossible for them to pay this contribution. No damage has been done to property or person in this village during the riots, nor did any Moors at any time live there.

Fear of armed soldiers made them sign bonds the contents of which were not explained to them.

Commissioner ordered petitioners to pay Rs. 4,000, then reduced the amount to Rs. 3,000, and finally to Rs. 900.

I come now to petitions from Alutkuru Korale South. These are from the residents of Rathmalwita and Makiulangomuwa in the Ragam pattu of

Alutkuru korale in the District of Colombo. They have been ordered to pay a sum of Rs. 4,000 as damages, which is far in excess of their humble means. The amount is not proportionate to the small number of the inhabitants living in the two villages. The memorialists took no part whatever in the disturbances, but deplore the acts of violence and crime which characterized the riot. The Special Commissioner, finding that Your Excellency's memorialists had declined to pay the amount, ordered them to meet him at Ja-ela resthouse on August 30 and altered the amount of the contribution from Rs. 4,000 to Rs. 3,000. They said they were not in a position to pay even the reduced amount. The Commissioner decided to have a final settlement, and ordered the villagers to be present on the following day and affix their signatures to a document promising to pay to the Ceylon Government the sum of Rs. 900. Your Excellency's memorialists are now informed that because of their failure to obey the orders of the Commissioner a punitive tax is about to be imposed on them. The villagers are very poor. Their lands are subject to periodical floods. Some of the houses which were destroyed by the inundation of 1910 have not yet been repaired, and the suffering and misery of the memorialists have become intensified by the floods of 1913. They have not taken any part whatever in the recent deplorable disturbances, nor has any damage been caused either to the persons or to the property of a single Muhammadan within a radius of four miles from these two villages.

Now they are threatened with a punitive tax.

They did not take part in the riots.

His Excellency the Governor (after conferring with the Hon. the Ceylonese Member) :—You will be as concise as you can, Mr. Rámanáthan.

The Hon. the Ceylonese Member :—Yes, Sir. This is from the poor Buddhist villagers of Tibbotugoda, Hambagama, and Horagolla in Ragam pattu of the Alutkuru korale in the Western Province. They have been ordered to pay Rs. 3,900. They did not take part, covertly or overtly, in the riots in their village or elsewhere. They did not take part in the riots.

This is from the village of Batagama South in Ragam pattu of Alutkuru korale. The Buddhist residents have been ordered to pay a sum of Rs. 5,200, and the Catholic residents a sum of Rs. 5,850. They did not participate in the breaking and looting of any Moorish boutiques or houses. Ditto.

This is from the residents of Kelanimulla and Belagama of Ambatalenpahala in Alutkuru Korale East. They have been ordered to pay a sum of Rs. 15,000 and to sign bonds under compulsion. Petitioners sign bonds under compulsion.

This is from the inhabitants of Galahitiyawa. It is a barren village. They have been obliged to sign a bond of indemnity for Rs. 9,960. They cannot bring themselves to agree with the Commissioner and call it after him " a voluntary contribution." Ditto.

This is from Kotikawatta and Angoda in Ambatalenpahala. The residents have been ordered to pay a sum of Rs. 12,000 as compensation. Ditto.

This is from the inhabitants of Wennawatta and Brendiyawatta in Alutkuru Korale South. They have been called upon to pay Rs. 11,000 under the pressure of a number of armed soldiers and to sign bonds under the same compulsion. Ditto.

This is from the villagers of Gotatuwa and Megoda Kolonnawa in Ambatalenpahala of Alutkuru Korale South, about five miles from Colombo. The damage claimed from them is Rs. 20,000. They No Moor boutique in the village.

submit that there is not a single Moorish boutique or any property belonging to a Moor in the two villages.

Petitioners great losers by floods and the war.

This is from the villagers of Peliyagoda and Paliyagodawatta near the Victoria Bridge. They are asked to pay Rs. 40,000. The losses they have suffered from the floods are immense. Thereafter came the war in Europe, and the vast majority of those who work in the city lost their employment and had to work as daily paid coolies.

Did not participate in the riots.

This is from the inhabitants of Gampaha and Ihalagama in the same korale. They have been asked to pay Rs. 5,000. No disturbances or looting took place in these villages. The inhabitants have always been law-abiding and loyal.

Ditto.

This is from the inhabitants of Bulugahagoda and Wewelagare in the Ragam pattu of Alutkuru Korale South. The amount claimed by the Special Commissioner is Rs. 3,750. These two villages are the poorest in Ragam pattu. They had absolutely nothing to do with the recent riots. Most of the inhabitants had been very helpful to the Moors of the adjoining villages, who entered their villages as refugees.

They have helped the Moors.

Levy on Christian Sinhalese smaller than on Buddhist Sinhalese.

This is from the inhabitants of Kuda Butgomuwa, Maha Butgomuwa, and Kohilawatta in Ambatalenpahala of Alutkuru Korale South. The amount demanded from the three villages is Rs. 20,750. The Christians in the villages, who, though fewer in number than the Buddhists, are certainly more wealthy, were ordered to pay only Rs. 750.

Then I come to the petitions of Salpiti korale. This is from the villagers of Mirihane in the Palle pattu of Salpiti korale. A sum of Rs. 25,000 has been fixed upon this one village.

His Excellency the Governor :—I would remind

the Honourable Member that conciseness does not consist exclusively in protracted pauses.

The Hon. the Ceylonese Member :—I am human, Sir, and am standing at great inconvenience to perform my duty. I must pause to see what is said in the petition. If you wish me to be more concise, I will not be able to do it.

His Excellency the Governor :—I beg that you will be concise and not pause unduly. If you do this, you will be following the desire of those who wish to hear you, and to see your point of view, and to sympathize with it as far as possible.

The Hon. the Ceylonese Member :—This is from the village of Nedimale in Palle pattu of Salpiti korale. The contribution demanded is Rs. 17,500.

Levy on Christian Sinhalese smaller than on Buddhist Sinhalese.

This is from the Buddhists of Dehiwala in the Salpiti korale. The amount claimed from the Christians was Rs. 4,000, and Rs. 22,000 from the Buddhists.

This is from the inhabitants of Rilawela and Wettera in Salpiti korale. The amount they have been called upon to pay is Rs. 3,240. Not a single man from these villages has been charged or convicted for any offence.

This is from the village of Dampe in Salpiti korale. The amount claimed from the inhabitants is Rs. 6,250.

This is from Kalubowilage Helena Perera of Malamulla in the Panadurebadda. She has been called on to pay a sum of Rs. 80 on account of her property in Malamulla, and Rs. 43.50 on account of her property at Mahawila.

This is from a woman of the name of Emelia Peiris of Galtude in the Panadurebadda. The Police

Vidane has demanded Rs. 120 from her as compensation, which she is utterly unable to pay.

This is from Maria de Silva Hamine of Panadure. The police have insisted on a payment of Rs. 200 as her contribution. Neither she nor any one of her family took part in the disturbances.

This is from Annie Elizabeth Kuruppu of Walana, Panadure, complaining of a similar contribution demanded.

Villagers are in terror of their lives.

This is from the residents of the village of Dodangoda in Pasdun Korale West. The villagers have been ordered to pay Rs. 2,000, and they are in terror of their lives.

Damages to the Moors done by fools and thieves.

This is from S. B. Kuruppu of Gorakapola in Panadure. He has been called upon to pay, together with some others, a sum of Rs. 10,000 as damages done to the Moors in other villages by fools and thieves.

This memorial is from the inhabitants of Wekada in Panadure. The memorialists are called upon to contribute a sum of Rs. 40,000 as compensation.

Did not take part in the riots.

The set that I am now going to present is from Hewagam korale, Sir. This is from the villagers of Rukmale in Hewagam korale. They did not participate in the recent riots nor commit any deed of wickedness. They have been called upon to pay Rs. 7,700.

Bonds signed in fear of life and imprisonment.

This is from the inhabitants of Dedigomuwa in Hewagam korale. A sum of Rs. 26,400 has been demanded of them. In fear of their lives and of imprisonment they signed bonds.

This is from the inhabitants of Kottawa in the Palle pattu of Hewagam korale. They have been called upon to pay a sum of Rs. 38,500.

This is from the inhabitants of Miriyagalla in Meda pattu of the Hewagam korale.

His Excellency the Governor :—Will you speak a little louder, please, Mr. Rámanáthan.

The Hon. the Ceylonese Member :—This is from the villagers of Miriyagalla in Meda pattu of the Hewagam korale. The demand made on them is Rs. 9,000. There are only 40 houses in that village, and 72 coolies working on rubber estates. The deed they signed was for Rs. 9,000, but the amount said to be due is Rs. 4,500. Deed signed was for Rs. 9,000, but amount said to be due was Rs. 4,500.

This is from the inhabitants of Kahawala, Mallagala, and Yatawatura in the Meda pattu of Hewagam korale. The amount demanded of them was Rs. 19,500. They did not participate in the recent disturbances, there were no boutiques belonging to any Muhammadans in any of these villages, and there was no riot or disturbance within a radius of seven miles from these villages. Did not participate in the riots. Scene of riots seven miles away.

This is from the inhabitants of Waga in the Meda pattu of Hewagam korale. Their village has been assessed at Rs. 16,500, and signatures obtained to a bond by intimidation. No Moor boutique existed in the village, and there was no disturbance within a radius of four miles from Waga. Bonds taken by intimidation. No disturbances within four miles.

This is from certain people of Uggalla in the Meda pattu of Hewagam korale. The amount demanded of them is Rs. 16,500. There is no Muhammadan boutique in the village, nor did any villager take part in the riots, nor was anyone charged. They are perfectly innocent, and their income is most meagre. Ditto.

This is from the inhabitants of Malabe in the Meda pattu of Hewagam korale. The amount demanded of them is Rs. 15,000.

Rioters were those who came in from other villages, given to gambling, drinking, stealing and highway robbery. Their boast.

This is from the inhabitants of a village in the Palle pattu of Hewagam korale. They are asked to pay Rs. 5,888, which, when divided among the 320 men liable to pay, works out at Rs. 18.37 per head. The rioters were lawless men who came from outside villages, and who spend their time in gambling, drinking, stealing, and highway robbery. It is reported that some of these lawless men say: "We are not afraid to do anything wrong, because the damage will be paid by the good and rich people."

This is from Pitumpe. The amount claimed is Rs. 12,000. The inhabitants had nothing to do with the riots.

This is from the inhabitants of Hokandara North in the Palle pattu of Hewagam korale. The amount demanded is Rs. 21,200.

Damages not Rs. 3,000, but compensation demanded was over Rs. 20,000.

This is from the inhabitants of Atigala in the Meda pattu of Hewagam korale. The amount demanded is Rs. 20,640. They are unable to meet this demand for the reasons narrated in the petition. The value of the property damaged or destroyed scarcely amounts to Rs. 3,000.

Through fear of the military they gave their deeds and signed the bonds.

This is from the inhabitants of Pore in Palle pattu of Hewagam korale. The amount demanded is Rs. 17,600. Through fear of military guards they gave their deeds and signed the papers put before them.

Ditto.

This is from the inhabitants of Arukwatta in the Meda pattu of the same korale. They were intimidated by the presence of military guards, and delivered their deeds and signed bonds.

If the bonds are enforced, petitioners will be reduced to beggary.

This is from the inhabitants of Hanwella Ihala in the Meda pattu of Hewagam korale. The amount they are called upon to pay is Rs. 23,000. They are quite unable to pay it. If their bonds are enforced they will be reduced to beggary.

This is from the inhabitants of Pitipana in the Palle pattu of the Hewagam korale. They have been called upon to contribute Rs. 36,000, and were compelled to sign documents on the threat that if they did not sign they would get lashes and two years' imprisonment. Bonds taken by threats of lashing and imprisonment.

This is from the residents of Galagedara in the Meda pattu of the same korale. The amount wanted was Rs. 11,000. It is significant that the rioters in this village were led by Moors, consequently two Moors were tried by Court Martial and sentenced to penal servitude for life, and two other Moors were given six months' hard labour and six cuts respectively after trial in the minor court. The petitioners are leading respectable people, and have had nothing to do with the riots. Rioters in this village were led by Moors who were afterwards convicted. Petitioners did not take part in riots.

This is from Bollatawa in the Udugaha pattu of the Hewagam korale. The villagers earn their daily bread by rowing padda boats to and from Colombo. They have been called upon to pay Rs. 9,450 as compensation, and deeds and signatures to bonds were extracted from these by display of force. Bonds signed by display of force.

This is from the residents of Himbulana in Adikari pattu of Hewagam korale, a village about seven miles from Colombo. The village is subject to an annual inundation, and the people are very poor.

This is from the inhabitants of Neluwattuduwa in the Udugaha pattu of Hewagam korale. They have been called upon to pay Rs. 10,000. Through fear they gave their title deeds and signed bonds. Ditto.

This is from the villagers of Hewagama in Palle pattu of Hewagam korale. They have been called upon to pay Rs. 12,600. They were put in terror at the sight of the Punjabis who had collected at the Kaduwella resthouse, and were forced much against their wishes to give up their deeds and sign bonds.

Bonds signed by display of force.

This is from the villagers of Jaltara in the Meda pattu of Hewagam korale. The contribution required of them they are utterly unable to pay, being very poor. Their petition is a long one, Sir, and goes into details.

Ditto.

This is from the inhabitants of Kahahena and Mabulla in the Udugaha pattu of Hewagam korale. The amount wanted was Rs. 18,000. This is also a long petition, Sir.

Ditto.

I come now to petitions from the Siyane korale. This is from the village called Wanaluwawa in Gangaboda pattu of Siyane Korale East. The amount required of them was Rs. 8,900. The orders were peremptory, and as they feared that anything short of instant and absolute compliance would bring them harm from the fierce soldiers who were present, they did just as they were ordered.

This is from Kinigama and Kimbulgoda of Siyane korale. The amount demanded was Rs. 3,600. Not a single memorialist was ever charged with the offence of rioting or looting. No damage whatever has been caused to the Moors or their property in these villages.

Ditto.

This is from the inhabitants of Utuwandogahawatta in Meda pattu of Siyane Korale West. They met the Commissioners at the Veyangoda resthouse, and were ordered to pay a sum of Rs. 9,000. Overawed by the military force, they had to deliver their title deeds and sign bonds. There were no Moors at all in the village, and therefore none suffered any injury, nor was there any rioting in the village, nor, again, was any one of the villagers concerned in any of the riots. In short, their village is far removed from the disturbed areas.

Village far from disturbed areas.

This is from the inhabitants of the village Wirangula in Meda pattu of Siyane korale. The amount demanded was Rs. 11,000.

This is from three villages called Keragala, Nakandapola, and Parakadamulla in Gangaboda pattu of Siyane korale. The Moors had no boutique, shops, or any other building in the said three villages, and they suffered no loss or damage at the hands of the residents of the said villages. The petitioners have been ordered to pay a sum of Rs. 22,700 as compensation. Thus, the share that each person will have to pay will amount to over Rs. 80.

Ditto.

This is from the village of Detemulla in Gangaboda pattu of Siyane korale. The amount demanded was Rs. 11,000 in respect of two villages. In neither of these villages is there a single house or boutique belonging to the Moors, and none of the petitioners participated in the disturbances. They are miserably poor.

Ditto.

This is from the inhabitants of Ellakkala in the Udugaha pattu of Siyane korale. They were asked to pay a fine of Rs. 11,000, and title deeds and bonds were got from them by force.

Bonds obtained by force.

This is from the villages of Paranagama, Galboda, and Beraunna. The villagers were called upon to pay Rs. 16,000. There was not a single Moorish boutique in any of these three villages, and none of the residents participated in the rioting.

Did not take part in the riots.

This is from Ihala Imbulgoda in the Meda pattu of Siyane korale. The amount demanded was

Bonds taken by force.

Rs. 19,000. Being in fear of military force they signed the bonds and delivered their deeds.

Petitioners are Christians. Took no part in the riots.

This is from the Christian residents of Uda Mapitigama in Gangaboda pattu in Siyane korale. The petitioners are members of the Baptist congregation at that place. They took no part in the riots. They have been called upon to pay Rs. 595 in four instalments.

Took no part in the riots.

This is from the combined villages of Alutgama, Widiyawatta, Galtotamulla, Morenna, Mahattuwa, Maipalagoda, and Mahawita in the Meda pattu of Siyane Korale West. The villagers have been called upon to pay Rs. 24,000. They are very poor, most of the high and low land belonging to outsiders. There are only 27 tiled houses in the five villages. None of the villagers were implicated or convicted in any case of riot, nor was any stolen article found in the villages.

Ditto.

This is from the inhabitants of Alutgama, Gampaha, and Morupola in Meda pattu of Siyane korale. They have been ordered to pay Rs. 12,000. The amount is too heavy for the petitioners. No disturbance or anything in the shape of looting took place in the village. There were no Moor boutiques there.

This is from the residents of Hubutiyawa and Udammita in the Udugaha pattu of Siyane korale. The amount they were required to pay was Rs. 16,000.

This is from the residents of Meti-debehera in Udugaha pattu of Siyane korale. They were called upon to pay Rs. 22,000. Only 200 people are paying poll tax. The residents do not hold even one-fifth of the lands in the village.

This is from the villagers of Kannimahara and

Indurugala in Gangaboda pattu of Siyane korale. They have been ordered to pay a sum of Rs. 17,000, and were intimidated by the presence of the Panjabis, who were always ready to pounce upon them with drawn swords. Villagers intimidated by armed soldiers.

This is from the inhabitants of Udugama in the Meda pattu of Siyane korale. This is a long petition, Sir. They have been called upon to pay a sum of Rs. 10,000 under similar circumstances.

This is from Dinapamunuwa in Udugaha pattu of Siyane korale. The sum claimed from them is Rs. 22,800.

This is from Wadumulla and Dalugama in the Adikari pattu of Siyane korale. The amount the inhabitants were called upon to contribute is Rs. 16,000. They were forced to part with their title deeds and to sign the bonds owing to the presence of the Panjabis. The petitioners were told that if they did not consent to pay the compensation it would be recovered by force. Ditto.

This is from the residents of Pelpita in the Gangaboda pattu of Siyane korale. The amount demanded is Rs. 5,400. The village is a small one, consisting of about 40 houses, and each family will have to contribute Rs. 135. They are not even able to pay the poll tax.

This is from the inhabitants of Wadurawa in the Meda pattu of the Siyane korale. They have been called upon to pay Rs. 12,000. Having no choice but to pay, they did exactly as they were ordered to do. Ditto.

This is from the inhabitants of Maimbula in the Udugaha pattu of Siyane korale. They were called upon to pay Rs. 13,000.

This is from the inhabitants of Bopagama in the Udugaha pattu of Siyane korale. The amount claimed is Rs. 8,000, and they were told that if they did not obey orders the amount of the indemnity would be increased.

This is from the residents of Pugoda and Pudukandana. The amount claimed is Rs. 6,000. They signed the documents and delivered their deeds through fear.

This is from the village Kirikittamulla in Meda pattu of Siyane korale. The amount they were called upon to pay was Rs. 4,000 under similar circumstances.

This is from the inhabitants of Narangaspitiya, Pingomuwa, and Dottuwilla. The amount that they are required to pay was Rs. 11,700.

Bonds signed by intimidation.

This is from the villagers of Akurumulla and Alubowila in the Adikari pattu of Siyane korale. The amount involved was Rs. 8,500, and there is the same complaint against the manner in which the papers were signed and the deeds obtained.

This is from the villagers of Nittambuwa and Nambadaluwa in the Adikari pattu. The amount sought to be levied on them was Rs. 35,000.

Ditto.

This is from the villagers of Belunmahara and Galoluwa. The amount claimed from them is Rs. 18,000 under the same circumstances. The people are very poor.

This is from the residents of Anuragoda in the Gangaboda pattu of Siyane korale. The amount claimed is Rs. 6,600.

This is from the village Mahara. The amount claimed is Rs. 32,000.

This is from the villages of Pasgammana and

Nilammahara. The amount claimed is Rs. 14,000.

This is from the village of Malwatuhiripitiya in Meda pattu of Siyane korale. The amount claimed is Rs. 10,000.

This is from the village of Veyangoda in the Udugaha pattu of Siyane korale. The compensation demanded was Rs. 6,000.

This is from Uruwala in the Meda pattu of Siyane korale. The amount demanded was Rs. 12,000. Through fear of the Punjabis the villagers signed the papers and tendered the deeds. They were in no way implicated in the recent disturbances. No Moors lived within a radius of two miles from the outskirts of the village. Bonds signed by intimidation.

This is a petition from Ambrose Perera and certain residents of the Roman Catholic Diocese of Pamunuwila in the Adikari pattu of Siyane korale. They are very poor people, who make an honest living by trade and cultivation. Not one of them was involved in the recent riots. There was no Moor boutique within a radius of two miles. They have been called upon to pay a sum of Rs. 9,600, which is unbearable. Petitioners are Roman Catholics. Did not take part in the riots.

This is from the villagers of Mahara-Padiliyatuduwa in the Adikari pattu of Siyane korale. The amount they were called upon to pay was Rs. 7,000.

This is from the inhabitants of Dambutuwe and Bonnuwe in Udugaha pattu of Siyane korale. They were called upon to pay a fine of Rs. 5,000, and their title deeds were forcibly taken, and bonds were also forcibly taken. Deeds forcibly taken and bonds signed under intimidation.

This is from the villages of Mudungoda and Henaratgoda. The inhabitants were called upon to pay Rs. 28,000. Their title deeds and signatures were forcibly taken. Ditto.

Rioters came in from other villages.

This is from the residents of Hakgalla in the Udugaha pattu of Salpiti korale. The amount they were called upon to pay was Rs. 10,000. The damage done to the Moors was by rioters who came from outside. Not one of the inhabitants was convicted of any offence during the disturbances.

No disturbance in these villages. Bonds taken by force and without explanation of contents.

This is from the residents of Welagedara, Walaliydda, and Kospelawatta in the Udugaha pattu of Siyane korale. The amount demanded was Rs. 10,000. No disturbance whatever took place in these villages. Their signatures to the bonds were taken from them by force, without their being told the contents of the bonds. Owing to the deprivation of their firearms they have been rendered defenceless. The last-named village contains only three houses and five men, one being a cripple, and it is impossible to raise the large sum of Rs. 10,000.

Ditto.

This is from the residents of Paddawala in the Gangaboda pattu of Siyane Korale East. The amount they were called upon to pay was Rs. 12,200. They produced their deeds and signed the bonds through fear.

Only an ex-convict looted and was sent to jail.

This is from the villages of Helummahara and Pananwala in the Gangaboda pattu of Siyane korale. The inhabitants took no part in the riots. The houses of the Moors were miles away from the two villages. There was an ex-convict who took part in the looting of a boutique, but he was promptly arrested, convicted, and sent to jail for six months.

Deeds signed under threat of being shot.

This is from Biyagama in the Adikari pattu of Siyane korale. Rs. 35,000 was the amount they were called upon to pay. It is impossible for them to pay it. They gave up their deeds and signed the bond as they were threatened to be shot.

This is from the inhabitants of Amunugoda in the Meda pattu of Siyane korale. The amount sought to be levied on them was Rs. 7,000. The documents they signed were not read or explained to them, and the signing was not done of their free will, but to escape the threats held out to them. Deeds signed under threat of being shot.

This is from the inhabitants of Pattigoda and Hindeniya. The amount of the levy is not given. They were asked to present themselves at the Veyangoda resthouse with their title deeds. They appeal to Your Excellency to exempt them from a levy which to people in their condition will prove entirely ruinous.

This is from the inhabitants of Mailawalana in the Gangaboda pattu of Siyane korale. It is impossible for them to pay the levy of Rs. 9,000.

This is from the inhabitants of Sinharamulla and Pilapitiya in the Adikari pattu. The amount claimed from them is Rs. 10,000. They signed the bonds and gave away their title deeds owing to the fear of armed Punjabis. Ditto.

This is from the inhabitants of Dadagomuwa in the Meda pattu of Siyane korale. They state how they came to sign the bonds and deliver their title deeds to cover the amount of Rs. 11,000 imposed upon them. They have no means to pay this sum.

This is a petition from certain persons of Bogomuwa relating to the sum of Rs. 7,000 demanded of them.

This is a petition from certain residents of Kalatuwawa and Pilankada in the Meda pattu of Siyane korale. The amount sought to be levied is Rs. 11,000.

This is from the inhabitants of Pahala Biyanwila

Deeds signed under threat of being shot.

in the Adikari pattu of Siyane korale. They have been asked to pay a sum of Rs. 19,000, and forcible possession was taken of their title deeds. They were also made to sign bonds by force. There were no Moor boutiques in the village, nor were there any disturbances in the shape of looting.

Ditto.

This is from the inhabitants of Kirikitta in the Meda pattu of Siyane korale. The amount sought to be levied on them is Rs. 15,500. There are not even two persons who are possessed of a block of land of 10 acres. It was by force that their title deeds and signatures were obtained.

This is from the village Mahara Nugegoda in the Adikari pattu of Siyane korale. The amount sought to be obtained from the inhabitants is Rs. 18,000. They took no part in the riots.

This is from the inhabitants of Dikpitigoda and Badalgoda in the Adikari pattu of Siyane korale. The amount claimed from them is Rs. 10,000. The major part of these two villages is covered by paddy fields, and a much smaller area is dry land, consequently the income of the villagers is very small.

It is now about 18 minutes after 5 o'clock, Sir.

His Excellency the Governor :—Any more petitions?

The Hon. Mr. Rámanáthan :—I have got some more, Sir, which I shall not present to-day.

His Excellency the Governor :—Any other petitions?

The Hon. the European Urban Member :—I have six petitions, Sir, and with your permission I will present them together. Five of them are from villagers in different korales, and one is from the Christian residents of Kelaniya.

His Excellency the Governor retired from the Council Chamber for a short while, and the Chair was taken by the Honourable the Officer Commanding the Troops.

## MOTIONS IN THE NAME OF THE HON. THE COLONIAL SECRETARY.

The Hon. the Colonial Secretary :—There are five motions standing in my name, Sir, but three of them are on routine matters, and I am sure that it will be the general desire of the Council that we should get to business. I propose, therefore, with the permission of the Council, to defer moving the motions standing in my name until after the Riot Damages Bill has been disposed of.

The necessary permission was granted.

---

At this stage the Council adjourned for a few minutes.

(4) *Mr. Rámanáthan's Motion for the appointment of a Select Committee of the Legislative Council to consider and report on the grievances alleged in the aforesaid and other Petitions (October 14, 1914).*

On resuming.

The terms of the motion.

The Hon. Mr. P. Rámanáthan (the Ceylonese Member) said :—In reference to the draft of the Ordinance to provide compensation for losses by riots, which proposes, *inter alia*, to validate and confirm all assessments, apportionments, and allotments made by the Special Commissioners appointed by the Officer Commanding the Troops, I move, Sir,—

1. That a Select Committee of this Council be appointed to consider and report on the complaints made in the numerous petitions presented to this Council, to the effect—

(*a*) That the assessment of damages caused by rioters was far in excess of the actual damages suffered.

(*b*) That the apportionment of the damages to headmen's divisions was made without regard to any rule of law.

(*c*) That the allotment of the apportioned amount among the residents and landowners of each village was grievously unjust.

(*d*) That though disturbances did not take place in villages, and though their inhabitants did not take part in the riots, yet compensation was imposed on them all.

(e) That the compensation imposed on innocent persons, whether living in undisturbed villages or living in villages where rioting and looting had occurred, is utterly beyond their power to pay.

(f) That the Special Commissioners, attended each by a number of armed soldiers, intimidated the villagers and so compelled them, while in terror of martial law, to produce their muniments of title to lands, and to sign mortgage bonds securing to His Majesty the King the payment of the oppressive compensation imposed on them.

(g) That the bonds signed by them in favour of their gracious King were not voluntary.

(h) That while the Special Commissioners called for claims for damages from the Muhammadans, and readily awarded compensation to them, no notice whatever was taken of the damages suffered by the Sinhalese (Buddhists and Christians) at the hands of the rioters and looters, even though such claims were pressed on them. And—

2. That until the report of such Select Committee upon the foregoing and other complaints is made, the consideration of the Draft Bill before the House be postponed.

For a week, Sir, between May and June, the people of this country were alarmed by the predatory invasion of the criminal and unemployed classes consequent upon the failure of the police, both urban and rural; and when these raids were subdued by military force, the people found themselves quaking through fear at the abnormal proceedings of Courts His speech.

Martial and of the Military Commissioners who had been appointed to inquire into cases of treason, house-breaking, and theft, and to assess and recover the damages caused by the rioters. My motion, Sir, just now is not concerned with the causes of the riots, or the failure of the police, or the Special Commissioners' preliminary investigation of criminal cases, or the trials held by Courts Martial. It is concerned with that part of the work of the Commissioners which relates to the assessment and recovery of the damages for losses incurred by the Moors and others. We know, Sir, that compensation is due where life, limb, or property has been injured, and we shall all rejoice if the damages suffered by the Moors and others can be made good. But from whom shall such compensation come is the question. For the present let us take as our guide the statement made by Mr. Bonar Law, the Secretary of State for the Colonies, in the House of Commons on July 27th last. He said that it seemed right that any village which did not take part in the riots should not be assessed for compensation, and that all villages in a district which have been concerned in rioting should contribute their respective share in payment of the damage caused.

The Secretary of State's instructions regarding compensation.

The question now is, Have the Commissioners done their work of assessment and apportionment in terms of the Secretary of State's exposition? You, Sir, have no doubt seen all the returns and reports made by the Commissioners, and you think that their assessment and apportionment, as well as the bonds of the villagers sent up by the Commissioners, should be confirmed. I speak under correction, Sir, for you may not think so at all, but I gather the intentions of the Government from the Bill that is submitted before

The question is, Have the Commissioners done their work of assessment and apportionment of damages in accordance with Mr. Bonar Law's instructions?

us, and I think I am right in saying that, howsoever much you may disagree with your advisers, it is possible that you have given your consent to this policy. Not only does the intention of the Government appear to be to enforce the bonds that have been signed, but also to continue the work of assessment and apportionment left undone since the withdrawal of martial law, and to make applicable the principles and procedure now followed when similar contingencies arise in the future.

The duty of the Government to table the reports and returns of the Commissioners not done.

But we, Sir, the non-official Members of the Council, have not seen these returns and reports of the Commissioners, and it is only right that, if you desire our advice and consent to the Ordinance read a second time to-day, you should give us an opportunity to study the returns and reports and judge for ourselves whether the Commissioners' assessments and apportionments and the bonds they have produced are worthy of confirmation. In the absence of such reports and return, we, non-official Members, will naturally feel that the duty which His Majesty the King has cast upon us of advising you as to the desirability of passing the Ordinance cannot be properly fulfilled, much less can we consent to it. According to our conception of our functions, it is our bounden duty to do our best to advise you, and, if possible, to consent to the policy that you may formulate in this Council. Every Ordinance that is passed here states, in explicit terms, that it is enacted by the Governor of Ceylon with the advice and consent of the Legislative Council thereof. If, Sir, we are to advise you, how are we to carry out our duty without the necessary papers being submitted to us? If we are to exercise our discretion and consent to any piece

The duty of the non-official members to study all connected papers and advise the Government.

of legislation, how can we honestly consent or honestly not consent without seeing any of the papers which the members of your own Government have been privileged to see? I sincerely hope, Sir, that Your Excellency will give us the satisfaction of being able to do our duty in the manner that is expected of us by His Majesty's Government. We are not called to do our duty here in a flimsy, superficial way. It is not right to enjoy the honours of the situation and be respected by the people, and be given the highest places in their communities in public or in private if we do not do our duty to the people. What respect can we have from the people, what from the King himself? You should help us to perform our duty. Some of us at least are willing to fulfil our duty and to undertake the responsibilities of our situation; but if we find that the Government for some purpose or other keeps back papers from us, and does not admit us into its confidence, we feel that we have no right to be in Council. Our people, however, will not allow us to resign our position. What are we to do, because the moment the elected members resign their position they will be re-elected, and put back again into the seat in no time.

The Government has not helped non-official members to perform this duty, which they owe to the King and the people.

Thus, we have to go to our beds with a groaning spirit, with a sense of duty undone to the King, undone to the people, and undone to you, Sir, because Your Excellency may often feel unsatisfied with the advice given by the members of your own Government in the Executive Council, and you may often like to have the benefit of our advice.

Well, Sir, if the Government will not take us into its confidence, and make us speak from our hearts with all the experience we have, what are we to do? We feel often that things are miscarrying, and that though we have been summoned by the grace of our King to this important office in the Legislative Council, we have not the chance of doing our duty as it must be done.

The allegations in the petitions must be considered with the reports and returns of the Commissioners.

We, the non-official Members of Council, feel that the duty of examination and consideration becomes all the more peremptory because of the petitions which have been presented in such large numbers to Your Excellency and the Legislative Council regarding the measures taken by the Commissioners in the performance of their duties.

The lamentations of the people deserve full inquiry—as regards the atrocities of the martial law, and the illegal and unrighteous acts of the Commissioners.

We, Sir, dare not turn a deaf ear to the lamentations of the people as expressed in their petitions before us. If we do, we shall lay ourselves open to the charge of betraying the trust reposed upon us by the King and by the people alike. I believe, Sir, the Legislative Council has received about 350 petitions already, and I know not how many more have reached Your Excellency, because I have a heap of them here on this side of the table addressed to you, and which I have not yet presented. When I read these petitions, Sir, I feel very sorry. I feel that I must do something for the people who are groaning under the misfortunes which they have suffered for no fault of their own. And I expect you, Sir, who have been so sympathetic and have extended to me your private friendship, to try and do something for the people on this extraordinary occasion. I have gone amongst them and I have seen grown-up men, women, and children weeping bitter tears owing to the untold sufferings that have been heaped on them by the atrocities of the martial law and by the illegal and unrighteous acts of the Commissioners on whom Your Excellency cast this sacred duty, not knowing how inexperienced and how wanting in the sense of justice ——

Governor's idea that high officers cannot do wrong.

His Excellency the Governor :—Mr. Rámanáthan, there are three of them here, and I am sure your words do not apply to them.

The Hon. Mr. Rámanáthan :—I wish them to stand up and answer, Sir.

His Excellency the Governor :—I am sure you do not mean to make any imputations against any member.

The Hon. Mr. Rámanáthan :—Sir, I have seen the work of the Special Commissioners, I have heard of their doings ——

Duty of the Government to inquire into complaints of oppression and injustice against high officers.

His Excellency the Governor :—I take it that your remarks do not apply to any members of this Council.

The Hon. Mr. Rámanáthan :—Private friendship, Sir, has nothing to do with public duty. That is my creed, and this is a most uncomfortable day for me. I have been called upon to do a duty that is most unpleasant, but which I must do at any cost, because the just cries of the people are dear unto God, and to the British throne, and to you, Sir. If any Honourable Members who have been charged with the duty of administering the Government have done wrong, it is for them to rise and say in the presence of this assembly, "I have done wrong. I desire that my work should be thrown away, and that others better advised than I have been should do the work in the manner in which it should be done." I beg Your Excellency's forgiveness and the forgiveness of my honourable friends who are sitting round this table if in the discharge of my duty I have to say some things painful to them, but far more painful to myself. I will ask them to bear with me, because in the complicated circumstances of the case there should not be a pronouncement upon only one side of it, but there should be a careful consideration and a sober pronouncement on the other side of the case, too, which is the case that I am trying to lay before Your Excellency. If all the hundreds of petitions which have been presented are to be thrown into the waste paper basket, or are to be superficially examined only to create the impression that they are receiving attention, but all the same the original intentions of Government are to be carried through the Legislative Council by means of the official majority, I say, Sir, that that will be an awful imputation on this Council, and I am sure that you, with your sense of justice purified in England, will not allow such a thing to be done here. I do believe that, whatever you may have said to the members of your Government, or to the officers concerned, you will from this very minute re-consider your conclusions and make a pronouncement upon the case which the people of the country have presented to you by their humble petitions in such vast numbers to-day and in days gone by.

I do not think, Sir, that human nature after all is bad. I believe that those who have been called by the King to do their duty to the people will do it when their eyes are opened, and make the contentment of the people their greatest concern. We may reasonably expect them to see that the rights and liberties of the people are conserved, and that nothing will be done to endanger their confidence in the Government.

The eight kinds of complaints made by the people may be reduced to five.

I have endeavoured to analyze the 300 odd petitions which have been sent to me for presentation, and I find that eight kinds of complaints have been made by the people against the Commissioners. I have set them out in my motion, but it is possible to reduce them to five. It is our duty to consider them in the interests of the good government of the country.

The first complaint is that the assessment of damages by the Commissioners is far in excess of the actual damages suffered.

The first complaint is that the assessment of damages is far in excess of the actual damages suffered. The petitioners say they had no opportunity of pointing out to the Commissioners the absurdity or the falsity of the claims made, and if the Commissioners had invited the co-operation of the leading Sinhalese, they would have induced the Muhammadan boutique-keepers in their respective districts to accept a much lower value than was found by the Commissioners for the losses they have suffered. Several petitions show that the original assessments of the Commissioners have been reduced by 50 or 70 per cent. That is what the petitioners say, and I heard quite recently that in the case of Panadure, which had been assessed to the amount of Rs. 495,000, a reduction is now proposed to be made of no less than Rs. 245,000. I am told that the Panadure people have been informed that, if they pay Rs. 250,000 now, the claim for Rs. 495,000 will not be pressed. I also learn, Sir, from Moratuwa that the assessment has been reduced equally low, and that the people are in treaty with the Government to obtain a fairly sufficient reduction in order to contribute their quota at least on grounds of humanity and charity. I have had petitions this morning from people speaking of such reductions. Here is a petition, Sir, from Kosgama dated October 13. I beg your pardon, Sir, it is a letter addressed to me. (Reads) "We, the undersigned, beg to bring to your kind notice that, owing to the recent disturbances among the Sinhalese

The assessment is admittedly wrong, and great reductions have been made, but reduced amounts are still heavy.

and Moors, all males over 18 years of age were expected to pay at the rate of Rs. 100 indemnity. The amount is now reduced to 30 per cent., which also is too high to be equally divided amongst the villages of the locality. The undermentioned is a list of the villages and what a single man in each village has to pay." The list is too long to read. In so paying, I beg to point out to you, Sir, that in some families there are four to six males, and if they are each to pay from Rs. 11.30 to Rs. 27, the amount from a single family would vary from Rs. 100 to Rs. 200, which amount it is impossible to pay.

Then, Sir, here is a list of villages in Siyane korale and Hewagam korale, showing the sums payable. They appeal to me, Sir, and say that, as I know the circumstances of the people in this country, I should not allow even this reduction to 30 per cent. to stand, but should interpose myself between the Government and the people and safeguard their interests.

Another petition, Sir, from Malabe in the Palle pattu of the Hewagam korale is much to the same effect. So you see, Sir, it ought not to be news to you that the Commissioners whom you have appointed have strongly misunderstood their duty, and have implicated the Government in what I may say a troublesome position.

Why the Commissioners went wrong in their assessment.

Now, if the Commissioners had associated with themselves men of experience in the country, both English and Ceylonese, they would have had a better chance of doing the duty imposed upon them. Why, Sir, even amongst the officials, I understand that Mr. Cumberland has, in association with some level-headed officials, done his duty of assessment very fairly. The people recognize it. Not that they admit that they are bound in law to give compensation to men whom they have never injured, but they appreciate the work of Mr. Cumberland, and say to themselves that he has by tactful means saved the city and their district from destruction of life and property; and when a man like that calls upon the people to stand by him and to help him to do something towards the injury done to the Moors, they respond generously; and I was quite prepared to hear what the Attorney-General said, that the amount of compensation fixed by Mr. Cumberland so carefully has been recovered. But where are the Provinces in which there has been the same careful assessment, the same tactful and sympathetic treatment, and the same responsiveness on the part of the people to conserve the efforts of the head of their district in the interests of peace and good order? I have not heard of any other Provinces, Sir, and in view of these circumstances you will see how important it is to thresh out the question at this table, so that Your Excellency may not lend yourself to the idea that everything has been done properly and righteously because it has been entrusted to able and honourable officers of the Government.

Their assessment in every case deserves careful revision, if contentment and respect for British Justice are to reign afresh in the hearts of the people.

Sir, I say do not for Heaven's sake assume any such thing. Look at the matter like a judge sitting in a court of justice, and bring to bear your own independent judgment upon each assessment, and if necessary send into the villages one or two disinterested officers—officers who have had nothing to do under the martial law or under the promptings of officers who do not know their business, and let them arrive at a finding. Then, only, Sir, will the people be satisfied. Contentment will reign in their hearts, and the respect for British justice will never slacken.

I say, Sir, that now that all the proposals of the Commissioners have come before this Council, it is time that we, ourselves, should take the matter in hand, you being our President, and make inquiries from day to day, and arrive at a finding which will stop the lamentations of the people. It is impossible, Sir, for anybody to be without giving his most earnest consideration to this matter. Supposing, for instance, an unfortunate man went before a court of justice and complained of intimidation, duress, etc., and says to the court that a bond had been taken from him by such and such a person and he wanted that bond to be cancelled. Supposing the Judge said: "Now, look here, that is all very fine, my good fellow. I know the gentleman against whom you are complaining. He is the soul of honour, and is a most able man. My friendship with him is lifelong, and I know that he is not the man to do what you complain of. Now, you get out of court, and I order that bond to stand."

What will not be tolerated in a Court of Justice must not be tolerated by the Government in its dealings with the people.

Would English law sanction such a decision? Would the Appeal Court allow that decision to stand for a minute? And would you, Sir, as the Governor of Ceylon, allow that Judge to continue to sit in the seat of justice and do similar harm to the people and make a travesty of justice, the sacred justice that has prevailed amongst us by the goodwill and strength of the British Government?

No, Sir, you will not do it. Why, then, should we throw to the winds these 300 petitions and more, and say to the people: "Now, my good fellows, this will do good to you. You know this is the best thing that can be done for you. Just pay the money demanded. If you do not pay, I shall see it wrung out of your pockets."

I say, Sir, that this is due to extreme want of the sense of justice. Give to every man his due. The Rs. 100 which it is attempted to pull out of the pockets of innocent villagers is to them as large a sum of money as, say, Rs. 100,000 to Your Excellency, or Rs. 50,000 to the members of Your Excellency's Government.

The people must be saved from the consequences of oppression by a full and particular inquiry into each case.

The amount is no concern of our's, but the principle of justice, the principle of righteousness, the principle of listening to the just complaints of the people and finding a remedy for them and restoring contentment in their hearts and respect for British justice, which has kept them in prosperity for more than a century—that is all-important, and by entertaining this sense of justice and saving the people from oppressions of all kinds, we draw ourselves nearer and nearer to God, and are the recipients of His reward in many a spiritual blessing that makes us happy for all time and under all circumstances.

Sir, both in regard to personal evolution and in regard to the righteous administration of the affairs of other people, this sense of justice is worth cultivating, and we must therefore do our very best to hearken to the complaints of the people, which I feel are true, and which in the course of my speech to-day I shall prove to you to be true. We should, Sir, do our very best in the unfortunate circumstances in which we find ourselves to restore peace in the hearts of the people, and to make them cease to entertain bitter hatred against the persons who are being favoured, and against those officers who have given cause for all this trouble by improper assessment of the compensation.

Your Excellency must now be convinced that a reduction is absolutely necessary, and that we cannot deal with this complicated question in a higgledy-piggledy fashion, in a pell-mell way, but should take every petition into our hands and deal with them as we would our own complaints or the complaints of our particular friends to be dealt with. Mistakes will happen, errors will be committed, but what a good man will do is to jump up from his seat the moment he sees that he has committed an error or a wrong, go to the offended man, seize him by the hand, and say: "My good fellow, I have unwittingly done you mischief, I will do my best to make reparation to you." That must be the attitude of the Government and the Government officials towards the people. I shall say nothing, Sir, about the past, but I have much to say about the future. Let us desist from wrongdoing any more, let us halt and examine the complaints of the people, and see what we can do to mitigate the horrors of the situation.

Let us desist from wrong-doing any more, and try to mitigate the horrors of the situation.

Now, Sir, the second complaint is that the apportionment and the allotment of the damages assessed to each headman's division was made without regard to any rule of law. According to law, which nobody knows more than the Attorney-General, damages are the pecuniary satisfaction due upon a breach of contract or for an injury caused to life, limb, or property by a person or by his agent. That is good, sound law which is not peculiar to Great Britain, but is the common property of all civilized nations. If such damages are not amicably agreed to and voluntarily paid, what is the remedy? For the person to go

The second complaint is that the apportionment of the damages is not according to law.

to a court of law and complain of the injury done, and ask the court to assess damages and pass judgment in favour of the plaintiff. But what is done here? Men who are no doubt good in their own routine work are sent out into the open country, made to meet people of all kinds and degrees, and asked to sit in judgment over the damages caused by persons, without a word of help or without any opinion expressed by the persons on whom the compensation falls. Is that justice, Sir? That is not justice. It is not even patriarchal Government. No, Sir, I do not think even a despot would do it, because he fears the wrath of the people and imposes on his own greed or passion some limit consistent with the aggregate strength of the people. He would ask himself, "Why should Peter be robbed to pay Paul? Why, in the assessment of damages, should not Peter have a voice?" No court of law would sanction this principle of making a man responsible for damages which he has not been given the opportunity to check, even though he is present and eager to check it. No court of law would sanction the principle of robbing Peter to pay Paul. We, of course, twenty or twenty-one members, can sit and glibly pass an Ordinance to give effect to it, and no doubt the great force of the King behind us will put it all through. But that, unfortunatetly, would not be consistent with the eternal principles of justice or with the ordinary law of the country. We may say, "Oh! it is a complicated question, the matter has arisen and continued for 100 long days, and now we must end it all quickly in this way. Let us bury it and put on the best face possible." But go into the country and see the people, Sir, sitting with a heavy

Why should Peter be robbed to pay Paul?

It is iniquitous to refuse investigation and deny justice, because the offence of the Government officers is too complicated.

heart and saying, "Oh! what is going to happen to us." See them crying. See them ask, "What has happened to our King? What has happened to our Governor? What has happened to the Legislative Council? Have we no protectors in this world? Are we to be made a football of by inexperienced and heartless men?" No, Sir, we have power to pass this Ordinance, but the good sense of this Council must assert itself, and with all the criticism that we are capable of we must analyze the whole question and once for all settle whether the complaints of the people are right or not. If they are right, I do not ask you, Sir, to punish your officers. Let them live. The world is broad enough for the good and the bad, but let justice be done to the poor innocent villagers. We need not be vindictive, Sir. But it is most important, for our own sakes, and for the trust that is reposed on us, for the duty that we owe to the King and to the people, that the petitions should not be thrown to the winds, and that there should be a pronouncement upon them in an authoritative way.

The people cry to the King for protection against the acts of inexperienced and heartless officers of the Government.

They call for a pronouncement on their case before passing the Ordinance.

The petitioners complain, Sir, that in defiance of the ordinary law of the country the Commissioners have made every able-bodied man residing in a headman's division liable for damages, without considering whether or not he caused any injury to any one, and whether or not he participated with the rioters. If their complaint is found to be true by the Council, neither Your Excellency nor the Secretary of State will sanction the apportionment and allotment of the Commissioners, and this Council cannot pass Chapter IX. of the proposed Ordinance.

The third complaint is that the compensation

The third complaint is that the compensation is quite disproportionate to the means of innocent villagers.

levied is not only out of proportion to the actual loss inflicted by the rioters, but also disproportionate to the means of the innocent villagers. Sir, many of us practise charity under compulsion. Many of us are afraid of public opinion, and it is not without a groan that many a subscription sees the light of day in the newspapers of Ceylon, and the subscription is not given out of real charitable feeling, but because other people expect us to do our duty, and we must rise to the occasion. All that is personal vanity.

The villagers of Ceylon are also much in the same predicament as we high folks in the world. They, too, will be prepared to do charity, if not freely and out of love for the Muhammadans, at least for the sake of being honoured by a certain class of people. Well, Sir, these persons say, "How can you expect me, a poor labourer getting only 50 cents a day, to lay down on the table, even in instalments, Rs. 100? How am I to do that? You know, Sir, that we have not enough to take two meals of rice and curry a day, that our meal consists occasionally of rice and mostly of jak and coconut and manioc and other roots. You know perfectly well that we have no oil to burn our lamps with, but we hurry up our cooking before it becomes dark, and eat our rice at about 6 o'clock in the evening, and go and sleep in the dark. All that is because we have nothing more than 50 cents a day to feed five mouths. How are we going to table Rs. 100 as compensation to the Muhammadans of Ceylon? It is out of all proportion to our resources. It is excessive and most oppressive, and if you put the screw on and expect us to pay, we must die in the attempt. There is nothing but ruin and beggary staring us in the face. What is to become

It will reduce them to ruin and beggary.

of our grown-up daughters? Improper proposals will be made to them. It is excruciating." We, who are feeding fat on our wealth, who roll along in motor cars and fine carriages, can have no conception of the grinding nature of the life which the people whom we have to deal with are labouring under. Europeans do not go to these places, except a few planters. I have spoken to a number of European planters—not to Mr. Huyshe Eliot, but to Mr. Sinclair and others—and they agree with me that the poverty of the country is our worst phenomenon, that the poor are very poor. I say that experienced planters are at one with the experienced Ceylonese as regards the impossibility of a poor villager paying Rs. 100 as compensation to the Muhammadans. Once you realize that fact, Sir, you will not be a party to this kind of legislation. You will say, "Hurry up, children, revise, revise, and remedy quickly."

The fourth complaint is the oppressive conduct of the Government officers selected for the work of assessment and apportionment, owing to their contempt of law and justice.

A far graver complaint, Sir, is the fourth, which, if true, reveals great contempt of law and procedure and much recklessness of mind on the part of the officers selected for the work of assessment and apportionment. The petitioners bitterly complain that Commissioners, attended each by a number of armed soldiers, forced them to produce their title deeds and to sign mortgages in favour of His Majesty securing the payment in four quarterly instalments of the fine imposed on them. They deny *in toto* that the bonds they were made to sign were voluntary. Before considering the terms of the mortgage bonds, let me call attention to some official documents which the petitioners have produced, and which throw a lurid light on the complaints made by them. Here is a printed notice, Sir, bearing date June 10, 1915,

Petitioners were coerced to produce their title-deeds and to sign mortgage bonds in favour of the King.

Official documents signed and widely published by such officers prove this statement.

purporting to be signed by a gentleman whose name I do not want to disclose, but I may say that he is a Government Agent and a Special Commissioner. That document runs as follows :—

"Whereas I, ———, have been appointed under the hand of the Officer Commanding the Troops, a Special Commissioner for the Western Province, for the purpose of inquiring into the recent riots, assessing damage, and levying compensation for such damage:

"I do hereby give notice, in the name of the military authorities, to all persons whomsoever in the said Province, that they are required to give every assistance, information, etc., to the military and civil authorities, and that *persons not obeying orders will be shot at sight.*

Persons not obeying the orders of military and civil officers will be shot at sight.

"All Moormen who have suffered damage should be ready with detailed claims for compensation. All Moormen are placed under the special protection of the headmen, who will be regarded as personal hostages for their maintenance and security."

I always understood, Sir, that the word "hostage" meant a person delivered to an enemy or hostile power as a pledge to secure the performance of conditions, and that the term "Government Agent" meant a superior officer appointed by the King to supervise headmen and other classes of Government servants in the work of administering a particular Province. I, therefore, fail to see how the Government Agent—the ruler and patron of his subordinates—converted himself into an enemy, and who delivered the headmen into his hands as hostages for the safety of the Moors. But let that pass, Sir.

The Hon. the Attorney-General :—Will the Honourable Member give us the name of the official who he says issued that notice?

The Hon. Mr. Rámanáthan :—Do you really want it? I will give you the printed document itself. It is Mr. Fraser. The notice is in black and white, Sir. Here is the document [hands document]. Similar notifications have been issued by other Commissioners also. No doubt, Sir, the Attorney-General is astonished, but I thought he knew all about it.

But let us consider the earlier part of this formidable notice. It enjoins upon all persons the necessity of giving assistance and information to the Commissioner in his work of assessing damages and levying compensation, on pain of being shot if the orders given were not instantly carried out. Therefore it cannot be denied that such notices, flung broadcast in the villages and towns of the Western Province, must have had a most enslaving effect on the minds of the villagers. Following this notice, Sir, came an announcement in the *Government Gazette* of June 25 last, intimating that the Officer Commanding the Troops in Ceylon had appointed as Special Commissioners twenty-seven gentlemen, all fully named, for five Provinces in the Island, and the functions entrusted to them were notified to be—

Such notices flung broadcast in villages and towns had a terrific effect on the people, since the 10th June.

(1) To inquire into all crimes and offences connected with the recent riots and disturbances in the towns and villages of the district for which they were appointed;

(2) To inquire into and assess all damage to

Then came the Brigadier-General's order, published in the *Government Gazette* of June 25th, appointing Military Commissioners invested with the power of District Judges and Police Magistrates, for assessing damages, arranging for payment of compensation and securing contributions from the inhabitants of the said towns and villages.

property caused by rioters and others in the towns and villages in the district;

(3) To arrange for the payment of compensation of such damages and for that purpose to secure contributions from the inhabitants of the said towns and villages.

All the twenty-seven Commissioners thus appointed were also declared by the Officer Commanding the Troops to be Additional District Judges and Police Magistrates for their Provinces and districts. Surely, Sir, the General has assumed too much power in creating District Judges and Police Magistrates.

The Hon. the Colonial Secretary :—I may perhaps correct a misapprehension in the honourable gentleman's mind if I observed that that circular merely stated that these gentlemen had been appointed District Judges and Police Magistrates. The appointments were made by the Governor. It was merely announced by the Brigadier-General as a matter of convenience.

The Hon. Mr. Rámanáthan :—My honourable friend has missed the point. I will explain.

The Hon. the Colonial Secretary :—The honourable gentleman distinctly said that the Brigadier-General has exceeded his powers by creating District Judges and Police Magistrates.

The Hon. Mr. Rámanáthan :—I shall not withdraw a single word of that. I have not erred, in fact. I was saying that soon after this notification by Mr. Fraser came a notification in the *Government Gazette* of June 25 last, which declares that the Officer Commanding the Troops had appointed these twenty-seven Special Commissioners to be Additional

District Judges and Police Magistrates for their Provinces or district. This notice, Sir, is signed by L. A. Northcote, Captain, D.A.A.G. Now, Sir, if the General Commanding the Forces had power to appoint District Judges and Police Magistrates, he may assume power to appoint the Supreme Court Judges and ourselves, Sir. A document of that kind going before the world carries some weight. A District Judge, Sir, has the right to send a man to jail for not answering questions, or for being contumacious in regard to his orders. So also a Police Magistrate. He might commit a man to jail on the spot. Well, when a *Gazette* notice like this goes from the General Officer Commanding the Troops, what are the people to do, but to feel themselves as slaves in the hands of the military authorities, just as they felt themselves enslaved by the Government Agent's notice to the people of his Province that they would be shot if they did not obey his orders.

The people felt themselves to be slaves in the hands of the military and civil authorities, with the fear of being shot if they did not carry out their orders.

After these terrifying notices and *Gazette* notifications came the Special Commissioners in motor cars bristling with the guns and bayonets of the Punjabis. The petitioners complain, and complain with good reason, Sir, that the Commissioners ordered the villagers to produce their title deeds and to sign the mortgage bonds. There is, Sir, a *primâ facie* case made out by these villagers in regard to the statements contained in the petition. We know that certain things, such as notices, notifications, and armed police, etc., had preceded the arrival of the Commissioners, and the petitioners say that, when the Commissioners went to the village, they ordered the villagers, sometimes directly by the use

Arrival of the Commissioners in motor-cars, bristling with the guns and bayonets of soldiers, and their order to produce title-deeds and sign bonds in favour of the King.

of the Sinhalese language, or sometimes indirectly with the aid of the Mudaliyars of the district, to produce their title deeds within so many days, and that if they did not do so, they would be dealt with under the martial law. The villagers say they were terrified, as they had had practical examples of the operation of martial law. When I come to the question of the operation of martial law some other time, Sir—not to-day—you will hear the doings of the officers concerned in the enforcement of martial law. The petitioners have seen with their own eyes men hauled up and shot without charge or without trial. They remember, they say, the treatment that such and such a man received at the hands of the Panjabis, who shot him dead. Such instances were quoted by some of the Special Commissioners at one or more of their sittings.

Petitioners who had seen innocent men hauled up and shot without charge or trial were terrified beyond measure.

In great terror the petitioners humbly produced their title deeds, because the idea was thrown out that the Panjabis would come and ransack their houses. It was no good concealing their title deeds anywhere, so they said: "Here, master, are our title deeds; what more do you want us to do? Sign documents? There is a halter round our necks. There is penury and beggary staring us in the face, and the desecration and destruction of our homes. If they will let us off with our lives, it will suffice," and they signed the bonds.

How can the Legislative Council of Ceylon shirk the duty of inquiring into these things?

Sir, if this Honourable Council has heard of such things directly from the people for whose benefit we have been appointed, can any member rise from his seat and say, "We shall not allow that complaint to be heard. We shall not allow ourselves to give a pronouncement upon the charges made against the

Commissioners"? That kind of nature is not in the hearts of any member of this Council. I believe that they are all gentlemen. If they have erred, they will be the first to stand up and say, "I have erred. I have exposed myself to criticism, and even the condemnation of Your Excellency, but let me do justice now and remedy the wrongs that have been done to the people."

The Police Headmen, Sir, appear to have been commanded by the Korale or District Mudaliyars, who in turn have been commanded by the Commissioners to force the people to surrender their title deeds, like the guns with which they protected their fields and plantations, to the Commissioners. Here is a typical order, Sir, by a Korale Mudaliyar to a Police Headman :—

"The amount of indemnity specified by the Commissioners is Rs. 7,900. You are therefore ordered to appear on ———, at ———, with title deeds in value to twice the amount in question as security. You are not required to bring the men on ———, but you should be ready with a list of the valuation of the lands on that day.

Written order of a Korale Mudaliyár to surrender title-deeds and bring a male goat for feeding the soldiers, on pain of a fine of Rs. 2,000 for not supplying the goat.

"You are further ordered by the Commissioner to bring a male goat for the use of the Panjabis, and if you do not bring the male goat as required, your amount of indemnity will be increased by another Rs. 2,000.

"(Signed) ———,
"Mudaliyar, ——— Korale."

A goat for Rs. 2,000! These and other atrocious proceedings, Sir, require to be sifted carefully. If true, they would vitiate every one of the bonds taken.

So far, Sir, as to what happened in the villages. As regards towns, here is a summons bearing the British coat of arms professing to be signed by a Government Agent and Special Commissioner, and bearing date of delivery July 17, 1915. It was served on a Sinhalese gentleman, and runs as follows :—

Another written order signed by the Government-Agent and Special Commissioner informing the people that, if title-deeds are not surrendered and bonds signed, the parties will be taken into custody.

"1. You are hereby ordered to appear at ——— Kachcheri on July 21, 1915, at 1 p.m., with the sum of Rs. 540, being damages due by you for losses caused to the Muhammadans of ——— palata by the rioters.

"2. In the event of your not being able to pay the said sum on the said date, you are requested to appear with a deed in your favour, or in favour of your surety, to sign a mortgage bond in favour of the Government as security for the payment of the said sum.

"3. If you do not obey these summons, you will be taken into custody."

This document, if true—I believe it is true, Sir, because I have got the original of it—shows that the method of levying compensation in towns was the same as that adopted in villages, viz., by intimidation and force.

Let us now, Sir, proceed to consider the wording of the mortgage bonds, which reveals the situation of affairs fairly well. I do not know if my honourable friend the Attorney-General had anything to do with the drawing up of the mortgage bond, but I have got copies of it in my hand. These are the bonds that we are asked to confirm by the Bill before us. They run as follows :—

"Know all men by these presents that *we, the undersigned persons of the village of* ———, are hereby jointly and severally held and firmly bound unto our Sovereign Lord King George the Fifth, his heirs and successors, in the sum of rupees ———, for which payment well and truly to be made we do hereby bind ourselves, our heirs, successors, and administrators firmly by these presents.

A copy of the mortgage bond which the people were forced to sign.

"And by way of further security for the due payment of the said sum of rupees ———, we do hereby hypothecate and mortgage unto our Sovereign Lord the King all our property, whether movable or immovable, wheresoever they may be situated.

"And by way of further security for the due fulfilment of the said bond, we do hereby specially mortgage the immovable properties set out in the schedule to this bond."

Before I proceed further let me say that the foregoing words acknowledge a debt to the King and create a special mortgage. Then the bond seeks to justify itself by these words, which are very significant, Sir :—

"Whereas in or about the beginning of the month of June, 1915, armed Sinhalese Buddhist mobs systematically attacked and destroyed sundry Moorish Muhammadan villages, houses, and boutiques, and looted the property of Moorish Muhammadans and *were guilty of other acts of lawlessness amounting to the offence of high treason against our Sovereign Lord the King:*

" And whereas martial law was proclaimed in the Province of ——— on ——— of June, 1915 :

" And whereas the General Officer Commanding the Troops, acting in pursuance of the powers vested in him, appointed ——— Special Commissioner, hereinafter referred to as the Special Commissioner, to make inquiry in each village and district, and assess the said damage caused to the said Moorish Muhammadans :

" And whereas the said Commissioner *has inquired into the damage caused in the said village*, and has assessed the said damage at rupees ——— :

" And whereas *we, the principal inhabitants of the said village*, with a view to the settlement of all losses sustained by *the Moorish Muhammadans of the said village*, and in consideration of an undertaking by the said Special Commissioner made on behalf of the Government of Ceylon, that, subject to the faithful performance of these presents, *the said village* shall be exempted from such punitive burdens as shall in such cases be hereafter imposed by Ordinance or otherwise, have agreed with the said Special Commissioner to pay him, or according to his order, the said sum of rupees ——— in four quarterly instalments, payable on ———, and to enter into this bond.

" Now the condition of the above-written bond is such that if the said sum of rupees ——— is duly paid in four quarterly instalments, together with the said interest, on the dates aforesaid, then this bond shall be null and void, but otherwise shall be in force and virtue."

Noteworthy points of the bond.

Now, Sir, the points to be noted in this document are as follows :—First, the signatories to the bond are described as persons residing in a certain village named. Second, the Special Commissioner is said to have inquired into the damage caused in the said village and to have assessed the said damage at rupees ———. Third, the signatories are described as the principal residents of the said village in which the damage was caused. Fourth, the losses are said to have been sustained by the Moors of the said village in which the signatories reside. Fifth, the Special Commissioner is said to have entered into an agreement with the signatories to exempt the said village from certain punitive burdens not yet sanctioned by the Legislative Council. Sixth, the signatories are said to have signed the bond in consideration of the Special Commissioner's promise to exempt them from impending punitive burdens.

The principal feature, Sir, that emerges out of the bond is that damages were caused by the rioters in the very village in which the signatories reside, and that the signatories voluntarily signed the bond in order to avoid the punitive burdens which the Special Commissioner said were impending. The punitive burdens, Sir, were non-existent. This Council alone can impose punitive burdens, and so long as a law to that effect is not passed by this Council, no man can hold in his hand a bond and say to the people that unless it is signed the punitive burdens will come, and that if they sign the bond he will see that they do not come.

Sir, what a demoralizing state of affairs does this disclose. Decency, the exigencies of public life, honour, and morality alike are against any such proposal being made by any officer of Government to the people who are entrusted to his care and protection. To misuse all the great power of his situation, to intimidate them by threats of impending burdens into signing a bond of the most oppressive character—why, Sir, if the matter went into a court of law, that august tribunal, which my honourable friend the Attorney-General has so feelingly spoken of as the soul of honour and as the one body that was fearless of the Executive Government, would condemn the action of the officer and cast that bond to the winds as utterly vain and ineffectual. And why should you, Sir, a greater person than the Supreme Court, sanction this proceeding when the facts are brought before you. From my experience of you, I say that you would be the last person to tarnish and desecrate the principles of justice, so carefully fostered by the British Government for a century or more, by allowing these proceedings to be confirmed by the authority of this Council.

Impossibility of recovering in a court of law the money said to be due to the King upon the bond.

Most of the petitions, Sir, say that the damages caused by the rioters were far away from the limits of the petitioners' villages, and that they are utterly innocent, and that it would be unjust to impose punitive burdens on them. It is not difficult to see, Sir, that the draftsman of the bond is a lawyer, that his opinion is that those who did not cause any injury to the Moors should not be liable in damages; that if the principal residents of the disturbed villages are to be asked to sign the bond for the payment of the damage caused by others, it should be for a con-

Allegations recited in the bond in justification of its obligations are wholly false.

sideration; and that the consideration of avoiding punitive burdens may be a good consideration for the agreement to pay compensation. Neither is it difficult, Sir, to see that the Special Commissioners, whose knowledge of legal procedure and legal documents could not but be scanty owing to their want of study and training, though the title of District Judge and Police Magistrate is given to them, completely missed the point of view of the lawyer-draftsman and made the inhabitants of undisturbed villages also to sign the bond that was not intended for them. If upon inquiry it be found that, as a matter of fact, the residents of undisturbed villages were made to sign the bonds made only for the residents of disturbed villages, the obligation in the bond would count for nothing, because both the parties to the bond were in error, even if no fraud was intended.

The last complaint of the petitioners is that the Commissioners have not taken notice of the claims made by the Sinhalese for damages suffered by them.

The last complaint, Sir, by the petitioners is that the Special Commissioners have not taken notice of the claims made by the Sinhalese (Buddhists and Christians) for damage suffered by them at the hands of the rioters and looters. There is no doubt, Sir, that, in the early stages of the riots, the Sinhalese Buddhist was grinding his axe against the Coast Moorman, called *Hambaya*, who had obstructed his procession in Gampola and Kandy. But within two days of the outbreak, during which the criminal classes had the time to observe the passivity and the paralysis of the police force and their opportunity for loot, thousands of Christian Sinhalese belonging to the criminal and unemployed population found it a paying business to join their Buddhist brethren in the general fray, and plunder the stores of not only

Changes in the course of the riots as regards the persons attacked.

the Coast Moors or *Hambayas*, but also of the resident Moors, called by the Sinhalese *Marakkalayas*. Why, they even occasionally looted the stores of the Sinhalese and Tamils too. Rioting and looting thus became general for four or five days. In these circumstances, the damage done to the Sinhalese and Tamils was as worthy of consideration as the damage done to the Muhammadans. I have read to you petitions showing that many a Sinhalese man has had his property damaged, and that he has been refused compensation, and the Tamils have also come forward with petitions saying that their claims have not been admitted by the Special Commissioners. On what principle can we deny compensation arising out of the same set of circumstances to one class of people, while we are giving compensation freely to another class of people? That will not be justice; that will not be fair.

If compensation is due to the Moors, it is also to the Sinhalese and Tamils.

An inquiry into all these complaints should be made by the Select Committee moved for.

Now, Sir, we who have heard these complaints directly made to us must not be callous or deaf. We owe it to them and to the King, who has called us in fair Ceylon to do our respective duties, to go into these matters in detail and once for all pronounce upon the situation that has been created by the unfortunate circumstances which were ushered in on May 29 last. Howsoever hard or unpleasant the work may be, we must take the petitions severally into our hands and go into them, even as a Judge would take into his hands a complaint from the meanest villager and make him call evidence, examine the other side of the case, and give a judgment that would satisfy the conscience of the country.

I beg, Sir, that you will not hesitate to appoint a Select Committee to inquire into all these complaints, and only after their report is tabled should you be prepared to take up the second reading of the Bill and make it live or die as the circumstances will admit of. My own feelings, Sir, are that you will do justice, and that even the officers about whom I have spoken will be prepared to do justice, by the appointment of a Select Committee. I move, Sir, for the appointment of a Select Committee.

The Hon. the Second Low-country Sinhalese Member seconded.

(5) *The Reply of Mr. Rámanáthan to the Hon. the Attorney-General's Speech on behalf of the Government of Ceylon opposing the Motion for the Select Committee (October* 14, 1915*).*

The misconceptions of the Attorney-General.

The Hon. Mr. Rámanáthan:—Sir, I was not surprised to hear my honourable friend say that I was living in an unreal world, implying that he himself was living in a real world. I was not surprised, because I know him to be earnest and strong in conviction, but, of course, convictions may often be wrong. He is convinced that the case he fathered on me was really my case. Having set up a case which I never set up, he bombarded and knocked it down, and feels happy that he has done a clever feat. Who lives in an unreal world, Sir? He or I? He charged me with not recognizing the great sufferings of the Muhammadans; with not taking note of the fact that from Kandy downwards to Matara much destruction of property had been caused, together with loss of limb and life. Why does he say that I have not taken notice of these things? I appeal to every one of my honourable friends and ask them if I ever said one word to that effect to-day or any other day. On the contrary, if the reporters in this chamber are called upon to examine their shorthand notes of my speech, my honourable friend will find that I acknowledged more than once the great sympathy I had with the Muhammadans, and I said that I would rejoice very much if by any possibility that was legal the wrong done to them could be righted.

Sir, I am not conscious of living in an unreal world. I believe the Attorney-General, in the intensity of his wrong convictions, has persuaded himself that he is living in a world of realities.

His defence does not touch the specific points raised.

The greater part of his speech was mere declamation. He did not meet squarely and fairly any of the specific points that I raised—quite apart from the statements that were contained in the petitions which it was my duty to read. I have not identified myself with the statements contained in the petitions. I summarized them because it was my duty to do so. I said that, independently of the petitions, certain official documents had come to my hands, and that when I examined them I found there was a *primâ facie* case against the procedure adopted by certain of the Commissioners which went far to disqualify the work of assessment and allotment done by them. My honourable friend has not met these points, and therefore I say that the whole of his speech is neither apposite nor just. Who denied the sufferings of the people? Who denied the desire of some people to pay compensation? But how does the Attorney-General know the universal sentiments prevailing in the hearts of four million people as regards their desire to pay compensation? Are they able to pay it, and when unable to do so, do they feel called upon to pay it? How can he speak for the four million people in Ceylon and say to us that he feels quite sure that the public of Ceylon are with him in his statement that compensation must be paid. He says too much. He is living in an unreal world. He takes his wrong convictions for facts. I am astonished, Sir, that my honourable friend has given himself away on such obvious points.

The falsity of his argument regarding the shower of artificially organised petitions.

Now, Sir, he says that he is obliged to reject my motion, first, because what he calls this shower of petitions is artificially organized, and is the work of professional petition drawers. This is another erroneous conviction in his unreal world. Has my honourable friend considered the work of the petition drawer in reference to the work done in his own department, and even by himself? As Attorney-General, he knows nothing of the things that have happened in the Provinces or been done by those Government officers who seek his help, some to bring an action against wrongdoers or breakers of contract, and some to defend them against private plaintiffs. A number of papers come to him, and some officers also go to see him in his chambers. When he utilizes the rich material of his brain and works out a case for them, and even dares to present it to a learned Judge in a way that was not contemplated by the Government Agent or other officer of Government, sometimes such officer has been known to say: "No, no, Attorney-General, that is not exactly what I mean. I would rather that you stated my case in the way I have indicated, because it is more in consonance with what actually happened." The Attorney-General replies: "No, you do not know the legal aspects of the case. The statement you have submitted to me means all that I have pleaded. I know my business and I must present the case, out of your material, in the way that I like." Can anybody, even a Judge of the Supreme Court, cry shame upon the Attorney-General for doing what the law of pleading permits him to do? He is there to prepare cases and defend cases on behalf of the Government, and he does it so dexterously that even his client, the Government of Ceylon, is astonished at the ingenuity of his arguments and pleadings.

Well, Sir, turn now your attention to the work of the petition drawer. The poor villager comes from the village burning with a grievance and goes to the best petition drawer in Colombo, let us say, Mr. Blazé, and tells him in his own language—that is, the Sinhalese language—all the facts that he knows. Perhaps the Sinhalese villager takes an intelligent friend of his from the village, or even a proctor who has studied the case from all points of view. The professional petition drawer—no shame to him, neither to the professional lawyer—receives the whole case from the lips of the villager and his friends, and prepares a petition which commands the respect of all enlightened men as a statement which bears the impress of truth. No point is missed that deserves the consideration of the Government of Ceylon. My honourable friend, forgetting the parity of things between himself and the poor professional petition drawer, throws vials of ridicule upon the petition drawer, puts his foot down upon him, and says, "I will not have you deluding the Legislative Council of the Island with your artificial story."

Sir, this is a clap-trap argument. There is neither truth nor justice in it. Nor does it hold up to our consideration the importance of the issues involved, or the proper way in which we should deal with them.

I am sure that, howsoever cleverly a petition drawer may have stated the case, there is only one question before the Legislative Council, and that is whether that petition, notwithstanding its artificial magnificence, contains an element of truth in it. Let not the Attorney-General fix his mind upon the poor professional petition drawer, or upon the language which is quite suitable to the lips of an M.A. of a University, but rather let him gather the grains of fact involved in the words. I ask him whether he can charge his conscience with the falsehood of those statements. Without investigation can he say for certain that the statements contained in the petitions are untrue. Have I not shown that official notifications and other documents actually signed and issued by responsible officers of Government reveal a series of most illegal and high-handed proceedings. If they are true what must he do? Must not he be the first person to advise the Government to make an inquiry into the case? But what does he say? "Some of the officers complained of are Honourable Members of this Council, great and glorious men. They and others who have assessed damages are perfect Trojans in work and examples of honour. What? Hear complaints against them by the people of the country, expose them to ridicule and imperil the work of the Government of Ceylon in regard to the attainment of order, peace, and authority?" He virtually says, "No; my affection for them is greater than that. I love them, I believe them, they are immaculate, they are incorrupt. They are quite unable to do any wrong, and, therefore, you brutes, get out of this. I will not have anything to do with you."

He is quite silent as regards the printed notifications of the Commissioners and these illegal and oppressive proceedings.

He says, in the teeth of written proof, that they are too immaculate to do wrong.

The Hon. the Attorney-General :—That is quite foreign to anything I have said.

The Hon. Mr. Rámanáthan :—I beg his pardon,

Sir, I believe that is the effect of his words, the extent to which his statements go. But I hear he disowns it. I am glad of that. I will accept his assurance. But I regret that without fixing his attention upon the statements of fact which are contained in the petitions, he has allowed his predilection for the officers at this table to be in the way of an inquiry upon the points urged in the petitions. He says, " We repudiate *in toto* the statements made by the petitioners against honourable officers." Supposing he was a Judge on the bench, could he say that? Could he say to the plaintiff, " I repudiate your statements, as an inquiry into your allegations would affect the dignity of the defendant. Therefore I will not hear the case." I do not think he would say so. I need not labour that point.

He refuses an inquiry because they are honourable officers, and the inquiry would affect their dignity.

Then he says that the work of inquiry suggested by me is impracticable. He says the Special Committee of this Council cannot do it. Why, Sir, Special Committees have before now done this kind of work in this very Council—not under your régime.

His argument that inquiry is impracticable is obviously an evasion of duty.

His Excellency the Governor :—Not about riots.

The Hon. Mr. Rámanáthan :—Not about riots, but about even more complicated things than riots. About riots too, Sir, now I come to think of it. There was a riot between the Roman Catholics and the Buddhists in Colombo. You will find that a Committee was appointed to inquire into the causes and consequences of the riots. They called evidence, and came to a verdict on many matters of fact and law. You will find their report in the Sessional Papers of 1883, I think. It is an important State document. Then, Sir, many Special Committees have sat in this very hall during the last forty years and dealt with questions similar to this. I do not see any practical difficulty about a Special Committee inquiring into the assessment. I recognize this fact, that when a person does not want to do a thing, it is easy for him to say, "Oh! it is impracticable, and therefore you cannot expect one to do it." I am not in the least impressed by the plea of the Attorney-General, by the justice of it, or by the correctness of the position he has taken up.

If the reports of the Commissioners are placed before the Select Committee, what more easy for the Committee than to read them and the papers on which the reports are founded, and settle in their mind how the course of things lies? What more easy than to summon a few witnesses in typical cases, and if it is found, by studying the map and the topography of the place, that the assessments as to disturbed and undisturbed villages and imposition of compensation on innocent persons as stated in the petitions are true, then it would be needless to go into detail in every case. We can say that a sufficient number of cases has been examined by us in reference to the proceedings of every one of the Commissioners, and we find such and such errors in them, and we make such and such recommendations. There is no impracticability about it, and we need not want thirty long months to prove the work which thirty able Commissioners have done in sixty days.

He leaves untouched the terms of the mortgage bond, which are not true, and the force used by the Commissioners to obtain the signatures of the petitions.

Well, Sir, my honourable friend has not dealt with the mortgage bond itself that I quoted from first to last. He has left that severely alone. I read to Honourable Members from first to last a typical mortgage bond, and I said, "Now, what is the standpoint of view of this mortgage bond?" It is that the damages took place in the place of residence of the signatory himself, and that the damages in that village were, as a matter of fact, assessed by the Commissioners. I pointed out that the petitioners complained that, though in very many cases no damages were done in villages, and though the signatories to the bonds did not participate in the riots at all, yet they were forced to sign the bond. I also showed that the allotment proceeding upon a promiscuous basis could not be just, and that in very many cases the amount of the assessment had to be reduced by fifty per cent. or more. My honourable friend the Attorney-General quibbled a little with the word "reduction," but at last he was forced to admit that he was obliged to alter the figures in the bond in terms of a revised assessment.

Sir, this is an astounding statement. A bond given by one person to another is usually in the possession of the latter, and does the Hon. the Attorney-General say to me as a lawyer that any alteration of the bond by the grantee, without the consent of the grantor, is legal or justifiable? If I granted a promissory note to my honourable friend with the amount inserted in it, he has no right to alter the figures in it in the secrecy of his own chamber. So also I say he has no right to alter a mortgage bond in favour of the Crown without reference to the person who signed it, and the admission he has made to-day at the Council table is a disgrace to the Government that cannot be easily forgotten.

The laxity in procedure and contempt of the principles of justice shown by the Government officers are amazing and discreditable.

Sir, there has been much backsliding in principle and much disrespect for law and legal procedure during the past few months.

His Excellency the Governor :—I do not quite

follow the Honourable and learned Member. I understand the point to be that a man entered into a bond for Rs. 100, and his creditor let him off with Rs. 30.

The Hon. Mr. Rámanáthan :—No, Sir. He altered the bond. The Hon. the Attorney-General said that. I have got his words. But let that pass. It is going on to 9 o'clock. I say the laxity in procedure and contempt for the principles of justice which I have observed during the last few months is amazing, and does not do credit to the officers who are entrusted with the duty of governing the country.

Sir, I think I have said enough to show that the points referred to by the people in the numerous petitions are worthy of consideration, and that we are asking nothing impracticable or unfair in begging the Council to halt a little before they obtain our consent to the retention of Clause 41 of the Bill which is before us.

I have not spoken a word about the second reading of the Bill, or about the other forty clauses of the Bill. I have got much to say about it. It will be my duty to refer to the main principles of that Bill at its second reading. Without expressing my opinion now about the different clauses of the Bill, I say that in justice and honour we are bound in duty to the people on one side, and the King on the other, to examine the complaints of the people and see whether the bonds sought to be confirmed by Section 41 of the Bill were obtained by intimidation and duress, and whether the signatories to the bond were participators or non-participators in the riots.

Bonds obtained by intimidation and duress cannot stand.

The motion was then put to the meeting and His Excellency the Governor declared that the "Noes" had it.

The Hon. the Ceylonese Member :—Divide.

A division was then taken with the following result :—

*For*—6.

The Hon. the Second Tamil Member.
The Hon. the European Urban Member.
The Hon. the Second Low-country Sinhalese Member.
The Hon. the First Low-country Sinhalese Member.
The Hon. the Kandyan Sinhalese Member.
The Hon. the Ceylonese Member.

*Against*—13.

The Hon. the European Rural Member.
The Hon. the Muhammadan Member.
The Hon. Mr. W. C. S. Ingles, Acting Surveyor-General.
The Hon. Mr. F. Bowes, Principal Collector of Customs.
The Hon. the Principal Civil Medical Officer.
The Hon. the Government Agent of the Southern Province.
The Hon. the Government Agent of the Central Province.
The Hon. the Government Agent of the Western Province.
The Hon. the Treasurer.
The Hon. the Controller of Revenue.
The Hon. the Attorney-General.
The Hon. the Colonial Secretary.
The Hon. the Officer Commanding the Troops.

His Excellency the Governor :—" Ayes " 6, " Noes " 18. So the " Noes " have it.

The motion was accordingly lost, at 9.30 p.m.

---

At this stage the meeting adjourned till 10.45 p.m.

## (6) *Mr. Rámanáthan's Speech opposing the Second Reading of the Bill to make provision for the Levy of Compensation on all the Sinhalese, irrespective of the question whether they participated in the riots or not.*

The Hon. Mr. Rámanáthan (the Ceylonese Member) :—In rising, Sir, to oppose the second reading of this Bill, permit me to acknowledge, Sir, the extreme attention which Your Excellency has devoted to the consideration of this complicated question, and also to say that I recognize that every word that fell from the Attorney-General in recommendation of the principles of this Bill has left the impression upon my mind that he is quite sincere in his conviction——

His Excellency the Governor :—Hear, hear.

The Hon. Mr. Rámanáthan :—And does not hold a brief only for the Government of Ceylon. In these circumstances my duty to the Council becomes proportionately more difficult in the endeavour to show that, notwithstanding all its care and earnestness, the Government has erred gravely in the analysis of the complicated facts before it, and in the reasoning adopted to solve the problems which it desired to settle. We, Unofficial Members, do not know exactly the methods by which the Commissioners have come to their conclusions, because we have not seen their reports and the papers on which

The Attorney-General is in error in stating that the bulk of the people in the Western Province have acquiesced in the Government assessment.

their reports depend. But the Attorney-General has given us a glimpse of the conclusions arrived at by the Commissioners appointed during the days of the martial law. He says that in the city of Colombo and the remaining parts of the Western Province the damages done amount to four million rupees. In the Central Province about half a million, in the Province of Sabaragamuwa about half a million, in the Southern Province about a quarter million, and in the North-Western Province about a quarter million, making a total of five and a half million rupees. He also says that the inhabitants of the disturbed areas in the North-Western Province have accepted the assessment of the Government Agent as correct, and have expressed their willingness to pay voluntarily the sum of a quarter million rupees, and that they have allotted it amongst themselves and have actually paid it. I heard of their willingness, but surely the Attorney-General is mistaken in supposing that the great bulk of the Western Province has followed the same course as that adopted by the North-Western Province, because I know, from the numerous petitions that have come into my hands, that the villages of the Western Province have bitterly complained, not only of the assessment of the Government Agent, but also of the manner in which the assessed amount has been allotted. The sums demanded of the petitioners, according to the petitions in my hands, most of which I have presented already amount to three million rupees, Sir. If four million rupees be the amount claimed by the Government from the Western Province, and three millions of it are vehemently objected to, it cannot be said that the bulk of the Western Province has acquiesced in the Government assessment and are ready to pay the amount as readily as the North-Western Province people have done.

The Hon. the Attorney-General :—May I interrupt the Honourable Member? What I said was that they had entered into bonds and followed the same course, that is, undertaken to make voluntary payments. May I also say that probably the three million rupees he has added up refer to the original estimate and not to the final assessment.

The Hon. Mr. Rámanáthan :—I am glad to have that explanation, Sir, if it be an explanation. But at present, for want of information, I am unable to draw a distinction between the estimate and the assessment. In my mind, and in the minds of the villagers and of everybody else that I know of outside the Government circle, there does not seem to be any difference between the assessment and the estimate, because the assessment itself is an estimate. It would not do for people to believe that, because a jury, for instance, has assessed the amount of damages, it means that the exact sum, which only God knows, has been found correctly by the jury. It is only their estimate; it is an opinion. The estimate is an opinion in the first place, and the assessment is also practically an opinion; though resting perhaps upon some more detailed information. Anyway, I am glad to be assured that there has been a reduction on the assessment or estimate of 70 per cent. That is something gained by the people, Sir.

His Excellency the Governor :—Yes, that is right. Gained by the people and given very freely and readily by the Government Agent.

The Hon. Mr. Rámanáthan :—Quite so. But still

I do not know whether the five and a half millions of rupees referred to by the Attorney-General mean the reduced amount or the original amount. I think the statement of the Attorney-General as regards Colombo and the Western Province was drawn in a roseate hue, whereas the truth, as I understand the sentiments of the people, is that they are weeping and gnashing their teeth over this estimate or assessment. And what they are concerned most about is this, Sir, that without any opportunity given them to examine the assessment as made by the Government Agent, they are called upon to pay the sums assessed as if they were not subjects entitled to the protection of His Majesty the King, but were the slaves of the Government of Ceylon.

The people are weeping and gnashing their teeth over this assessment.

They feel that they have been treated as if they were the slaves of the Government of Ceylon, and not the servants of the King, entitled to his protection.

If I am called upon to pay moneys, I certainly will ask—I think Your Excellency would ask if the same demand was made upon you—"Please explain why you call upon me to pay this amount, and how you have made up your bill against me." Is that wrong or impertinent? And if the man who makes the demand be a gentleman who loves his own honour and has a sense of justice, isn't it his duty to say, "Here is my bill, look at it. I shall be very glad to show you how it is arrived at." But the Government of Ceylon is determined to have its own way of no explanation and stand and deliver. The people think that it is utterly wrong, and that it is unrighteous to rob Peter to pay Paul. The villagers are Peter, the Muhammadans are Paul, and somebody is robbing Peter to pay Paul.

"No explanation; stand and deliver," is the attitude of the Government.

It is unrighteous to rob Peter to pay Paul.

Neither, Sir, do I understand the Attorney-General's statement that, after all, the damages claimed from the villagers is very little, because if

The incidence of the allotment is far more burdensome than the Attorney-General thinks.

the amount of the damage is worked on the basis per head of the population liable to the road tax, the damage per head in the Colombo District would be Rs. 15.16, in the Western Province Rs. 3.56, in the Province of Sabaragamuwa Rs. 1.35, in the Central Province 80 cents, in the Southern Province 55 cents, and in the North-Western Province 36 cents. I feel sure, Sir, that this is a very misleading statement, which my honourable friend has taken as gospel truth from a wily official who is trying to screen a brood of wrongdoers and throw dust in the eyes of the public. If the Council will study the petitions presented to the Governor and the Council, it will be seen how enormous and crushing is the allotment to each villager. I read to you about four hours ago two petitions from two different villages showing what the actual amount is that falls on each villager even on the basis of the reduced amounts. It is several times beyond the amounts mentioned by the Attorney-General.

The Hon. the Attorney-General :—Does the Honourable Member realize that Rs. 3.56 is per head of the population? The figure I gave, Rs. 15, is per road tax payer for the Colombo District.

The Hon. Mr. Rámanáthan :—What is the value of this explanation, Sir? My contention remains true that the incidence of the allotment is unbearable. It is very different from the figures quoted by the Attorney-General.

And may I ask, Sir, whether you have personally considered the grievances of the people in regard to the mortgage bonds which were taken by the Commissioners and which we are asked to confirm to-day? You assured us that you would give your most careful

The Governor's assurance to the Council that he would give his own personal attention to every Petition presented has not been fulfilled.

consideration to every petition presented, and if that be so, I thought the people would be safe. But up to this day, neither I nor any of my honourable colleagues on this side of the house have received any intimation from you, Sir, or the Hon. the Colonial Secretary, that the complaints of the people have been examined, and what the results of such examination are. In the meanwhile, the feeling has grown far and wide that the Government may grant a reduction in the amount of compensation, but will certainly not wipe it out altogether even in the case of those villages which have not been disturbed by riots and in which the inhabitants have not done wrong to anybody. It has been represented to me, Sir, by a recent letter, that in one of the petitions presented to you it was stated that though not a single person had done any wrong to any Muhammadan or taken part in the riot anywhere, my informant's village being situated three or four miles away from any of the disturbed villages, the Commissioner ordered the male adults to pay no less a sum than Rs. 6,000. I understand that this petition was referred by Your Excellency to a deeply interested Commissioner, who is himself charged with oppression and intimidation, to consider and dispose of the petition against the Commissioner who assessed the village in a similar way, and that the former Commissioner informed the petitioner that he saw no reason to re-consider the decision arrived at by the other Commissioner. There is no doubt about the truth of this representation, Sir, for I hold in my hands the reply of the Commissioner to the petitioners, which runs as follows. It is dated August 9, 1915 :

Petitions referred for consideration and disposal to the officer himself who is charged with oppression and intimidation.

"With reference to the petition of the villagers of Tammitta, addressed to His Excellency the Governor, and sent to me for disposal,"—not for report—"I have to say that Mr. Moore, Special Commissioner, has fixed a very reasonable amount to be paid by the village. If it is found possible, the amount will be ultimately reduced, but no promise to this effect can be given at present.

"(Signed) J. G. FRASER,
"Special Commissioner."

Sir, I ask, how can this inquiry and decision be considered just and proper? How can it produce satisfaction in the hearts of the complainants and respect for British justice which our people have loved so long?

Then, Sir, I come to another feature of the compensation. It can never be put upon the right shoulders unless the causes of the riots are ascertained and responsibility fixed upon the persons who perpetrated the riots and permitted the continuance of them. What strikes me, Sir, is this, that the Government does not appear to have consulted the most experienced residents in the country, Europeans or Ceylonese, about the question of the cause of the riots. Not even the Unofficial Members of this Council have been consulted in proper time, so that their advice might fructify and be of some use to the Government in the disposal of the question of responsibility for the riots, and other questions that have arisen as a consequence of the riots.

The question who should pay compensation depends on the question who caused the riots.

The Government did not confer in due season with the leading men of experience on the subject.

His Excellency the Governor:—Mr. Rámanáthan, I think there are only two Unofficial Members whose opinion I do not personally and confidentially know on the subject of the origin of the riots. It so happens that I do know the opinion of the rest of the Unofficial Members by personal conversation with them, though it is confidential.

The Hon. Mr. Rámanáthan :—I appreciate Your Excellency's difficulties as regards the ascertainment of the causes of the recent riots. They cannot be easily settled. It is a profound subject, which at its inception required very serious consideration for days, and therefore I admit that, with your Excellency's numerous and important engagements, which cannot be postponed, it was difficult for you to sit down and hear persons——

His Excellency the Governor :—Not at all, Mr. Rámanáthan. It is a great pleasure to me. I do sit down and hear their opinions very frequently and at great length. I have heard you, for instance, and it has been a great pleasure to me.

The Hon. Mr. Rámanáthan :—But that was long after the introduction of your remedies for the riots and their consequences. I was going to say, Sir, that persons who have taken the trouble to dive deep into these questions are very few in the Island, so that Your Excellency's remark is true that no two persons are agreed upon the cause of the riots.

His Excellency the Governor :—I said there are not more than two Unofficial Members whose opinions I did not confidentially know. I am sorry I did not make myself clear.

The Hon. Mr. Rámanáthan :—I regret I have misunderstood you, Sir. But as regards the remedy of compensation and the other drastic measures which appear on the face of this Bill, I think justice cannot be done unless the true causes of the riots are probed into. In India, Sir, there is a vast accumulation of experience as regards riots, both in the official and the unofficial mind.

His Excellency the Governor :—The Honourable Member does not suggest that we should rival India in the wealth of our experience of riots? I hope not, Mr. Rámanáthan.

The Hon. Mr. Rámanáthan :—I was going to say, Sir, that the method by which the riots have been dealt with in India are worth noting by our officials here, because such a study would dispose of a number of ugly features that are worrying the hearts of the people here. One of our riots in Ceylon took place in 1847, and another in 1883, and the third is that of the present year. The intervals are about a third of a century. Riots are novel to us in Ceylon, and our knowledge of remedies for them is very meagre. You must have observed, Sir, that while the present riot was in progress, and even for many weeks afterwards, every one was in a maze about it. Nobody understood the situation, and therefore could not assign the proper remedy for it. How is the appropriate remedy to be found? The Indian Government says it is discoverable only after conference with those persons who are in every-day touch with the thoughts and feelings of rioters. We are not to run here or there, nor sit in our chamber and spin out a fancy remedy, but quickly confer with the most experienced natives and unofficial Europeans in the country, who are in constant touch with all classes of people, and they will tell you where the sore is, how the riot happened, and what the remedy is.

Riots few in Ceylon, and our knowledge of remedies scanty.

Not so in India.

Causes of riots are ascertainable by Government conferring with experienced and reliable leaders of the people.

Sir, in 1911 riots occured in Calcutta between the

Example of Lord Hardinge, in the case of riots between Marwari Hindus and Muhammadans in Calcutta in 1911.

industrious Marwaris, who are Hindus, and the Muhammadans, in consequence of the latter objecting to the religious procession of the Marwaris passing their mosque. The riots were very severe. The action taken by the Lieutenant-Governor of Bengal was almost similar to that taken by the Ceylon Government, viz., by setting armed policemen and soldiers to suppress the riot, but the orderliness of the city could not be maintained without the patrolling of armed men for several days. The Viceroy, Lord Hardinge, was not satisfied with this remedy. He said that a more appropriate remedy than brute force should be found, because, said he, the ruling of a people by physical force would engender hatred in their hearts and cause more dissension and trouble. He insisted on finding out the actual cause of the ferment. So he invited the leading people of Calcutta—both Hindus and Muhammadans—to his own palace and spoke to them, and by such conferences he learnt that the riots were not due to disloyalty, or to a contempt of the Government of the country, or even to devilry or absolute wickedness, but to a personal quarrel that had taken place between one Muhammadan trustee of a mosque and one Hindu trustee of a Hindu temple. One trustee had insulted the other trustee, and the Muhammadan trustee put up all the other trustees of his mosque and their people to oppose the procession from the Marwari temple. The city was in a furore at once. The Muhammadans collided with the Hindus, and the people did not understand the sudden outburst. The rioters themselves had each his own notion and motive, and broken heads and even murders were the result. The Viceroy, in the presence of the leaders

The fruits of his policy of conference, patient research, and final discovery of the true cause of the riots.

of Calcutta, sent for these two sets of trustees and spoke to them seriously, and they acknowledged the cause of the differences between them. He made peace between them, and from that day forth there was no necessity for patrolling the streets with armed men, and the Muhammadans and the Hindus lived in peace. The Viceroy said : " If in the metropolis of India we do not know the hearts of the people, how can we govern a country so vast as India, whose population amounts to nearly that of the whole continent of Europe without Russia, and how are we to find armed men to parade the whole country? That is impossible. Our rule cannot have any other basis than actual knowledge of the conditions, wishes, and even idiosyncracies of the peoples we govern, and we must take more trouble than we do in keeping ourselves in greater touch with at least the leading men of the country, and not be satisfied with the little official experience we have. Till we reach the hearts of the people and know the secret workings there we shall never be able to rule the country wisely and well."

Sound administration will not be satisfied with the experience of officials only, but will keep itself in constant touch with those un-officials who possess the confidence of the people.

Then, Sir, some eighteen months ago, in the year 1914, Calcutta was thrown into a state of terror by an influx of highway robbers going armed in motor cars and taxicabs and robbing the people in the streets, whether on foot or in carriages, in broad daylight. Especially those who were returning from the banks with moneys were attacked. It was a mysterious outbreak of violence, and it was so well organized that the police found themselves powerless to cope with it. It was believed that a secret conspiracy had at last manifested itself to the endangerment of the Government and the Empire. Well, Sir, with great

The example of Lord Carmichael, in the case of the Calcutta riot of 1914.

perseverance Lord Carmichael, after conference with the leading men of the city, discovered the cause of the sudden outbreak to be the work of some university students dissatisfied with some police officers who had roughly handled them on a previous occasion. The students subscribed money, engaged motor cars, manned them with stalwart armed ruffians——

His Excellency the Governor :—Mr. Rámanáthan, you might put me off from starting a University College in Ceylon if you proceed on these lines.

The Hon. the Ceylonese Member :—No, Sir. Our student population are much wiser. They do not use bombs. The Calcutta students made the city quake. Lord Carmichael did not punish the people promiscuously, nor did he levy contributions on them for the damages done by the students, but he dealt with the ringleaders and the police who goaded the students to rise and discredit them. He said, "The students shall be students, and the police shall be the friends of the people, not their oppressors," exactly as in England, where the police have been taught by the authorities to be on the best terms with the people, and do nothing to irritate them.

The Example of the Viceroy of India, in the case of the great Cawnpore riots of 1914.

Then, Sir, last year too occurred great riots in Cawnpore, because the Collector of the district acquired a piece of land which was part of the ground of a mosque, and made a road through that piece and so separated the mosque from the tank used by the Muhammadan congregation on the other side of the new road. The Muhammadans begged hard of the Collector not to separate the tank from the mosque, but he would have his own way. "Oh! nonsense," he said, "we know what a tank is, and it does not matter if you have to cross the road to get to the tank or to go to the mosque? You ought to be satisfied with my ruling." The result was that many thousands of Muhammadans poured into the city of Cawnpore from different directions, effaced altogether the road made by the Collector, pulled down the municipal building put up by him, and attacked with brickbats, sword, and gun the police and soldiery who were sent against them by the Collector. Seven hundred persons were killed and wounded, and many more hundreds were incarcerated. The Collector reported the circumstances to the Commissioner of his Province, and the Commissioner agreed with him that very severe measures must be imposed upon all the Muhammadans, and sent up the papers to the Viceroy for his consideration and disposal. The Viceroy was not at all satisfied with the proposals, and the extreme tension produced in the circumstances of the case, so he himself came down from Simla, after making an appointment with the leading Muhammadans and Hindus of Cawnpore, and conferred with them for three days. He at last found a remedy, and settled the serious dislocation, with the consent of the Collector and Commissioner, by the expedient of making a new road over a causeway or raised bridge, so as to enable the Muhammadan congregation to wash their feet at the tank and proceed straight to the mosque on sacred ground, without having to tread on a dusty or dirty public road. After devising this remedy, Sir, which gave contentment to everybody, both official and unofficial, the Viceroy directed a great public meeting to be called, and attended by the Commissioner of the Province and the Collector his lordship addressed the people in a most remarkable speech, which disclosed the secret of good gov-

The narrow views of the Collector and the Commissioner overruled after conference with the leaders of the people.

And a happier remedy found.

The Viceroy's exposition of the true principles of good Government.

ernment treasured in the hearts of our Gracious Sovereigns, and the way how to administer a country without oppression or causing discontent. He said that King George V. was the ordained ruler of the whole British Empire, and was the father of every person ushered into life in it as his subject; that he had appointed him as his Viceroy to rule in India; and that he stood there as the father of all the people of that country. They were all his children. He said, that just as a father rebukes and punishes refractory children, he proposed that day to speak severely to those persons who had misbehaved themselves in the city. In impressive terms he said that, though punishment had been meted out to the rioters and those directly concerned in the riot, it was not the duty of a father to continue to be vindictive. The recalcitrant sons should be given a chance of improving themselves and of becoming good citizens. He therefore said that, after conference with the Commissioner of the Province and the Collector of the District, he had arrived at a conclusion which it was now time to disclose to the public. He said that he had resolved to be clement towards all the rioters, except those who had been proved by indubitable evidence to have killed or caused grievous hurt to others, and that he would direct them to be released from jail. Accordingly a large number of persons were discharged, and great was the joy in the city, both in the hearts of the Muhammadans and others, for the clemency shown to them. That clemency was not at all undeserved in the circumstances of the case. The King of England and his Viceroy looked upon the people of India as his children, and would govern them accordingly. This sympathetic message and treatment deeply touched the hearts of the people, and the most amicable feelings thenceforth prevailed, not only among the different classes of the people, but also between the officials and non-officials.

I will state only one other Indian case which is applicable to the affairs which have occurred in Ceylon, and that happened also last year in Arra in the United Provinces, where a great riot suddenly occurred in one of the thoroughfares of that city. The Governor of Allahabad met the mob in the street personally, unattended by any official, but attended by only leading unofficials, and addressed the crowd and asked them if they were not ashamed of themselves in behaving so riotously in the streets without coming to him and stating their complaints. They might have preferred their complaints to the Collector, but if they were not satisfied with his decision, why did they not send their leaders to wait upon him at Allahabad? Now he had come into their midst, unarmed and unattended by any local official, ready with a free mind to consider their grievances. He would consider them if they peacefully went back to their homes and appointed a few of their leaders to wait on him at such and such a place in the city. He then asked some of the high and trusty leaders of the people who stood around him to address the people, and that being done, the people quickly dispersed.

The example of the Governor of Allahabad, in the case of the riots in Arras, who went amongst the rioters, unattended by officials, but attended by non-officials, addressed the crowd and made their own leaders speak to and turn back the people.

Need there be any doubt now that the ascertainment of the real causes of riots by conference with the mob leaders and the rightful leaders of the people, and a determination to be just and sympathetic are essential principles for the restoration of order and peace?

I say that the Government of Ceylon has signally

The Government of Ceylon has signally failed to confer with the rightful leaders of the people, and to settle the trouble justly and sympathetically.

failed in both these respects. It does not know even to this day the real causes of the riots. It has not yet taken any steps to ascertain those causes, and yet it is blindly determined upon a remedy which is crushing the very life of the people and quenching all their regard for British justice.

If the Government knew the causes of the recent riots in Ceylon, they would not have done many of the things they have done to the dismay of every right-minded person in the country, and this Bill, so crude and so unrighteous and oppressive, would not be attempted to be forced through the Council with the aid of the official majority.

From inquiries I have made from all classes of men, I gather that Government officers have not borne in mind the duty of upholding the constitutional rights of the people, but have gone about thinking that, because they had a vast amount of power in their hands they should exercise it in full force, even as an angry person is wont to use a knife which he has in his hands. That is not good government. A good father remembers that one of the objects of his existence in the world is the improvement and reformation of his children (laughter). My honourable friend the Colonial Secretary laughs.

The Hon. the Colonial Secretary :—Only at the idea of your reformation.

The Hon. Mr. Rámanáthan :—Well, Sir, what am I to do? Things that are apparent to one class of thinkers are not apparent to another class of thinkers, owing to their density. But what I mean is that any one who has lived long enough to be a father or grandfather and thought seriously of life could easily understand the principle of living for the people and treating them as his own children. I know that with the years of experience in me I must live for the happiness of my descendants and my countrymen, and that I must control myself and use the power which Providence has put into my hands with the least possible friction in order to improve and reclaim those who are under my control and set them on a principled footing. Government officers must guide themselves by the principle that the people, whom the King has appointed them to govern, must be treated like their own children, with sympathy and yet firmly. If they sit down quietly and think the matter over, they will see the correctness of the conclusion that the power in their hands is given to them for a sacred purpose, and that those who are called upon to govern the people must be very considerate and tactful in the use of their power. If power is to be enforced on the people, it must be for their happiness and well-being, and not for the glorification of the officers or to prove the might of the Government.

Government officers must govern the people as if they were their own children, and must not misuse their power for vainglory.

Well, I cannot help thinking, Sir, that our officers have not gone about with that spirit. The doctrine is new to them, but not new to the Sovereigns of England or their wise ministers, and other high officers of State in India. We may well learn at their feet and have them as our models.

Let us now consider the causes of the riots in Ceylon and see whether the measures proposed in the Bill are appropriate or just in the circumstances of the case.

The causes of the riots.

It must be admitted, Sir, that the riots of June last are rooted in things that happened in Gampola in

The ill-advised action of the Government Agent in refusing the Buddhists the celebration of their great national festival in the usual way in Gampola.

August, 1912. The first cause is the ill-advised action of the Government Agent in refusing to the Buddhists the celebration of their great national festival in the usual way in Gampola. The Basnayake Nilame of the Kataragama dewale at Walahagoda in Gampola wanted to take his procession, as of old, through a certain street in Gampola along——

His Excellency the Governor :—I must not be led away by the fascination of listening to your silvery tones, Mr. Rámanáthan, but shall you approach the second reading of this precise Bill?

The Hon. Mr. Rámanáthan :—Oh, yes, Sir. What I am saying has a distinct bearing on the Bill. I am right in it. The first cause of the rioting of June last is the denial of the Government Agent of the Central Province to the Buddhists of Gampola to have their procession conducted, as of old, from their temple with music right through Ambagamuwa street to a particular part of the Mahaweli-ganga. An application was made to the Government Agent by the trustee or Nilame of the dewale, but he refused to grant his permission on August 27, 1912, on the ground that the *Hambaya* Muhammadans, who had built a mosque in Ambagamuwa street, objected to the Buddhist procession passing their mosque with music. The trustee of the dewale let the preparation for the procession slide, and went into the District Court of Kandy in September, 1913, and complained that the Government Agent had wrongfully and in breach of the Convention signed in Kandy in 1815 by the British Government and the Kandyan Chiefs refused plaintiff permission to conduct the procession through that portion of the Ambagamuwa street within one hundred yards of the *Hambaya* Muham-

The obstruction of the Hambaya Muhammadans.

madans' mosque to the accompaniment of musical instruments. The judgment of the District Judge, Mr. Paul Pieris, was delivered in June, 1914. He found that, instead of binding the *Hambaya* Muhammadans of the mosque to keep the peace, the Government Agent directed the police to plant pipes fifty yards away from each side of the mosque, and to inform the Buddhists that they should not sound their music while going over these one hundred yards.

Neglect of the Government Agent to bind the Hambayas to keep the peace in Gampola.

The facts of the case are undisputed. The procession was the Esala Perahera, celebrated throughout the dominion of the King of Kandy as the greatest of the national festivals of the Sinhalese. It related to the worship of the generalissimo of the celestial forces named Kattragama Deva by the Sinhalese, and Karthikeya by the Hindus. The procession, so far as the Walahagoda dewale was concerned, went for centuries from that dewale to the Mahaweli-ganga at Parutota for the cutting of the waters in great pomp and ceremony, and returned by the same road, during all which time the people have been in the highest state of enthusiasm and devotion to that powerful Deva. There are four mosques on the route of the perahera. Three of these mosques belonging to the permanent Muhammadans of the town do not object to the perahera, but the trustees of the fourth mosque, built a few years ago by some immigrant Muhammadans from South India, objected to the procession. The Government Agent did not see the political danger of forcing the Basnayake Nilame into court to discuss the constitutional question about the interpretation to be given to the Kandyan Convention. It was sure to irritate hundreds of thousands of Buddhists, and bring them into conflict with the *Hambaya*

The failure of the Government Agent to see the political danger of forcing the Buddhists into court to discuss their rights under the Kandyan Convention of 1815.

Muhammadans all over the Island. The District Judge points out that if the trustees of that one mosque belonging to the immigrant Muhammadans from South India had been bound over to keep the peace nothing would have happened. But the Buddhists being forced into Court, obtained judgment from the District Judge. The Supreme Court upset the District Judge's judgment on February 2, 1915. The plaintiff went to the District Court in Kandy almost a year after the refusal of the license.

The Hon. the Colonial Secretary :—The license was refused in 1912.

The Hon. Mr. Rámanáthan :—That is so. The Basnayake Nilame's complaint was that on August 27, 1912——

His Excellency the Governor :—This happens to interest me very much, but I must protest in the interests of order. We must not go too deeply into this. It happens to interest me, but I must go counter to my inclinations. We will come on to the second reading of the Ordinance to provide compensation for losses by riots.

The Hon. Mr. Rámanáthan :—Well, Sir, I have repeatedly asked, on whom are you going to saddle the compensation—upon the causers of the riots or upon someone else?

His Excellency the Governor :—Who did cause the riots?

The Hon. Mr. Rámanáthan :—I say the wrong move of the Government Agent in regard to the Gampola Basnayake Nilame was the earliest of the causes of the recent riots. The fault is on the part of a Government servant. Then comes another fault of a Government servant on May 27, 1915, in connec-

Another neglect of the Government Agent, to bind the Trustees of Hambayas' mosque in Kandy.

tion with the carol procession in Kandy on the Wesak Day. The Government Agent granted a license to those who wanted to have the procession, but said, "Don't go to Castle Hill street, where these immigrant Muhammadans have a mosque, till after 12 o'clock midnight, when their mosque must be closed." The Government Agent did not bind the trustees of this mosque to keep the peace. The Buddhist procession did not go there till about 1 o'clock. But the *Hambaya* Muhammadans were ready for them then and there, hooting and jeering at the Sinhalese, whose patience was exhausted. They chased the Muhammadans, damaged a part of their mosque and some of their boutiques also, and brought their procession abruptly to an end. Nothing further happened in the night in Kandy, but on the following day people from the villages came into Kandy and were hanging about the streets, wishing to protect their Dalada Maligawa or Great Temple of the Tooth Relic from the attack which was expected to be made by the Muhammadans coming by train from Colombo and from South India. They stood opposite the house of the principal *Hambaya* in Trincomalee Street at about 7 o'clock in the evening, together with some policemen who did nothing, because they were in fear of the people. While they were so standing, a *Hambaya* from the upper storey fired a shot on the crowd of people standing opposite the house, and a Sinhalese youth was wounded. Then the people cried, "There is the murderer; why don't you constables go and seize him?" The constables did not seize him. What they did was to carry the corpse of the youth to the mortuary. The crowd waited and called upon the constables to seize the *Hambaya* who was still in the

The Hambayas hoot and jeer at the Buddhists when the first riot begins, 29 May, 1 a.m.

A Hambaya kills a Sinhalese youth.

Second riot takes place in consequence, 30 May, 9 p.m.

boutique. Nothing being done, they vented their anger by raiding that and some other boutiques, and gradually the crowd melted away. The next morning ushered a momentous day. The crowd came back again in greater numbers, seeing the inactivity of the police and hearing that the Maligawa was in extreme danger. The leading people of Kandy—Burghers, Christians, Buddhists, and even Muhammadans—went to the Government Agent and told him that he could easily send away the mob if he only came near the Town Hall and said to the mob that he would inquire into the grievances of the people. The Government Agent refused to go, Sir, unlike the procedure followed in India. The first thing done there was for the chief official to go amongst the mob undefended, unprotected, but with the leaders of the people. The Government Agent of Kandy would not go and meet the mob, and the consequence was that in a little time there was a collision between the Sinhalese and the *Hambaya* Muhammadans, and there were two murders in the street. The crowd who witnessed this street fight were controlled by the unarmed cadets of Trinity College. Then came the Inspector-General with a few Panjabi soldiers. A few stragglers, who seemed to resent the bigotry of the *Hambayas* more than the rest, ran in different directions, some towards Katugastota, some towards Gampola, some towards Matale, and some towards Kadugannawa, and raised false cries that the Muhammadans had destroyed the Maligawa, had cut and mutilated Sinhalese women, and that the *Hambaya* boutique-keepers must be sent out of the villages before the Indian and the Colombo Muhammadans could join hands with them. So the feeling of self-

The Government Agent, though called upon, refuses to meet the crowd and assure them that their grievances would be inquired into.

A street fight and two murders ensued.

Crowd dispersed by soldiers.

defence and necessity for immediate action being roused in the hearts of the Sinhalese villagers, riots did take place, which soon extended to Colombo.

In Colombo, again, Sir, one of the principal causes of the riots was the passivity and even paralysis of the police. The people by themselves are not so foolish as to defy the great force that lies in the hands of Government and behind it. They are not so stupid as that, nor do they care to be caught red-handed and sent to jail. There are people in every nation who wait for opportunities to do wrong deeds, and if the police is found to be ineffectual, what more natural than for the criminal classes and the villains of the country to come out of their dens and prey upon the country? It is not disloyalty; it is not treason; it is not contempt for Government; but it is a rush upwards of evil desires consequent upon the inactivity of the police.

Passivity and paralysis of the Police.

Necessary rise of the criminal classes and the hungry poor.

The rise of dissension and animosity in the hearts of men can never be stopped. Timely discussion and peaceful persuasion may often allay them. But the power that keeps them down is the power of arrest vested in the hands of the police, and the power of imprisonment vested in the hands of Magistrates. If these powers are in abeyance, dissensions, animosities, and evil desires of all kinds will break out and throw social order into wild confusion. Thefts, grievous hurt, gang robbery, riot, and murder will be the result of the police and the magistracy not doing their respective duties. I say the principal cause of the riots of June last and the consequent loss of property and life was the failure of the constables and the Magistrates and Government Agents to do their respective duties. What was once a religious

Riots not due to disloyalty or treason.

riot soon converted itself into a general loot on the part of the criminal classes and the hungry poor, who saw their opportunity, and it went on extending up to Matara. The question now is, now that we know the causes of the riots, and now that Government have conceded that they have not found any evidence of conspiracy between the upper classes and the lower classes of the Sinhalese—who is to be saddled with responsibility for these deeds? Are you going to punish the criminal classes and the villains of the country? Are you going to saddle the responsibility upon the police and the Magistrates and Government Agents who neglected to perform their duties, which were the arrest of offenders *flagrante delicto*, the dispersion of the crowd by the methods prescribed by law, and the prompt punishment of the guilty. If the custodians of the public peace failed to conserve it, if they neglected ordinary prudence and the prompt exercise of the power vested in their hands, why should we go and saddle the responsibility of the riot on the shoulders of what my honourable friend the Attorney-General has called the "innocent and irreproachable Sinhalese"? I do not see any reason whatever, Sir, for passing the responsibility of the Government officers on to the "innocent and irreproachable Sinhalese."

Why should innocent Sinhalese be made to pay for damages caused mainly by the criminal classes and the hungry poor.

To quote from a great authority on this subject: "It is the duty of a Magistrate at the time of a riot to arm the subjects of the realm—either civil or military—for the purpose of quelling it. It is his duty to keep the peace. If the peace be broken, honesty of intention will not avail him if he has been guilty of neglect of duty. The question is whether he did all that he knew was in his power and which

Duties of magistrates at times of riot.

could be expected from a man of ordinary prudence, firmness, and activity." The law thus stated is gathered from the opinion of the Judges who tried the Lord Mayor of London and the Mayor of Bristol on indictment for neglect of duty during the Gordon riots of 1780 and the Bristol riot of 1831. In addition to his liability to an indictment at common law, a defaulting Magistrate is subject, under the provisions of the Acts of 1411 (Henry IV.) and 1414 (Henry V.) to a penalty of £100 for every default, the default to be inquired into by a Commission under the Great Seal.

Such is the responsibility which fall upon the shoulders of Government officers entrusted with the keeping of the peace. I now ask, why should innocent citizens be charged with the burdens which the actual rioters themselves and the defaulting Police Magistrates and Government Agents of the country must bear? I repeat that dissensions, animosities, and evil desires will arise in the hearts of the people from time to time, but they must not be allowed by the guardians of the peace to break out and destroy the life, limb, and property of others. Those who illegally take away life, limb, and property must certainly be punished, as also those officers of Government through whose neglect of duty the riots broke out.

Dissensions will arise in the hearts of men, but the Police must not allow them to break out and destroy life, limb and property of others.

Let me now come, Sir, to the idea of compensation recoverable from anybody but the rioters. The Attorney-General says that the idea came into the head of the Government from three channels: firstly, the common law of England; secondly, the Riot Damages Act of 1886; and thirdly, the Repression of Crime Ordinance, No. 3 of 1903, and that the present

Bill is an adaptation of those laws to local circumstances. Sir, my study of these laws does not enable me to bear out the opinion of the Attorney-General that they justify the present Bill.

The Common Law of England does not support the Ordinance relating to compensation;

It is a wrong premise, in the first place, to believe that the common law of England supports the Bill. According to the common law, damages are not payable by anybody but the rioters themselves. The idea of collective responsibility for a crime done in a village was a part of the obsolete Anglo-Saxon law. It was done away with. Then came the Acts 7 and 8 of George IV., Chapter 31, which provide that the compensation for damage by rioters should be levied on the hundreds, so that it should fall in the neighbourhood where the riot occurred. But this Act, Sir, was found to be wholly unworkable, because under its provisions it was necessary to prove that the houses were not only partly or wholly demolished by the rioters, but also that it was their intention to wholly demolish the premises. The Act of 1886, instead of recovering damages from the hundreds, empowered a levy from a wider area only for the purpose of making the taxation less onerous than it would otherwise be. The point I now make is this, that under the English Act of 1886 the damages are leviable on an already existing fund, called the Police Fund, raised to pay the maintenance of the police.

Nor can it be justified by the Riot Damages Act of 1886;

In England there is a Police Fund for the City of London, for the Metropolitan police, for the Counties, and the Boroughs, and these Police Funds are under the control of the City Council, the County Council, and the Borough (or Municipal) Council. It is a fact, Sir, that these Police Funds consist of not only rates payable by householders, but also of contributions made by the Government from the general revenue of the whole United Kingdom. The public exchequer pays 44 per cent., and the remaining 56 per cent. is subscribed by the ratepayers. Villages which have not been given Municipal organizations have no such Police Fund. Thus, if the analogy of England is to be observed here, the collective responsibility will fall only on Municipalities and Local Boards. Villages will not be touched at all. But what the Ordinance strives to do here is to cast the compensation upon the villagers mostly, and where it casts the responsibility upon Municipalities and Local Boards, the Government takes care not to contribute a cent towards the damages. It is therefore altogether wrong to believe that the English Riot Damage Act supports the levy of damages from villages.

Nor by the local Ordinance No. 3 of 1903.

Then, Sir, I come to the contention that the Repression of Crime Ordinance, No. 3 of 1903, supports the present policy. I have no hesitation in saying that this idea is also wrong. That Ordinance sanctions the quartering of police in a village, or the payment of compensation in money or labour by the villagers for the damage done only when murder, grievous hurt, or other offence has been perpetrated by some unknown offender, on the principle that the villagers may know who the offender is, but do not like to divulge his name or bear witness against him. In such a case, the Government Agent is empowered to go into the village and assess the damages suffered by the injured parties, and to allot the compensation to the different villagers in the special way indicated by the Ordinance and under the safeguards provided therein. The Ordinance does not apply to any village where murder, grievous hurt, or other offence has been committed by a known person, or where such crimes do not exist. I say, Sir, emphatically, that it is wrong to believe that the Repression of Crime Ordinance, No. 3 of 1903, justifies the application of its principles to cases of sudden riots, such as the one which we have in view, where offenders may be easily seen, identified, and brought to book before a court of justice. Do riots now exist in these villages from which compensation is claimed, or does the Government apprehend any more riots there?

Having now shown, Sir, that neither the common law of England, nor the English Riot Damage Act of 1886, nor the Ordinance No. 3 of 1903 for the Repression of Crime in Ceylon justifies the most inequitable principle of robbing Peter to pay Paul insisted upon in the present Bill, I now come to the doctrine of racial responsibility propounded by it.

The doctrine of racial responsibility propounded in the present Bill is utter foolishness.

I can only say, Sir, that I am astonished that my honourable friend the Attorney-General has stood up for racial responsibility and has the boldness to say as a legislator that, if "the innocent and irreproachable Sinhalese" do not accept responsibility for the acts of the habitual criminals and other ruffians of the country, the good name of the Sinhalese will be eternally tarnished, and that to be national one must pay, not only for the upkeep of lofty ideals, but also for compensating the damage done by the rascals of the country. I desire to ask the Attorney-General, Sir, whether he as an Englishman has ever paid one single farthing as compensation for any villainies practised by the villainous classes in England.

The Hon. the Attorney-General :—No; but I would if my community wrecked any quarter of this city. I will pay my share.

The Hon. Mr. Rámanáthan :—Your willingness to pay is not the question. The point is, whether you have ever paid it in England when class collisions occurred, and whether you once thought that the fair name of England was sullied by the fact that villains have lived in England and have continued to live and flourish there.

Sir, the doctrine of racial responsibility, I make bold to say, is utter foolishness, and commends itself only to those whom St. Paul has described as corporeal men. Does not the Attorney-General know that the law knows no colour, creed, or language? Has he not heard that the law is spiritual; that it makes no difference between Jew and Gentile, Greek and Roman; that all nations are made of one blood; that we are all the children of God; that we address ourselves to the one and only God, the maker and protector of all nations, as our Father; and that we should not walk after the flesh but after the spirit? The Attorney-General and the other members of the Government who have sat round the table in the Executive Council Chamber and worked at this wonderfully strange Bill, have, I am sorry to say, labelled themselves as very corporeal men, ignorant of the spiritual truths of the great religion to which they belong, truths which are alike common to all the great religions of the world. They have forgotten all these true sayings, and, alas! they have forgotten the express teachings of those great and glorious Sovereigns of England, Sovereigns who have graced the British throne since 1837. They have forgotten

It is condemned in the New Testament;

And is opposed to the declaration of Queen Victoria, King Edward VII., and King George V.

the proclamation of Queen Victoria in 1858, which states :—

"We declare it to be our Royal will and pleasure that none be in anywise favoured, none molested, but that all shall alike enjoy the equal and impartial protection of the law. It is our earnest desire to administer the Government for the benefit of all our subjects resident in it. In the prosperity of our subjects is our strength, in their contentment is our security, and their gratitude is our reward."

They have forgotten, too, Sir, the proclamation of King Edward VII. in 1908, which states :—

"We survey our labours of the past century with a clear gaze and a good conscience. Errors have occurred. The Agents of my Government have spared no pains or self-sacrifice to correct them. If abuses have been proved, vigorous hands have laboured to apply a remedy."

They have also, Sir, forgotten the exhortation of our Most Gracious King George V. :—

"I cannot help thinking," said His Majesty, "from all I have seen and heard, that the task of governing India will be made the easier if we on our part infuse into it a wider element of sympathy. I venture to predict that to such sympathy there will be an ever-abundant and genuine response."

I need not say more, Sir, upon the principles of this Bill. I have carefully touched upon all that fell from the Hon. the Attorney-General in his exposition. I do not think that it can be said with any degree of truth that either the common law of England, or the English Riot Damage Act of 1886, or the Repression of Crime Ordinance, No. 8 of 1908, can be construed as authorities for the new, unrighteous, and inequitable principles which appear in every page of this Bill. I do not want to go into the smaller principles of the Bill or the details of it, because when it comes into Committee we shall have an opportunity of dealing with them and making the Bill as little objectionable as possible in the event of the Government forcing it through the Council with the aid of the official majority. I submit that the needs of good government do not require a Bill so drastic as the one before us, and that it is a serious reflection upon the fair name of a people who have always been loyal and grateful to the British throne and to the officers of the British Government in this Island. Such gratitude as theirs, and such loyal feelings as theirs, should not be violated by thrusting on them an Ordinance so fearful and unrighteous as this, and I can only hope that wiser counsels will prevail and lead the Government to withdraw this Bill altogether. I oppose the second reading of it *in toto*, because it is a tangled mass of wrong thought and wrong principle from beginning to end, and is the outcome of gross ignorance of the causes of the riots and the true remedies needed. It discloses the extreme self-sufficiency and precipitate action of the Government.

The Bill is a tangled mass of wrong thought and wrong principle.

The motion for the second reading of the Bill was then put to the Council, and His Excellency the Governor declared that the "Ayes" had it.

The Ordinance was then read a second time.

The Hon. the Attorney-General:—I move the Council into Committee on the Ordinance.

The Council then went into Committee.

In Committee,

The Hon. Mr. Rámanáthan :—May I rise to ask whether, as Your Excellency told me, this Bill should not be sent before a Select Committee?

His Excellency the Governor :—We have passed into Committee, Mr. Rámanáthan.

The Hon. Mr. Rámanáthan :—We have, Sir, but we may still appoint a Select Committee to deal with the Bill, because I should like very much to discuss many things in it.

His Excellency the Governor :—I am afraid that is out of order at this point. I paused carefully when the Attorney-General had proposed to go into Committee in case you would take just that point, but as you did not, I said we pass into Committee.

The Hon. Mr. Rámanáthan :—Well, we are in Committee, but we might discuss the propriety of sending the Bill before a Select Committee.

His Excellency the Governor :—You cannot do that when you get into Committee, you can only deal with the details on the basis that the principles have been passed on the second reading.

The Hon. Mr. Rámanáthan :—That is true. The principles have been passed on the second reading.

His Excellency the Governor :—And we can therefore only go into details.

The Hon. Mr. Rámanáthan :—The details I submit, Sir, should be considered by a Select or Sub-Committee. You will see, Sir, that according to our old procedure it was only when a Bill had got into Committee that we could appoint a Sub-Committee.

The Hon. the Colonial Secretary :—It is not in accordance with our present rules and orders. A Bill shall be referred to a Committee of the whole Council or to a Select Committee—not to both.

His Excellency the Governor :—That was what I was feeling. A Sub-Committee, I am bound to say, is a thing foreign to my experience. It must be on a question of detail. Does the Honourable Member see that?

The Hon. Mr. Rámanáthan :—It is open to Select or Sub-Committees to deal with questions of detail.

His Excellency the Governor :—Let us go on and see whether you want a Sub-Committee, and I will order on that.

The Hon. Mr. Rámanáthan :—The time is now 11.30 p.m., and it is an unheard-of proceeding our sitting so late. Why are we hurrying so fast? What is the urgency of this proceeding, Sir?

His Excellency the Governor :—That is scarcely in order on the question of the Committee point.

The Hon. Mr. Rámanáthan :—I move the adjournment of the Council, Sir. I hope you will meet us on this point.

His Excellency the Governor :—Council is in Committee; if any question of a Sub-Committee arises, you will raise it at a given point, and I will give you a ruling whether it is in order or not on the precise clause on which you urge it.

The Hon. Mr. Rámanáthan :—May I urge the adjournment of the Committee, Sir?

The Hon. the Colonial Secretary :—It is open to you to resume, Sir.

The Hon. Mr. Rámanáthan :—Resume after we have gone through the Committee stage? That is not what I want. It is going on to 11.45 p.m., and is it right that you should work us like this?

His Excellency the Governor :—Mr. Rámanáthan, you must remember that I gave you every latitude as regards the reading of the petitions, and I followed the rules very carefully and jealously. Whether you feel that you had exactly followed the spirit of the Standing Orders is a matter which I leave to your own reflection. I let you speak for over two hours.

The Hon. the Ceylonese Member :—What am I to do? I have a duty to perform.

# CHAPTER IV.

## STATEMENTS OF RESPONSIBLE WITNESSES REGARDING SOME OF THE EVENTS OF THE PERIOD.

## (1) STATEMENT *of* Mr. D. B. SENEVIRATNA, *a Master of Trinity College, Kandy.*

Heard nothing of intended rising of the Sinhalese.

THE teachers and boarders of Trinity College heard nothing of any intended rising of the Sinhalese. Over 150 of the boarders, including boys of seven years of age, went at about 8 p.m. on Friday, 28th May. The children saw a good deal of the carol parties in many streets. They were sent back to the College about midnight with the prefects and some teachers. One of the teachers, D. B. Seneviratna, and two or three friends stayed behind, and saw the first carol party just about to turn from King Street into Castle Hill Street. They were behind the second carol party and heard the Moors hooting, and saw stones being pelted from the upper storeys of the Moor boutiques, and from the mosque into the streets, and from the streets into these buildings. They heard the stones fall on the glass panes of the mosque windows. This was about 1.30 a.m. They returned to their residences, D. B. Seneviratna to Trinity College, and George Pereira of Galaha and P. L. S. Jayawardena to their apartments.

How the collision began.

The next day, about 7.30 p.m., D. B. S. went on a bicycle to the railway station to see Muhandiram B. P. P. Seneviratne. On the way he saw a crowd of about 30 persons collected at the junction between Colombo Street and Brownrigg Street. He got off the bicycle and saw the dead body of a Sinhalese youth. He saw a Muhammadan shop, from which the shot had been fired, broken into, and the goods,

Saw the corpse of a Sinhalese youth lying on the pavement.

such as camboys, books, etc., burning low in the street. There was not a single policeman here, nor near the corpse; but about 150 yards away, there were about 40 constables with two superintendents, Thornhill and Tranchell, drawn up at the Castle Street Junction.

D. B. S. then went into Trincomalee Street, observing a number of people there, and saw Mr. Stace (Police Magistrate of Kandy) and some constables coming out of Jeweller Casie Lebbe's shop, with three or four Sinhalese men taken into custody. The shop appeared to be broken into. D. B. S. learnt that Casie Lebbe had removed the best part of the jewels before the shop was broken into. A few other boutiques were attempted to be broken into in Colombo Street, but, the police appearing, the crowd ran away.

Looting of shops

At about 10 p.m. D. B. S. saw the Government Agent (Mr. Vaughan), the Kacheri Mudaliyár Jayawardena, the District Judge (Mr. Dias) and many other gentlemen at the fountain near the Police Court. The rowdies had collected there to rest, and the Government Agent ordered them to go away, and they went away in different directions. There seemed to be about 300 people, of whom about 50 had sticks and clubs. These were Kandyan and Low-Country people.

D. B. S. went back to the College, as he found the bicycle lamp was going out, and left it there. He started again at about 12.30 a.m., and met the Station Superintendent (Seneviratna) and Proctor J.P., Amaratunga of Colombo, at one end of Trincomalee Street, near the Queen's Hotel, and they all walked on to Colombo Street to see the damage done. They saw the corpse of the boy on the pavement just as it was some hours before. A candle light was burning near the body, but no persons were about, not even the police. In all they saw about five boutiques damaged, namely, Cador Saibo's and two other boutiques in Colombo Street, Casie Lebbe's in Trincomalee Street, and the "Young Turks' Tea Kiosk" opposite the Planters' Association Hall.

A large body of Moors coming from Colombo by train stopped at Kadugannawa.

When the Station Superintendent and his two friends were opposite the Queen's Hotel, he received a message from the Government Agent to stop the night mail train at Kadugannawa, as a large body of Moors was coming in that train from Colombo.

The Station Superintendent telephoned to the station-master at Kadugannawa, who had the carriage in which the Moors were travelling detached, and the rest of the train came into Kandy. D. B. S. slept at the Station Superintendent's bungalow and went back to Trinity College at 8 a.m. on the following day. On Sunday, when the train came to the platform with the carriage in which the Moors were, about forty Sinhalese men were waiting outside the station gate, and the Station Superintendent, fearing a collision, had the gates shut; and the police gave the Moors the option of staying at the station and returning to Colombo by the next train at 11 a.m., or being marched to the Police Station. They preferred to go back, and so they were entrained and despatched to Colombo.

And sent back to Colombo.

Cadets of Trinity College, Kandy, sworn in as special constables.

At 11 a.m. on Sunday the Cadets of Trinity College (part of the Cadet Battalion of the Ceylon Light Infantry) were ordered by the Principal (Rev. A. G. Fraser) to fall in at 2 p.m. to march to the

Police Station and be sworn in as Special Constables. On going there at 2 p.m. and being sworn in, they were ordered to assume patrol duty at 6 p.m.

While they were at the Police Station, Mr. Ratwatte (cashier of the Mercantile Bank), Proctor Weerasurya and two or three influential Moors came in and were speaking to the Inspector-General or the Superintendent of Police. On our way back to the College with Rev. Mr. Fraser and other teachers, the Cadet Corps saw, at about 3 p.m., a motor-car with two Moors in it dashing towards the Police Station, and as the Cadets reached the College they witnessed a riot between the Sinhalese and Moors in Trincomalee Street. The Cadet Corps, though in civil suits and unarmed, went into the crowd, which immediately dispersed, leaving behind three Sinhalese men and one Moor severely wounded.

They disperse the crowd, though unarmed and in civil clothes.

It appeared that a crowd of Sinhalese coming from the direction of Mahaiyawa (where the General Cemetery is) knocked at a Moorish tailor's door, and an old Moor came out with a club and whirled it about madly among the crowd till he was struck down. Then his two nephews jumped out and stabbed three Sinhalese men, one of them being a Kachcheri clerk (Mr. Dissanayake), who was an innocent passer-by. The two Moors who stabbed the Sinhalese were also beaten and wounded, and one of the Sinhalese men who had been stabbed expired while being conveyed to the hospital. These two Moors were afterwards tried by Court Martial and sentenced to penal servitude.

Cause of the street fight.

The Cadet Corps arrested the two nephews, who had hid themselves in their house after wounding the Sinhalese.

Arrival of Government Agent and Inspector-General of Police, and dispersion of crowd by soldiers with butt-ends of their rifles.

The Inspector-General of Police and the Government Agent (Mr. Vaughan) came on the scene in their motor-car and alighted on the pavement of Trincomalee Street while the riot was going on. The Inspector-General got into the car and went to the Police Station, and returned with about 50 Punjabi soldiers and some constables. They dispersed with the butt-ends of their rifles a crowd which had gathered near the Town Hall.

The Cadet Corps did patrol duty from 6 p.m. to 2 a.m. for several nights. The Punjabis were picketed at important centres.

## (2) LETTER *of* Mr. F. R. SENANAYAKE, M.M.C., *Colombo.*

"*Kewstoke*," *Gregory's Road*,
14th June, 1915.

Honourable P. Rámanáthan,
"Sukhasthan,"
Ward Place.

Dear Sir,—As requested by you, I am jotting down for your perusal my experiences during the recent disturbances in and around Colombo.

One night, I believe it was the first day of the rioting, at about eight p.m., a Moorman living in a boutique adjoining my brother's residence (Mr. D. S. Senanayake's) came over to his bungalow looking thoroughly scared, and begged for protection. He informed us that mobs were attacking all Moor boutiques, killing the Moors and looting everything in them. At the time we thought the man was unnecessarily alarmed and asked him to go back to his boutique, and that he need not be afraid of anything. Shortly after the man had gone back, we noticed a crowd of about forty or fifty persons making a rush at the boutique. But when we ran to the man's rescue the crowd disappeared. It seemed to me that the mob had some fear of the law and were anxious to avoid recognition. Shortly after this incident I returned home. Subsequently I learnt that a large crowd attempted to attack the same boutique. My brother then thought it expedient to remove the inmates of that boutique, as well as those

Fifty rowdies attack a Moor's boutique in Gregory Road.

The rowdies run away at sight of rescue party.

How Mr. S. protects the boutique-keepers.

of another boutique near by, to his own bungalow. All their belongings were also removed to his place.

The following day I thought it my duty to offer my services to the Police. With this intention I proceeded with some difficulty to the Maradana Police Station. On my way thither I noticed boutiques being attacked and looting carried on in the very presence of the Police, and, so far as I could see, no attempt was made either to prevent it or to arrest the criminals. At the Police Station I met Mr. Altendorf, who informed me that the situation was very serious, and, having no orders, he personally did not know what could be done. I was informed that the Inspector-General of Police was not in Colombo, and that it was not known where the Colombo Superintendent of Police (Mr. Daniel) was. After some time, noticing I could be of no service, I returned home. That same afternoon Mr. H. L. de Mel sent his car for me. When I went over to his place he suggested that we address the crowds and make an attempt to disperse them. I proposed inviting Mr. Martinus C. Perera to join us.

Mr. S. sees looting going on in the presence of the Police and near the Headquarters at Maradana.

No one in command there.

Riot at Grandpass.

When we were at Mr. Martinus Perera's, Mr. J. A. Perera and Dr. Rutman, noticing us, stopped their car. Then we agreed that Messrs. de Mel and M. C. Perera should go towards Slave Island, while Dr. Rutnam, Mr. J. A. Perera and myself, with, if possible, Nanissere, high priest, were to go towards Grand Pass. The high priest joined us. But by the time we reached Grand Pass the mob had already been dispersed by the military firing upon the crowd. After despatching some of the injured to hospital we returned to our respective homes.

The next morning, when Mr. J. A. Perera and I

were with the Chairman of the Municipal Council, information reached us that there was trouble in Ferry Street. The three of us then motored to Ferry Street, left Mr. J. A. Perera there, and the Chairman took me with him to Dematagoda Junction, where we learnt that Mr. Thyne had brought information that about four thousand persons were marching on Colombo. I suggested to Mr. Allnutt, who was there at the time, sending some influential Sinhalese to meet the mob. Mr. Allnutt could not think of any better person than myself. Then I requested Mr. Byrde to ask Mr. D. B. Jayatilleke to accompany me. Mr. Byrde saw Mr. Jayatilleke, and immediately afterwards Mr. Jayatilleke and I, with Mudaliyár Rajapakse and my brother, started along the road to Hanwella. At the Kollanawe Temple we were informed that a gentleman who called himself "Agenta Hamuduruwo," informed the people that the Moors were coming in their thousands to attack the temple, and that numbers of women and children had been mutilated and murdered. This story of an attack by the Moors we found had preceded us everywhere. All the way to Hanwella we found crowds of armed men in groups. At every group we stopped the car, inquired the reason for the gathering, and were always told of this attack by the Moors. We always informed them that the rumour was false, and succeeded in dispersing the groups. At Hanwella the gathering numbered thousands, with an elephant leading. Among the crowd I noticed a large number of Tamils and a few Eurasians or Burghers. After addressing them for a considerable time we succeeded in making the crowd give up their clubs and disperse. Those of

Trouble in Ferry Street.

Mr. S. and two others are sent off to meet a large crowd advancing on Colombo from Hanwella, to ward off attack by Moors.

Spread of false rumours dissipated.

Crowd turns back, on hearing the Sinhalese in Colombo were safe.

the crowd who had armed themselves with guns discharged their weapons in the air and dispersed. Some of them handed over their clubs to us. In a short time we found the car loaded with clubs, and we had to sit on them. On our return to Colombo we unloaded the clubs at the Borella Police Station. While returning we found the roads perfectly quiet, and there were no men to be seen with weapons.

Another crowd advancing from Battaramulla.

On our return to Colombo we were told that crowds were approaching the town along the Cotta Road. Immediately we received this information we started off in that direction, and met a few groups, but the only gathering of any size that we came across was at Battaramulla Junction. While some were addressing them I made inquiries of the whereabouts of Mr. A. A. M. Salim, who I knew lived in the neighbourhood. At first the only information I received was that his house was burnt down and that nobody knew where he was. But when I told the people that Salim was a good man, who had to my personal knowledge been of good assistance to them during the last floods, one man got on to the car, and after we had left the crowds behind agreed to take us to the jungle in which Salim with his family had taken refuge. He further informed us that there were over ten persons in the jungle. Mr. D. S. Senanayake and Mudaliyár Rajapakse were then sent back to Colombo to bring another car. Mr. Jayatilleke was left at the end of the footpath to keep the crowd from following me while I walked towards the jungle. At about 7.30 that night Mudaliyár Rajapakse and my brother returned with a motor lorry and a military escort. It was only then that we felt fairly safe. While returning we

Rescue of Mr. Salim and other Moors from concealment in jungles.

came across other Moors, who had been protected by neighbours, and these, too, we brought with us. We returned to Colombo at about 10.30 that night. Next day Messrs. D. B. Jayatilleke, J. A. Perera and myself, encouraged by our success so far, started along Negombo Road. There we found the story had reached the people that the Moors were pulling down the Roman Catholic churches.

Report on the Negombo Road that the Moors are pulling down the Roman Catholic churches, and mutilating Sinhalese women.

At Wattala the parish priest informed us that he was solemnizing a marriage, and that during the service he noticed a commotion in the church, immediately followed by the ringing of the church bells. He hurried the service, and on inquiry he was informed of the rumours that the Moors were pulling down the churches and mutilating women. The crowds gathered there, and although he tried to stop them some could not be persuaded. All the way to Ja-ela, whenever we made inquiries, we learnt that this same story of the destruction of churches, temples and the mutilation of women had incensed the crowds.

At Mabola we found over 100 Moorish men and women, who had taken refuge at Mr. Goonetilleke's residence. At Ja-ela we found some twelve or fourteen Moors.

Moors protected by Mr. Goonetilleke at Mabola.

The Mudaliyár of the district, with whom we were at the time, took the necessary steps to protect them. From Ja-ela we came back to Colombo, and after a hasty meal we started to do similar work on the Kandy Road, but we were not allowed to cross the Victoria Bridge, so we returned home. These are some of the incidents that I at present remember.

Yours faithfully,

(Signed) F. R. SENANAYAKE.

## (3) *Further* STATEMENT *of* Mr. F. R. SENANAYAKE, M.M.C.

I AM a graduate of Cambridge University, a Barrister-at-Law, and the elected member for the Colpetty Ward of the Colombo Municipality.

Until the 8th of June, when my house was searched, I was ignorant of my being suspected in connection with the riots. Next day I called on the Chairman of the Municipality and informed him that I was not prepared to do anything to help the authorities on my own responsibility in future, but I assured him that I would gladly carry out any instructions.

In the search of my house no incriminating documents of any kind, firearms, or other dangerous weapons were found. Notwithstanding the absence of any complaint or evidence against me, and in spite of the services I had rendered, on 21st June, at about 5.30 in the morning, my house was searched once again, and I was arrested by a Town Guard and removed to Welikada Jail.

At the jail entrance I was taken charge of by Mr. Daniel, the Colombo Superintendent of Police, who ordered a jail guard to search me, and then handed me over to the jail authorities with the remark that he was to remember I was a " cell " prisoner. Inside the jail I noticed a number of other gentlemen under arrest.

We were taken inside the jail and locked in bare cells. Some hours afterwards I was taken before

Mr. Allnutt, a Special Commissioner, who questioned me and took down my statement. I was then taken back and locked in another cell. These cells are known in the jail as "penal cells," and are certainly worse than the ordinary convicts' cells. In the ward in which we were placed there are 150 cells, usually occupied by 150 convicts, but owing to the extraordinary circumstances the jail authorities, seeing the accommodation insufficient, found themselves compelled to shelter during the night over a thousand persons in this building. The temporary sanitary arrangements made for such a multitude and the overcrowding naturally made life almost unbearable.

We were kept in solitary confinement, locked inside these stinking cells, for about twenty hours each day.

During the first two days we were not permitted to have our usual food, but were supplied with ordinary convicts' food. Neither convicted nor even charged with an offence, I was not given the diet usually given to European criminals, nor was I given even that of long-term convicts. After the second day, however, public opinion asserted itself, and we were permitted to procure our meals from outside.

To add to the horrors already described, we were placed in charge of Muhammadan Somalis brought from Aden, who understood neither English nor any other language spoken in Ceylon.

For forty-six days, for no offence committed, and in spite of the fact that there was no evidence or complaint against me, I was kept in close confinement. *During this period the authorities were actually suggesting evidence to possible witnesses, and attempting to procure my conviction.*

Thanks to my having had no enemy among the Moors or among my own or any other community in this Island, I am alive and free to-day.

On the 5th of August I was released on my entering into a bail-bond, conditions of the bond being the deposit of Rs. 10,000 in cash and Rs. 50,000 personal, my binding myself to appear before any Commissioner if called upon, and not to leave Colombo for a period of one year without the permission of the military authorities or Inspector-General of Police. The bond has since been cancelled.

F. R. SENANAYAKE.

Colombo, 30th October, 1915.

## (4) LETTER *of* MR. C. P. DIAS, M.M.C., *Colombo.*

The Hon. Mr. P. Rámanáthan, K.C., C.M.G., M.L.C.

Dear Sir,—I venture to submit to you, as the elected representative of the educated Ceylonese in the Legislature of the Island, a statement of facts which I have gathered from my own observations, and also from information I have received from friends for whose opinions I entertain great respect.

Recent riots not directed against the Government or the Europeans, but against Coast Moors, owing to their exactions and insolence.

The recent riots cannot even by a stretch of imagination be termed "sedition." The rioters did not appear to be actuated by any hostility to the Ceylon Government or the Executive Officers. No churches, chapels, schools, Hindu temples, Government, Municipal, or private buildings belonging to the English, Sinhalese, Burghers, Tamils, and Malays have been damaged, nor have any Government, Municipal, or Police Officers been intentionally assailed. The disturbances appear to me to have been a sudden outburst of feelings of resentment on the part of the lower classes of Sinhalese, the artizans, and the unemployed in the villages and towns against the Moslems, particularly the Coast Moors. There has always existed a feeling of amity between the Sinhalese and the Moslems in all parts of the island. Since, however, the war began and many working people were thrown out of employment, the Coast Moors began to be too exacting and insolent towards those customers, especially women, who were not regular in their payments; and the relations between the lower classes and artizans and the Moors with whom they have dealings became strained.

Irritation of the Buddhists against the Coast Moors due also to their obstruction of the religious processions of the Buddhists.

A month or two ago the Gampola perahera case was decided in appeal against the Buddhists, who are mainly composed of the peasants and the labouring classes; and this incensed the Buddhists more against the Coast Moors, who objected to the perahera procession passing their mosque. Then the irresponsible Buddhist open-air preachers, who live on the collections made at the preaching places, began to preach against the Moslems. When things were settling down, the Wesak festival was celebrated, and the carollers were prevented from going past the mosque even after 12 p.m. by the police. The Moslems, looking upon this interference on the part of the police as a triumph of their cause, took to jeering and pelting stones from the steps of the mosque at the large crowd of Buddhists who accompanied the procession. This, on the other hand, inflamed the Buddhists all the more, and thousands of the lower and ignorant classes were burning with the spirit of revenge for what they considered as an insult to the founder of their religion. This idea was conveyed from mouth to mouth and district to district, and spread all over the Provinces, where Buddhism prevails, and confirmed the belief that a decided attempt was being made chiefly by the Coast Moors to insult and ridicule the Buddhist religion and its ceremonies. The rioting and looting were not simultaneous. The Rehalwatte riots were caused by the news which was spread that the two Buddhist temples in Achar's Lane and Dias Place were being attacked by the

Moors. I have been daily visiting the different streets and lanes of the San Sebastian Ward, which I have represented during the last 23 years, and am satisfied that the respectable and educated Sinhalese have had no sympathy at all with the mischief-makers, but, on the other hand, rendered the Moslems every help. In my own house I harboured seventeen Coast Moors —boutique-keepers—some of whom were taken to the Maradana mosque in motor-cars by my Sinhalese friends in this part of the city, and the others were removed to the Borella Police Station under police escort. I have often visited the Moslem refugees (from San Sebastian Ward) now in the Maradana mosque and Old and New Moor Streets, and have questioned them about their misfortunes. They cannot give me the name of any respectable Sinhalese resident in their midst who has not sympathised with them in their distress. It would certainly be most desirable to find that a large percentage of the three thousand habitual criminals supposed to be in Colombo have been arrested and punished. There is no doubt that 90 per cent. of these rowdies were the actual ringleaders of the movement in Colombo and the suburbs, and instigated the ordinary ignorant Sinhalese to follow their example and participate in the looting. I am strongly of opinion that had the police done their duty at the very outbreak of the disturbance (although unarmed), and showed a bold front, instead of listlessly looking on, the disturbances might have been put down without any recourse to martial law.

Respectable Sinhalese have no sympathy with those who took revenge on the Coast Moors.

No injured Moor knows of any respectable Sinhalese who has not sympathised with him.

Three thousand habitual criminals in Colombo, ninety per cent. of whom instigated the looting.

If police had done their duty, martial law would have been unnecessary.

I am, dear sir,

Yours faithfully,

C. P. Dias.

## (5) Statement *of* Mr. H. L. de Mel, M.M.C., *Colombo.*

Looting of a Moor boutique in Barnes Place, on 31st May.

On Monday, 31st May, at 8 p.m., Lieut. Vandersmagt, of the C.L.I., who is a neighbour, brought me information that a Moor boutique in Barnes Place was looted. I immediately tried to get the Cinnamon Gardens Police Station. Exchange informed me police 'phones were busy. Both of us set out to the boutiques and found the mob had left. We stopped one man running away, and were satisfied that he was attracted by curiosity. He was the cook of Mr. Robertson. We let him go. He had no arms or loot. Shortly after, the Town Guard (Lieut. Carver) ordered to bring up my car to the Colombo Club for military duty, also asked me to direct Sir Ponnambalam's car. I was detained there for about three-quarters of an hour and discharged without any duty. Several Town Guard turned up, and eight cars had assembled when I left.

Dispersed little mobs near the Eye Hospital and in Regent Street.

On 1st June, at 6.25 a.m., I left for the Chilaw Railway opening. On our return journey we learnt of rioting in Colombo. I got home at about 5.15, and saw signs of mischief. I sent my car to fetch Mr. F. R. Senanayake, a prominent Buddhist, and M.M.C., who lived hard by, and we set out to try and quiet the mob. We dispersed some people opposite the Eye Hospital and also in Regent Street. I then got Mr. Martinus Perera, also a Buddhist, into my car and Mr. Senanayake; went with Mr. J. A. Perera and Dr. Rutnam to fetch the High

Priest Nanissere to the Town Hall or Grand Pass. I saw Mr. Godfrey in civil clothes on horseback in Regent Street. I passed Union Place, when I saw six or seven boutiques of Coast Moormen already looted. I addressed a crowd near Stag's Head Bar. All of them agreed to be quiet by show of hands. Mr. Perera asked all Buddhists to behave, and not join in shameful acts. At Malay Street Junction there was a crowd of 500 to 700 of all races. I stopped the car; so did Mr. Perera. Dr. Bannerjee also got into my car. I addressed the Moors, Malays, Tamils, etc., in Tamil. One of the crowd said, "We are getting costs in the Gampola case from the Coast Moors." Another said, "These Coast Moors are killing our carol parties in Kandy." I was surrounded by some Moors and Sinhalese; a stone was thrown, which struck and injured a Sinhalese. I got the injured man into my car. I also took in another rowdy, as I knew he was drunk. Yet another injured man came up to me, and I took him also. Just then the Mounted Town Guard came up and handed me a notice from the Mayor that everybody was to keep indoors after six. I explained this in Sinhalese and Tamil, and several left for their houses. I saw a number of Moors individually, asked them to be quiet, and took the injured to the City Dispensary and got their injuries attended to. I returned again through Malay Street. I warned a few people outside to get in, asked the Castle bar to be closed, and the tavern-keeper to do so, and went to the Town Hall, then to Armour Street Junction. There J. A. Perera, F. R. Senanayake, Dr. Rutnam, and the high priest were. I again addressed the crowd and asked them to go home.

Looting in Union Place.

Ideas of looters.

Crowd fired on by military.

They were mostly people returning from work. They did so willingly. I was then told that the military had fired and injured a few. A man called Cornelis Appu, of Demetagoda, working at Framjee Oil Mills, appealed to me. I took him in my car. He was shot by the military and bleeding badly. I gave him water to drink and brought him to an ambulance party. I saw at the Town Hall Dr. John Rockwood, who then took over the man. I returned to Slave Island again, then to the dispensary, sent the two injured men with money in two rickshaws to their homes, put Mr. Perera down at his house, and came home at 9 p.m. for my dinner. After dinner I left again *via* Kolluptiya. The Town Guard were then on duty in the streets. I went through Slave Island. All was quiet. I returned home at 11 p.m.

Good work of Mr. de Mel.

On Wednesday I again visited almost all the streets in Slave Island, from Wekanda to Java Lane. I saw two leading Coast Moors in their houses with a large force of men armed: (1) Meeran Pulle, and (2) Kache's brother. I spoke to both, and warned them as J.P. and M.M.C. not to commit a breach of the peace. They assured me they were prepared only to defend themselves, and would do so if attacked by the Sinhalese. I then warned all the Sinhalese in the neighbourhood, the dhobies especially, who are Buddhists, and lived in the vicinity of Wekanda. T. W. Roberts, Additional Magistrate, heard me when I was addressing the crowds. He stopped his car for a while.

Scarcity of food supplies.

On Wednesday I visited the Slaughter-house and Cattle Mart with an idea of getting the butchers to work and seeing to the food supply. I saw Mr. Byrde, also Mr. Fraser, with some Sinhalese shopkeepers of the Pettah, who complained of the Punjabis. Mr. Fraser asked them to be quiet inside their houses, and spoke severely of the shameful attacks on Moors by the Sinhalese. I interpreted, and added warning myself. Later on I visited, with Messrs. J. A. Perera and Senanayake, X Street, Pettah. Had a long talk with the leading Coast Moors of the Pettah, and some Sinhalese. I saw a house was on fire. I got some Sinhalese standing by to help and extinguish it. Some of the S.Y.M.A. helped. I got 20 bags of rice, and took them to Slave Island boutiques that were open and doing business. The price of rice had been raised to 20 cents. I ordered those boutiques that were opened not to sell over 15 cents, the usual price.

That night some looted property was taken up by the police with the possessors. I was informed, and visited the station. Among the accused I found some Malays had been arrested, besides several Sinhalese men and women. They were tried the next morning and sentenced to imprisonment.

There are nearly 18 to 20 Coast Moor boutiques in the Slave Island Private Meat Stall. I spoke to them to be quiet, and so they were. I wrenched a lead pipe from the hand of a rowdy at Slave Island.

On the Thursday I was able to induce the carters to take their carts to the railway and to the produce stores to engage in transport work, in order to assure people that order was restored.

On Tuesday morning, before I arrived in Colombo, several small curry stuff boutiques and tea boutiques of Coast Moors had been looted in Hyde Park Corner, Hunupitiya, Union Place, and Vauxhall Street. Besides the rowdies and bullies of Hunupitiya some of the Sinhalese labour forces of the Commercial Company, Walker and Greig, Victoria Mills, and other European firms, did the damage. Some were prosecuted and imprisoned. After that evening no damage was done or any mischief by the mob, nor had the police any trouble with the crowds.

I was since Wednesday looking after food supply, getting butchers to work, arranging terms with owners of cattle; and as far as possible a fair supply of beef and mutton was available. Apart from assisting the Mayor and the members in feeding the poor, attending to the wounded, visiting the wrecked houses, taking down the statements of people who were looted, I kept a close look-out on Slave Island and the various places of the riot in the town and the villages just outside. I can detail many events and facts which will throw light on the disturbances.

Protection of Moors.

I harboured for three days four Muhammadans at my office in Grandpass, and as they wished to join some of their relations at Bankshall Street, I obtained a Town Guard escort and took them there by car. They were my tenants, and their boutique was looted on Tuesday, the 1st. I saved some of their rice, etc., of which I got a list made. They have since left for the coast and promised to return.

Who are the looters?

I saw several acts of mobbing, and noticed that the crowds were composed of the labouring classes, bullies, habitual criminals, and the unemployed. In two cases they were wreaking religious vengeance and trade animosities owing to alleged malpractices by the Coast Moors. Since the rioters have been arrested, tried, and imprisoned, the mischief has subsided; loot is being surrendered, or looters seized. There does not seem to be any reason or intention to harm the Ceylon Moors, but more evil-disposed people in certain areas, and especially villagers encouraged by the impunity with which lawless acts were done, damaged wantonly a few houses and estates belonging to Muhammadans of all classes. In the village, apart from the growing feeling of animosity against the Coast Moors, a rumour was circulated that, the British being at war with the Turk, the Ceylon Government did not object to the expulsion of these Islams. Such a rumour encouraged people to carry away looted property. In all towns and villages respectable and more educated people protected and befriended the Moors, and took all precautions to save them bodily injury till military aid arrived. Most people did this at the risk of their lives. The police and authorities were weak in dealing with the situation on Tuesday. The rioters and looters were not taken into custody or arrested promptly, and this created a wrong impression in the minds of the mob. Under the Police Ordinance those present should have been called upon to assist in arrest.

In all towns and villages Moors have been sheltered by the respectable Sinhalese.

Rioters and looters not arrested by the police.

The train and newspapers took the news of mob and mischief from town to town, and the idea was promptly put to action by rowdies robbing boutiques. The Buddhists returning from Kandy and Kelaniya by train carried the news to their villages far and wide.

How news of mischief was carried from place to place.

The better classes have few dealings with Coast Moors, save as tenants of their smaller houses or lessees of certain tenements in two or three Wards.

It is necessary to have a statement of all the damage done throughout the Provinces, and also to analyze the various accused who are in jail as a result of this mischief by race, creed, and previous character, and much light will then be thrown on the whole affair.

More destruction of property than looting.

Considerable damage has been done to Sinhalese property and house property of Sinhalese, while injuries have also been inflicted on Sinhalese. The damage done by the Sinhalese mobs is undoubtedly much greater. As far as I know, in Colombo the Crystal Palace shop and two houses that contained costly jewellery and cash in Punchitiawatta, belonging to Ceylon Moors, were looted, and I learn that the perpetrators of these crimes can be traced. Otherwise the mob seemed to aim at destroying Coast Moor boutiques, but not to injure them.

Injury to persons even less than looting.

In Kochchikade on Thursday a faction fight ensued, during which some Moors were killed. Otherwise in Colombo I did not see more than six people grievously wounded during Tuesday evening and Wednesday, and actual death resulting from violence by the mob is small, comparatively speaking.

Why the poor carried away looted property.

In the Sinhalese villages the economic conditions had been reduced, and after ten months of war people were in poor circumstances. The larger the population the greater the misery. With these facts and circumstances the ignorant mind was quick to carry away looted property, more so edible articles. This was openly done in the presence of constituted authority, and carried away in carts. From Borella, women took away large showcases, etc. In the Pettah, iron safes were carefully ripped open. In Maradana, 200 yards from the Police Headquarters, in broad daylight two iron safes were forced, and all the household furniture and clothes of respectable Moors were removed with impunity.

Looting in presence of the Police.

On Friday, the 4th, the Government Agent,

Kurunegala, wired me to see that mine labourers did not join the looters. I wired instantly to my managers, and also wired reply to the Government Agent. In Kurunegala I deal largely with Coast Moors. My rice contractor is one. I have built for him a large boutique 16 miles from Kurunegala, and he has traded up to to-day unmolested. A boutique at the fifteenth milepost saved itself by the protection of my manager and others. When the mob mischief spread to other towns from Kandy, the Coast Moors in Kurunegala gave over to my manager's custody 500 bushels of rice for fear of same being looted by mobs; the Government Agent, Kurunegala, acted with great foresight, and took preventive measures early to safeguard the town. If most other responsible officials had done the same, and called out the Volunteers and armed Special Constables, much mischief might have been averted. It appears to me that in each area the mischief was over in a short time, and it spread from village to village. In the far distant villages in the North-Western Province I learn Coast Moor boutiques were set fire to. That shows, if I may say so, that there was a feeling against that class of trade aggravated by the perahera case and the fate of the carol party. In Kurunegala there had been a riot some months back between the Buddhists and Coast Moors.

Sinhalese protection to Moors in the villages.

Surrender by Coast Moors of their property to the Sinhalese gentry for safe custody.

If Volunteers and Special Constables used in time, mischief would have been averted.

The action of these mobs is deeply deprecated by all respectable people, and, whatever grievance, religious fanaticism cannot justify the method or means by which the Coast Moors were molested.

In attempting to address the crowds our experience invariably was that, if a few in the crowd recognized the speaker, they gave same heed. Where there were no such, they were angry, and argued or refused to hear, and taunted or insulted the speaker.

Looters in Slave Island Ward of Colombo Municipality were mostly habituals, bullies and workmen of the big European mills.

Speaking of Slave Island Ward, the looters were all habituals of all races, bullies, and workmen of the big European mills. Several have been arrested and convicted, and warrants are out for 48 of that type in Slave Island. I know of my own knowledge that in Hunupitiya all the rowdies have left and are evading arrest. The whole place is now free of these undesirables. I made inquiries from refugees in Colombo, and a good many acknowledged the safety of their lives and property to respectable Sinhalese. (I annex an affidavit from Madarsa, referring to the services of Mr. D. S. Ranasinghe, of Slave Island; several others can be submitted).

Claims of Coast Moors for damages highly exaggerated.

While already in the mosque, as refugees, I read on the 6th June last written statements in the hands of the Coast Moors, in English, showing list of damages sustained by them. In my opinion they were highly exaggerated and spurious. I mentioned some of these cases to Mr. R. W. Byrde.

On Sunday, the 6th, I was distributing rice in the New Bazaar Ward with other members. I was surprised at the number of refugees from Gampola, Kandy, Kadugannawa, Veyangoda, Moratuwa, Panadura, and other places. A few of them had injuries.

I heard several commendations of the English Town Guards. Everybody wanted them to be pickets in their neighbourhood. They acted fairly and dealt tactfully with people during the disturbances.

H. L. de Mel, M.M.C.

15/6/1915.

## (6) Statement *of the* Rev. G. A. F. Senaratne, *of the Colombo Wesleyan Mission.*

*Y. M. C. A.,*
*Racquet Court,*
*Colombo, June 15th,* 1915.

First disturbance in Colombo over the price of a cup of tea, in a boutique at Maradana, on 31st May.

When the riots broke out in Colombo, on the evening of Monday, the 31st, I was residing at "Sweden Bank," Alexandra Place. The servants brought me the news that at Maradana the Moor tea boutique-keeper had raised the price of a cup of tea by one cent and the shop was attacked. It was after 8 p.m. when I was told this. On Tuesday morning I came to the Y.M.C.A. and found that rioting had broken out in the Pettah. I proceeded at once to Dam Street, which was the centre of various mission activities. One of the first things I did was to send away all the girls who had come to school. Then I went into "The Rest" (the social institution of the mission), and warned the rickshaw coolies and other Sinhalese of the lower classes who had gathered together there not to go out and take part in the rioting or the looting. I told them that there was no meaning in this outbreak, and that it would serve no purpose whatever. I managed to restrain that lot almost completely. Then I kept watching, standing on the steps. I saw several wounded, mostly Sinhalese, were being brought from the Fort end of Dam Street. I was told that they were coming from Bankshall Street and Wolfendahl, where the Moors

Rioting at the Pettah.

Many Sinhalese wounded at Bankshall Street and Wolfendahl by Moors taking the offensive.

took the offensive. Another thing I observed was police lenience, which perhaps was caused by a sense of helplessness. Two Sinhalese men were brought under arrest by four constables. At the very gate of the Police Station a gang of rowdies got round the policemen and demanded the release of two men, and the police shamefully gave in to the mob. This, I am sure, gave a very mischievous notion to the rowdy element of the hundreds who had gathered round about. Then when I saw that crowds were forming all round in the streets near the Police Station, I asked a sergeant to disperse these groups and ask them to move on. The police simply kept gazing as if they were mesmerized, and showed great weakness. At about 12.30 I came back to the Y.M.C.A. In the Racquet Court there was a gang of rowdies headed by one Noor, who for all purposes appeared like a Sinhalese. They were marching along Front Street with clubs and iron bars in their hands. Most of them were the well-known Pettah rowdies and "habituals," with a sprinkling of the workmen class. Once the police were driving the crowds from Main Street towards Norris Road. Somehow the crowd took to flight across Racquet Court in all directions. Then Noor—against whom I have already given information to the police—ran forward and confronted the constable and began to beckon the spreading crowd with his hand to come together again. He was able to speak a little English, and he began to cry out, "Go ahead, boys." They came back again, and a number of us from the Y.M.C.A. began to speak to the men. Somehow in a little while the company was broken, and Noor, with a couple of his friends, came and laid himself down under the Bo-tree.

Supineness of the police, who kept gazing as if mesmerized.

Looters in Front Street, Pettah, were rowdies and habituals and some workmen.

Noor, a Muhammadan, rallying the Sinhalese.

A little later we saw scores of people going through the Racquet Court with looted goods, especially from the Crystal Palace. Noor and his friends, too, brought some booty, and then they began to demand from every looter who crossed the Racquet Court a share of the things that were being carried away. There were four constables in Front Street who kept watching and did nothing. This action (rather inaction) of the police gave encouragement to the riff-raff, and even street boys began to run towards Keyzer Street, and they brought loads of crockery, etc. At about 3.30 or 4, I went again to Dam Street, and saw that things were fairly quiet. Then I walked towards Price Park and began to speak to the people who had gathered together in small groups here and there. I continued, in the kindest yet most persuasive language I had command of, to pacify the feelings of the mob. With the single exception of an old man (whom I later found in the lock-up), all listened to me well, and agreed not to begin a fresh disturbance. Here I heard from the people stories of Moor atrocities towards Sinhalese women in Moor Streets and Wolfendahl. I did not want to believe any of these, and said that "they can't be true." While I was yet there Messrs. E. G. Jayawardane and Batuwantudawe came in and tried to pacify the crowd.

Loot of Crystal Palace stores.

Police do nothing. Even boys took courage to carry away looted property.

Sinhalese gentlemen trying to pacify the crowd.

On Wednesday morning I went back again to Dam Street. The same morning I visited the secretary of the Workmen's Provident Union at Maligakanda, and asked him to use all his influence over the workmen who were rioting. He said he had tried his utmost, and they were beyond control. I saw a large number of women and children within the Police Station premises, so I went and inquired why they came there, etc. They said that they were come from Wolfendahl, Siripina Lane, New Moor Street, Silversmith Lane, and Alutkade. The Moors, who were quite strong in these places, had driven them away from their tenements. I made inquiries whether they were ill-treated. Except for a hit or two, they had not been badly handled. These people, who numbered between 150 and 200, in a little while were all turned out of the police premises. This, I thought, was most cruel. Then I invited them to "The Rest," and made arrangements for them to cook their meals. In the evening a good many of them moved themselves to a godown of a Sinhalese merchant near by. In the afternoon a number of Moor women and children came rushing in from the side of Price Park. These were, under police protection, housed in the verandah of the Girls' School. In the evening this company was escorted to the Old Moor Street by their co-religionists. By night the number of refugees who came for shelter at "The Rest" increased to 130. At noon on this day I saw and heard firing taking place at Price Park. The police, under the leadership of some European official and Superintendent Attygalle, fired at the crowd. I saw a Moor with a bullet wound on his right chest come running into the Police Station. At noon I rang up Mr. H. L. de Mel on the 'phone and suggested the idea of getting together several of the leading residents for the purpose of going out to the disturbed localities to plead with the people. Mr. de Mel told me that various people of position had already gone and were going in all directions trying to pacify the people. He wanted me to meet him at the Municipal Office at 3 o'clock. I did so, and was

Expulsion of Sinhalese tenants by Moor landlords.

Police fire at the crowd near Price Park.

Further activities of Sinhalese gentry to allay the disturbance.

informed that nothing further was possible just at that moment, and he wanted me to do all I could individually to calm the people. Between three and five I walked through Old Moor Street, Quarry Road, Messenger Street, Kurwin Street, Peer Saibo's Lane, St. Sebastian Street, Dias Place, and Price Park, speaking both to the Moors and the Sinhalese I came across. They all listened to me well, and I was able to persuade many that it was useless to fight any more. Next I paid a social visit to Dr. Solomon Fernando at Bagatalle Road. I found that he was protecting a Moor in his house.

In what parts of Colombo the Moors took the offensive, and in what way.

On Thursday I held an inquiry at "The Rest" as to the conditions that obtained in the localities from which the refugees who were under our protection came. They were all from those parts where the Moors predominated, namely, New Moor Street, Siripina Lane, Wolfendahl Street and lanes, Quarry Road, Silversmith Lane, and Wilson Street. In all these places the Moors had taken the offensive first by attacking the Sinhalese passers-by and then by turning out the resident Sinhalese. In one lane in Wolfendahl Street a Sinhalese man had taken the first steps.

False reports of mutilation by Moors.

Mr. Allan Vandergert, of the Presbyterian Sinhalese Mission, testified to me the truth of the Moor offensive in Wolfendahl Street. He had taken several Sinhalese men to the Municipal Dispensary. Mr. S. Sathasivan (who lived at "Rajagiri," Hultsdorf Street, when the riots broke out, and is presently at the Y.M.C.A.) told me that he saw two Moormen in Wolfendahl Street catching hold of a Sinhalese woman and mutilating her nose. A lad told me that he saw some Moors cutting a Sinhalese boy into bits. I made inquiries as to the atrocities said to have been committed in Moor Street, and found that they were groundless. I saw, when I walked through on Wednesday, Sinhalese women in the Moor houses, and observed no indications of violence. But my refugees complained that the Moors had broken their property and taken away their clothing and some money. Of course, I heard of many cruelties committed by the Sinhalese, too.

This week I have been interesting myself in finding new houses for these unfortunates, and in one case paid the house-rent for this month.

Sinhalese refugees curse the Sinhalese rowdies.

Another point on which I questioned the refugees was as to their view of the riots. They all deplored them, and in some cases they said that the curse of God ought to come down on the Sinhalese rowdies.

Conclusions of Rev. Mr. Senaratne.

Perhaps it will be useful to put down some of my impressions, too :—

1. The Sinhalese Press is responsible for preparing the ground for this outbreak, and the Buddhist street preacher also has contributed a good deal in rousing the spirit of the people. But in all that was said in the Press or by the preachers no violence of the type that happened was meant.

2. The perahera case plays the most important part it in.

3. In Kandy trouble was anticipated, and all concerned, including the police, knew it. All that was anticipated was a row in front of the mosque. A Muhammadan mason in Colombo told me four weeks ago that Moors in Kandy were preparing for it; that there was a rumour of the Moors having imported 300 men from India.

4. There seems to be no central organization that devised this almost simultaneous outbreak. The

Wesak crowds in Kandy and Kelaniya, where people from all Sinhalese districts had come on pilgrimage, carried the news back to the villages, and also perhaps some of the riotous spirits. This accounts for the sudden spread. On the whole, it was a work of rowdies and habituals. In the looting others, the unemployed and the poor, were tempted.

5. The reading of war news of all kinds has to some extent created the spirit of fighting in many minds. Rowdies are reported to have used war terms in rioting.

6. In many villages there have been attempts to resist the rowdies. Respectable Sinhalese people of various parts have been even risking their lives and property in protecting the Moor.

7. This outrage does not receive the approval of the Sinhalese as a race, nor of the vast majority of the Buddhists. Of course, there was a widespread feeling against the Moor, but to commit lawlessness in giving expression to it was far removed from the minds of self-respecting people everywhere.

8. Police lenience and incapacity to deal with a difficult situation are largely responsible for the huge extent of the damage.

9. The influential people everywhere have been trying to put down the mobs.

10. Whilst approving all the severity with which repressive measures were enforced during the first two days after the military were called out, I strongly feel that the military authorities have exhibited an unpardonable thirst for blood. They do not seem to think that the life of a Sinhalese man is worth anything.

11. The Government does a great injustice to the

Sinhalese nation by holding us all responsible for the outrage committed by the riffraff. The Government attitude is seen through the following :—

(*a*) The indiscriminate way in which the houses of respectable law-abiding citizens have been searched, thus casting great indignities upon them as suspects.

(*b*) The fact that the motor-cars and guns of Sinhalese gentlemen have been kept back whilst others are being returned.

(*c*) The refusal on the part of the Governor to interview any Sinhalese or a representative of the Sinhalese.

12. The proposed levy in Colombo upon 300 wealthy Sinhalese, and in villages on all within a five-mile radius of any damage, is utterly unreasonable and unjust. There is more reason in opening a relief fund. If it be necessary for the Government to pay compensation, then the properties (or a part of them) belonging to the rioters and others who have been convicted in the courts can be confiscated. There is some reason in that.

GEO. A. F. SENARATNE,
Wesleyan Methodist Minister, Colombo.

## (7) LETTER *of* DR. W. P. RODRIGO, M.M.C., *Colombo.*

*The Shrubbery,*
*Bambalapitiya, Colombo.*

17*th June*, 1915.

The Chairman,
Municipal Council and Mayor of Colombo,
Colombo.

SIR,—With reference to your letter No. 127 on the subject of the "Special Meeting of the Municipal Council" held on last Thursday (the 10th instant), I have the honour to inform you that I myself deeply regret my absence at the meeting, due to my absence from town.

2. As requested in that letter, I saw you on the following day at your office and expressed to you my views in regard to the measures you said are going to be adopted to compensate for the damage done to the Coast Moors during the recent riots. I now think it is my duty to put my views on paper, so that you may place them before the authorities if you think it necessary.

3. With regard to the question of compensation for the damage done during the recent disturbances, I have to inform you that, to my mind, the idea of compensation is both impracticable and, in the manner you suggested, unprecedented. Difficulty of estimating damages and allotting compensation.

4. There have been riots both in Ceylon and in other British possessions, particularly in Ireland and

India, at various times, but in no instances have I heard of compensation being paid to the sufferers in the manner suggested by you. Besides, with a people like the Moors, the Coast Moormen in particular, I think it is absolutely impossible to estimate the extent of loss each party has sustained, and therefore any attempt at compensation on equitable lines will result in total failure.

5. I therefore suggest that no attempt be made to compensate, but all measures be directed towards affording relief to the sufferers.

The idea of the Sinhalese paying compensation in order to avoid the stigma that would otherwise attach to them, is unreasonable.

6. Now, with regard to the methods proposed to be adopted, you said there is a stigma attached to the Sinhalese race on account of these riots. I entirely disagree with you in this opinion, and strongly resent it. As I said the other day, rioting against the Germans and looting of their properties have been going on in various parts of England in recent times, and if a stigma is to be attached to the Sinhalese on account of the scum of the race indulging in rioting against the Moors, you must admit that there is a worse stigma attached to the good name of the English people on account of the riots against the Germans, for, when one considers the two cases, everything palliates in favour of the Sinhalese rioter.

7. On account of this stigma, you said an opportunity is going to be given to the Sinhalese to redeem their name by voluntarily contributing 50 per cent. of the estimated loss, and in default it is proposed to levy a tax on the race for that purpose.

8. As I said above, I deny that there is a stigma attachable fairly to the name of the Sinhalese race, and therefore a tax of the kind suggested will be universally opposed by the whole race; and my advice

is to leave it severely alone. A voluntary contribution, if it is to be confined to the Sinhalese race, will also be equally resented, and to my mind the only equitable way of meeting the present situation is by heavily fining those individuals found guilty of aiding, abetting, or participating in the riots, in addition to a term of imprisonment, and if that were not sufficient to afford relief—and it is relief alone that is called for—a fund should be opened for that purpose, and all races asked to contribute to it.

The proper remedy is to fine heavily the rioters, and to open a voluntary relief fund.

9. As I said during my interview with you last Friday, the proposed levy sounds more like a fine than anything else, and I ask you, Sir, in the name of justice, why I and hundreds of other Sinhalese people who have done all that lay in their power to help the Government and the Moors in this unfortunate incident, and that at the risk of losing their lives and their property, be asked to pay a fine simply because they belong to the same race as a pack of vagabonds who have offended both the laws of the land and of society?

Why should hundreds of Sinhalese who have done their best to protect the Moors pay compensation to them?

10. I explained to you during my interview what I did during the riots, and as this is intended to be placed before the authorities, I will recapitulate the details, so that they may also know what the Sinhalese have done.

11. Although rioting had commenced in Colombo on the 31st ultimo, I knew nothing of it till I saw it on my way to the Town Hall on the 1st inst., and you might remember the discussion Mr. J. A. Perera and I had with you on that afternoon. After leaving you, I went round my Ward begging of the Sinhalese not to disgrace me by molesting the Moors, but protect the strangers in our midst, as such a dastardly

act would be a serious offence against the Government, for which they would be severely punished. At the same time I advised the Moors to take their goods and go to my house if they had any fears. About the end of my journey, about 7 p.m., to my greatest dismay I saw that rioting had already commenced, and the crowd was breaking the boutiques opposite Dr. Rode's residence. Single-handed though I was, I arrested three of the rioters and handed them over to the police, who came upon the scene after I had dispersed the crowd, and I understand that the mob assaulted the police and rescued these three men also.

12. On coming home I found that a large number of Coast Moormen had taken my advice and were awaiting me in my house with their bags and baggage, including large sums of money; and having undertaken to protect them, I had to mount guard over them overnight. On the following day, Wednesday, the 2nd inst., large crowds, certainly 400 to 500, collected opposite my house and threatened to kill me and demolish my house if I did not surrender my *protégés* with their belongings. This I refused to do under any circumstances, and kept the mob at bay with threats to shoot them if they entered my premises; and as the crowd was getting unwieldly I wired to the Colonial Secretary for help. I thus protected 86 Coast Moormen and their belongings until help came, and despatched them to India, some at my own expense, and am yet keeping here eight head of cattle, several carts, boutique goods, etc., belonging to some of the men who have left the Island.

13. The above is a short description of the part I played in regard to the disturbances, and I am

certain there are several others of my race who have done even more for the Government and the Moors than myself.

14. I will continue this communication at a future date, and forward to you my general impressions on the present disturbances, and in the meantime

Remain,

Yours faithfully,

W. P. RODRIGO.

## (8) LETTER *of* MR. S. A. GOONETILLEKE, *Millowner.*

*The Mabola Oil Mills,*
*Wattala, Ceylon,*

*17th September*, 1915.

To the Honourable Mr. P. Rámanáthan, K.C.,
C.M.G., M.L.C.,
Colombo.

The belief of Government officials that all the Sinhalese were in sympathy with the rioters is unmerited defamation.

Sir,—During the recent riots I had the pleasure of meeting several Government officials, and I observed that their general impression *re* the recent riots was that the whole Sinhalese population was in sympathy with the rioters.

So I have decided to write this letter to you, since you are so interested in our behalf, for I feel it my duty as a Sinhalese to help you to exonerate the Sinhalese people of this unmerited odium. I think that a mere superficial glance into the glaring facts perpetrated during the riots will be sufficient to convince one of the fact that these riots were only a sudden outburst of some Buddhists against the unfortunate Moors in some parts of the Island.

Moors have often sought refuge with the Sinhalese, and were protected by them.

Even among the Moors themselves, all whom I know do not hesitate in the least to assert this fact. There are even many instances where these unfortunate Moors sought refuge and were protected by Sinhalese people.

What happened in Mabola, and how the Moors were helped.

When the riots spread to Mabola, all the Moors of the place, with their wives and children, 187 in all, rushed into my bungalow for refuge. They came in a pitiful state of mind, and were continually crying out that they would become Christians, etc., if only I would protect them from their enemies. On the 3rd June the Mudaliyár of the korale, with Mr. J. A. Perera, M.M.C., and two other gentlemen, paid a visit to these Moors in their refuge, and also got the Government to send motor-lorries under military escort to take them to Colombo. But these Moors profusedly thanked the Colonel in charge, and most pathetically begged of him to leave them with me, saying that they preferred to stay under my care and even die, rather than leave my premises. The following day Mr. T. P. Attygalle, the Superintendent of Police, came here, and, seeing that it was impossible to get them to leave Mabola, sent armed police to guard the place.

Another proof that the Sinhalese of Mabola were not in sympathy with the rioters is shown by the fact that they felt such resentment against those miscreants who went in motor-cars spreading false rumours, with intent to excite the Sinhalese against the Moors, that they themselves gave the police the necessary information and gave evidence at courts, with the result that these rebels against the public peace were convicted and sentenced to ten years.

I may add that even before the Government sent me rice and curry stuffs to be distributed among these unfortunate Moors, the korale Mudaliyár, and, following his example, many other Sinhalese of this and the neighbouring villages, came to my place and distributed to them money and rice and other necessaries.

My brother, too, the Rev. F. F. M. Goonetilleke,

the parish priest of Gampola, on the 30th of May, hearing that the rioters were mustering strong there, himself went out to them and invited to his schoolroom the leading Buddhists of the place, as well as the Buddhists that were assembled in the town; and there, with the R. M. of the place at his side, he tried his utmost to pacify the rioters. He held a meeting of the Moors, too, and did his very best to settle amicably their differences.

If these few instances of my personal knowledge be of any help to the just cause you have at heart, I give you full liberty to make use of same.

Thanking you for so nobly and generously espousing our cause,

Yours faithfully,

S. A. Goonetilleke.

## (9) STATEMENT *of* MR. D. B. JAYATELAKA, *Barrister-at-Law.*

*Latila, Kynsey Road,*
*Colombo.*

*Trouble at the Temple Road Junction on and June.*

I WAS away from home from Monday (31st May) evening till Tuesday night. I have, therefore, no personal knowledge of what happened on these two days. On Wednesday morning I had to go to Henaratgoda for a case. At about 8.30 a.m. I left home for the Maradana Railway Station in order to catch the 9.15 a.m. train. But I could not proceed beyond the Maradana Post Office. There was trouble near the Temple Road Junction, and I was told that it would not be safe to proceed further. I returned home, and sent a telegram to the Magistrate requesting him to postpone my case.

*Road impassable.*

*Sinhalese chasing Moors in Rosmead Place.*

About 10.30 I heard a disturbance, and, coming out, I was told by Mr. Sanmogam, my next-door neighbour, that eight Moors who had been hiding in his premises were running along Rosmead Place in order to get to the mosque; and that they were being pursued by the mob. Sure enough a few minutes afterwards I saw a crowd of about 25 Sinhalese and Tamils approaching dragging along a young Moorman (a Hambaya) with them. Though I could not recognise any one of them I walked up and spoke to them, and with some difficulty induced them to set free the young Moor, who ran away in the direction of the mosque.

Mr. S. and Mr. J. give shelter to the Moors.

Then Mr. Sanmogam told me that he had three Moorwomen and a child in his house, and that it might not be safe for them to remain under his roof. I at once got them into my house, and sheltered them the whole day, until late in the evening they were removed to the Maradana Police Station.

The Mayor requests three Sinhalese gentlemen to go to Hanwella and turn off the advancing crowd.

At about noon, Mr. Byrde (the Mayor) came to my house and requested me to go along with Messrs. Senanayake and Mudaliyár Tada Rajapakse towards Hanwella, as a report had been received that a large crowd was assembling, and try to dissuade them from coming towards Colombo. I readily agreed to go, and we started at once. On the road at almost every half-a-mile we met crowds of people, most of them armed with clubs and sticks, and in a greatly excited condition. On enquiry we learnt that they had heard that 3,000 Moors had attacked Colombo, murdered the Sinhalese, outraged and horribly mutilated Sinhalese women, destroyed temples, and were pouring out into the villages around. In some places we found that the women and the children had gone into the jungle, while the men stood on the road prepared to meet the approaching enemy. We spoke to these people, showed them the absurdity of the stories they had heard and believed, reassured their minds as to the condition of things in Colombo, and asked them to return to their homes in peace. We further told them that they must on no account attempt to come into Colombo for a day or two until everything quieted down. Where the men were not drunk we found our assurances were readily accepted and our advice acted upon. When we got nearer to Hanwella the crowds became thicker, and the excitement was greater. Near the "Rest House" we met

The false reports heard by the crowd, as to the outrages of the Moors.

the Korale Muhandiram (Mr. J. A. Perera). Here we addressed the crowd that had already assembled, and advised them to disperse to their homes, and were about to turn back when we noticed a large procession advancing towards us. There were about 2,000 men in this procession. They were armed with sticks, clubs, and other weapons, and some of them had guns too. I distinctly noticed at least two Burghers armed with guns, and a large number of Tamils. We managed to get this procession to halt, and, having with difficulty obtained a hearing, addressed them. Here, too, we found it was the wild rumours referred to above that drew this huge crowd together. Fortunately these men were not drunk, and were, therefore, willing to listen to us. We were thus able to convince them of their folly and the serious consequences that might ensue if they proceeded any further. Acting upon our advice, the procession at once turned back, and was out of sight when we started homewards. On the return journey we found few people on the road, and they had thrown away the clubs and other weapons we saw in their hands when we were going up.

Their fears being dissipated, they turned back.

Returning to Colombo at about 5 p.m., we were asked at the Borella Police Station to go along to the Bottarmulla Road. So we did. Here we found only small groups of men (unarmed) until we came up to Bottaramulla Junction, where there was a large gathering. Here also we found the same wild stories current. At this place we learnt from one of the men present that a Moor family was hiding in a jungle a few miles away, and their position was very unsafe. The man undertook to take us to the place. So we got him into the car, and driving along some

Mr. J. and others requested to go to the Bottaramulla Road.

Measures taken to hunt up Moorish men and women who were in hiding in the jungle, and to take them safely to Colombo.

branch roads came to the village of Walpola. There we met the Headman, who told us that the number of people hiding in the jungle was 14, and that there were several women. It was, of course, impossible to bring all these people in our motor-car, and it was not at all safe to leave them in the jungle for another night. Mudaliyár Rajapakse and Mr. D. S. Senanayake then undertook to return to Colombo in order to fetch another motor-car, and Mr. F. R. Senanayake and I to remain behind until they returned. Our arrival was noticed by the villagers, who began to gather round us. We were not sure as to their attitude, so I remained with the crowd while Mr. Senanayake went with the Headman in search of the refugees. One hour passed, two hours passed; it was now completely dark, but still no signs of the motor-car. I was feeling very uneasy. Though I found that the villagers were generally in sympathy with the object of our errand, I was not quite sure of all who were about the place. One man distinctly said that what had happened was due to the wrath of the gods incensed at the insult offered to the Tooth Relic, which had been taken by the Hambayas and trampled in the mud. This man was quite convinced of the truth of this story, and it took me some time to show to this man and his friends that it was an utter falsehood. At last there was the sound of a hooter, and in a few minutes a motor-car came containing Captain D. Dyes and two Town Guardsmen and Mr. Senanayake. They had brought a motor-lorry also, which was left on the main road in charge of Mudaliyár Rajapakse. The refugees were soon brought out from the place of hiding, the ladies and the children were put in the motor-car, and the rest of us walked up to the main road, about a mile, in the dark. All the refugees were then transferred to the motor-lorry, and were safely brought to Colombo late in the night.

On Thursday, Messrs. J. A. Perera, M.M.C., F. R. Senanayake, and myself went along the Negombo Road, as far as Jaela. On the other side of the Victoria Bridge we met Mr. R. J. Fenando, a Wesak Sinhalese, who assured us that he would lose not less than Rs. 500 a month in the shape of house-rent in consequence of the riots. We advised the people all along the road not to get in the road, not to carry any kind of weapon, and above all not to attempt to get into Colombo. At Wattala we went to the Catholic Church and saw Father Boyer. He told us how on the previous day, when he was performing a marriage ceremony, the church bell was suddenly rung; how the people assembled, excited over a rumour that had spread that the Moors had destroyed the Catholic churches in the city; how he had to keep up till midnight in order to pacify the people, whose excitement grew stronger owing to the ringing of bells on the Mutwal side of the river. Thence we went to see the Mudaliyár (Mr. Sam Perera), and with him proceeded to Mabole (seven miles distant), where we found Mr. Goonetilleke, a wealthy resident, was sheltering and protecting a very large number of Moor people. We passed on to Kandana, where at the request of the tavern-keeper, the Mudaliyár sealed the arrack-tavern. Here, too, we heard quite a novel excuse for the attack on the Moors. We were solemnly assured by one of the large crowd present that the Moors sent contributions to Turkey to aid the Sultan against the British Government! When

Mr. J. and others go to Jaela on the Negombo Road, assuring the people of safety.

Rumours of Moors destroying Roman Catholic churches.

State of things in Mabola, Kandana, and Jaela.

we reached Jaela we found about 16 Moors in a house. Their boutiques had been looted on the previous day, and they appeared to be in great fear. The Mudaliyár took all the necessary steps for their immediate protection, and wired to the authorities about their position, as well as about those at Mabole.

Search for Hon. Mr. Abdul Rahiman's daughter and her husband in Homogama and beyond.

Returning home in the afternoon, we repaired to the Town Hall, where we met the Mayor and gave him a brief account of what we had seen and done. On our way home we met the Hon. Mr. Abdul Rahiman in the Fort. He stopped us and told us that his daughter and her husband, who had left Homogana in the morning, had not reached Colombo, and that there was a rumour that they had been taken out at Ramapitaya. He asked our help to find them. We offered at once to go in search of them if he could get us a pass. He at once went to Mr. Stubbs and brought us a letter of authority from him. With this we went to the barracks and obtained a military pass. Leaving at once, we went to Ramapitaya at about 8.30 p.m., where we learned from the stationmaster that the lady and her husband had passed through safely in disguise. With this good news we at once returned to Colombo and repaired to Mr. Abdul Rahiman's, where we found the missing party had safely arrived.

Their safe arrival in Colombo.

D. B. JAYATILAKA.

## (10) *The* STATEMENT *by* CHARLES BATUWANTUDAVE, *Barrister-at-Law and Advocate of the Supreme Court of the Island of Ceylon, with 14 years' practice; President, Colombo Buddhist Theosophical Society, and present Manager of about 400 Schools in the Island; President of several Total Abstinence Societies in the Island; Member of the Oriental Studies Committee, and the Royal Asiatic Society, Ceylon Branch; Member of District School Committee, Colombo.*

MY house was searched on the 8th of June, one week after the riots broke out, and not a scrap of paper connecting me with the riots was found; in fact, nothing was discovered in my house.

Search of Mr. B.'s house, on 8th June; nothing found.

On the morning of the 21st June, at 5.30, a European Town Guardsman, accompanied by a Punjabi private, came to my house and took me away in a motor-car direct to Welikada Prison, and I was lodged there for 46 days in a convict cell about 9 ft. by 9 ft., where I remained locked in for about 21 hours. I was given about one hour in the morning for exercise and one hour in the afternoon for the same purpose. I was locked in every evening at 4.30 p.m., and let out at 7.30 a.m. the next morning. No light of any kind was provided, and I had to be in darkness the whole evening and night. I was given the diet provided for convicted criminals for nearly three days. Being unable to eat the food given, I lived on a few ounces of bread and water during the three days. On the third day I was

His arrest and removal to jail, on 21st June.

What happened there.

allowed to get my food from home, but the hours of locking in remained unchanged.

One hour after my arrest a Special Commissioner sent for me and wished me to make a statement, if I could, as to the causes which led up to the riots, etc. I made as full a statement as was possible in the circumstances, and I was then informed that I was under arrest under martial law, and that I would be remanded for a period of 16 days.

I was next sent for to the Maradana Police Headquarters, which were then called the Military Headquarters, and taken before the Special Commissioner, who recorded my statement, and I was called upon to explain a perfectly harmless telephone message I had sent to Mr. D. S. Senanayake on the 3rd of June. I found the message had been wrongly recorded by the operator, who said it was her duty to observe my line along with some others. However, there was nothing in that, but I was again remanded for a further term of 16 days.

When I was next produced the police called the secretary of the Buddhist Theosophical Society, and proved that I was the president of the society, and also that a paper called the *Sarasavi Sanderesa* was the organ of the society, and that two communicated articles appeared in that paper regarding the Moorish traders and their tricks.

Then I was given a further remand of 16 days, but a few days after that I was again produced before the Special Commissioner, and a Police Inspector was called as a witness to produce two copies of certain English newspapers containing some account of meetings of temperance societies at which I was present or presided; but not a word of evidence was there as to what business had been transacted at those meetings. If the authorities were honest about their business, I take it that the secretaries of the societies and their books would have been produced. In no single instance was this done, but in every case the police kept on calling all but the right witnesses. Finally a charge of sedition was framed against me, under the Army Act, and the proceedings were forwarded to the Attorney-General. The charge was in respect of the two communicated articles in the newspaper referred to as the paper which belonged to the Theosophical Society. I was charged as president of the Society, although a copy of the rules and constitution of the Society was produced, from which I was able to establish that I had no control over the paper as president. The editor and the manager of the paper are responsible for anything appearing in the paper, as the editor is the man who is required by the law in Ceylon to take his oath as such, and the police keep a record of the affidavits, which are called declarations. The editor was also charged in respect of the articles mentioned above. I have every reason to believe my arrest was not due to anything which appeared in the paper referred to, but it was entirely due to my work among the people, particularly my work in the temperance movement.

The Police engaged in fishing for evidence, and Special Commissioners giving them every unfair opportunity.

On the 31st of May I was called up by the Government Agent of the Western Province, and my aid was asked to quell a threatened disturbance at the railway workshop; and I readily consented, and went with him and remained at the workshops for some time, pacified the people, and went away. I was always ready and willing to help the authorities.

I applied to be released on bail from the 15th day

Kept in jail for forty-two days, and then released—

of my arrest till the 42nd day, but each time my application was refused on the ground that the Inspector-General of Police had further evidence. In fact, what I believe the officials were up to was trying their utmost to fabricate evidence during my incarceration.

Not without further acts of impotent rage.

On the 2nd of August I was sent for by the Special Commissioner, and was informed that the Brigadier-General had no objection to my going out on the following terms: I was asked to pay down Rs. 5,000 in cash, and also to enter into a bond for Rs. 10,000 to be of good behaviour. In order to get out of the trouble I furnished this security and got my discharge. I was then given several dates to appear before the Special Commissioner to hear the Attorney-General's orders; and finally I was informed that my security money would be returned. All these high-handed acts were done, but the most surprising part of it all is that not even a word of regret has been expressed since I underwent so much inconvenience and suffered immense loss.

29th October, 1915. CHAS. BATUWANTUDAVE

## (11) Statement *of* Mr. D. S. Senanayake, *Planter and Merchant.*

I am a proprietary planter and plumbago mine-owner.

On the 8th of June, at about 12 o'clock, I was in my bungalow in Cinnamon Gardens, Colombo, when a Town Guardsman, an Inspector of Police, and two Panjábi soldiers came in a motor-car. The Town Guard informed me he had orders to search my house, and requested me to assemble all the inmates of the house. Some of us were permitted to be in the drawing-room, with a Panjábi soldier to guard us. The servants were made to stand just outside the house, with another Panjábi soldier in charge of them. The Town Guard and the Inspector of Police then made a careful search of the premises, but found no incriminating documents or firearms. After about two hours' search they departed.

A fortnight after this search, in the early morning of the 21st, I was awakened by a Town Guard, who informed me I was under arrest, and would not permit me to answer a call of nature. He took me, guarded by two armed soldiers, to the Welikada Convict Establishment, where I noticed quite a number of prominent gentlemen. After searching me, I was taken inside the jail and locked in a bare cell. For want of a chair or bench, I had to stand inside this for some hours, when I was taken before Mr. Allnutt, who, after informing me that I was at liberty to make a statement, proceeded to question me, obviously for the purpose of getting some statement likely to incriminate myself and others. Since I was aware of nothing to incriminate any respectable person, I was not in a position to help him.

Immediately after this examination, I, with the others arrested on the same day, were removed to a more uncomfortable ward, and were locked inside cells that are known in the jail as "penal" cells. Having no one to speak to, and nothing to read or do, each one of us had to remain in these cells. Our midday meals were pushed inside the room. The very sight of the dirty food and the vessels in which it was served disgusted me, and naturally I was unable to take that food. After two days, however, we were permitted to get food and books from outside.

On several occasions we were taken to the Police Headquarters, and a farce of an inquiry was gone through. All the evidence called that in any way concerned me was that I had sent a message to Mr. Advocate Batuwantudave, on behalf of the Honourable P. Rámanáthan, requesting me to come over to see him; that I was on one of my estates on the 27th, 28th, and 29th of May; that I was a temperance worker; and the fact that I had helped to disperse a very large mob of armed men on the 2nd of June—*i.e.*, during the time of the riots. None of the witnesses called proved anything against me.

On the 5th of August, after forty-six days of incarceration under as unpleasant circumstances as one could imagine, I was let out on my entering into a bail-bond. The conditions of this were that I should be of good behaviour, that I should not leave Colombo for a period of one year, and that I should appear before any Commissioner if called upon. I had also to deposit Rs. 10,000 in cash and enter into a personal bail for Rs. 50,000.

This bond, however, with its severe restrictions, which entailed considerable loss to me by confining me to Colombo, was subsequently cancelled.

I ought to mention I have always been on good terms with the Moors; I have never entertained any feeling of animosity towards their faith or race. During the days of trouble I was actually engaged, either as a Town Guard or in my private capacity, in doing everything in my power to help the Government to suppress the disturbances.

The Mayor of Colombo had given me a letter, addressed to all military officers, to render me any assistance necessary to quell the disturbance. I had exerted myself not only in Colombo, but also outside, at the request of Government officers.

D. S. SENANAYAKE.

30th October, 1915.

## (12) LETTER *of* MR. FRANCIS D. STUART, *Merchant.*

*S.S. "Paul Lecat,"*

*17th November*, 1915.

The Hon. Mr. Rámanáthan.

Dear Sir,

It is with pleasure that I accede to your request to communicate to you what I know about the riots that occurred in Ceylon in the months of May and June of the present year. I do so all the more readily as I am in sympathy with those who consider that a strict inquiry should be made by unprejudiced persons into the cause of the said riots and into the extraordinarily severe measures that were afterwards adopted by the Ceylon Government.

As you are aware, I have been a resident in Ceylon since 1908, and the exigencies of my business have placed me in constant touch with the Sinhalese, Tamil and Moorish races forming the population of the Island, of whose qualities and defects I am perhaps better able to judge than many other European residents, owing to my intimate knowledge of their domestic and social life.

On Wesak day, 1915 (May 31st), I was at Nuwara Eliya, and I have a perfect recollection of the same. The carol carts went round the town as usual, and everything was perfectly quiet. It was only on the following day that I heard about what had occurred at Kandy, and a day or two afterwards I learned by the newspapers that riots had taken place elsewhere. I almost immediately went down to Colombo, and, visiting the quarter of the town where the greatest damage was said to have been done, my impression was that it had been exaggerated by the newspapers. Certainly some shops belonging to the Moors had been broken into, but I saw nothing of the " ruin " that had been described.

At about this time I received a telegram from Galle telling me that the caretaker of my bungalow at that place had been arrested in connection with the riots, some Moorman living in the neighbourhood having caused his arrest. I thereupon wired to the Superintendent of Police for particulars, and was told that he could be liberated if bail to the amount of Rs. 100 was forthcoming. To this I immediately agreed. I may add that the charge against him was afterwards found to be an absolutely false one, some personal feeling of revenge being the sole motive, and the case was withdrawn.

Another telegram from Galle subsequently reached me, after I had returned to Nuwara Eliya, from the proprietor of my bungalow, telling me that his brother-in-law, a highly respectable, harmless and peaceful man, whom I have known since 1909, was to be tried by Court Martial, and imploring of me to do what I could for him. On the day preceding the trial I left Nuwara Eliya at 8.30 a.m., and, travelling through to Galle, reached it about 11 p.m.

Typical opinion of a Court Martial Officer.

An incident occurred during my journey that I think worth while to relate, as it gives a fair idea of the sentiment prevalent among most of the Europeans at the period of which I write. I made the acquaintance in the train of an English officer, who, upon

His firm belief that the Sinhalese had entered into a conspiracy to massacre the Moors, Burghers, and Europeans; and that the more Sinhalese are got rid of the better it would be.

hearing that I was going to Galle as a witness for the defence of a Sinhalese, expressed much astonishment, adding, "Leave the rascals alone; the more that are got rid of, the better." He subsequently told me that he had assisted at Courts Martial in the Ratnapura district, and that it had been clearly proved that there was a conspiracy of the Sinhalese to massacre first of all the Moors, and then the Burghers and the Europeans; that it had been discovered just in time, and that "sacks full of treasonable correspondence with a certain foreign State had been found secreted among the rafters of the bungalows occupied by the Sinhalese gentlemen who had been arrested.

I reached Galle, as before stated, at about 11 p.m. The Court Martial was fixed for the following morning at 7 a.m., but in truth it was not assembled before 8 o'clock. Major Andrews, of the British Army (I think, of the Devonshire Regiment), was the President. After taking the usual oaths to administer justice, etc., he addressed a few words to the advocates who were counsel for the accused, and told them that there was no need for their services, which could be dispensed with altogether; that he was, however, willing to allow them to remain; but that he hoped that the proceedings would be curtailed as much as possible by the elimination of anything like a display of eloquence, etc. The trial then commenced. The six accused men were brought in under the guard of armed Panjábis. Three Moors were called as witnesses for the accusation. They declared at first that they had seen three of the accused (including the brother-in-law of the proprietor of my bungalow) armed with a sword and in their mosque at 4 o'clock in the afternoon on the day when the riots took place, but on cross-examination by Mr. Elliot, the well-known advocate of Colombo, the hour was gradually extended to 4.30, to 5, and finally to 6 or 7 o'clock! In a word, their depositions were said by Mr. Elliot to be quite different from what they had stated in the police court. Several witnesses were then hurriedly heard for the defence. The proceedings ended at about 11 a.m. The six accused were then taken back to jail under escort as they had come. No judgment was pronounced for some days afterward. Then it was made known that the accused had been condemned to seven years' penal servitude.

My personal impression of the whole affair was one of the greatest astonishment that such things could occur in a Colony of the British Crown, for without in any way calling into question the good faith of the officers who were called upon at a moment's notice, and without any previous study, to hear and determine criminal cases, it must be admitted by all unprejudiced persons that a very grave probability exists that by reason of their ignorance of Asiatic character and the ordinary subtleties of law, to say nothing of local jealousies and animosities that were undoubtedly the motive of a large number of accusations, much gross injustice must inevitably have been the result.

Mr. Stuart's opinion of the gross injustice done by Court Martial;

The Sinhalese are both loyal and peaceful, but they naturally expect to be treated with justice and with no greater severity than what is displayed towards other races under British rule. This is my fixed opinion of them after over seven years' experience. That a certain number of Sinhalese, irritated by no small amount of mischievous interference in the free exercise of the Buddhist religion, committed

of the loyalty and peacefulness of the Sinhalese;

of the causes of the riots;

many unlawful acts of violence, there can be no doubt, but the measures taken for their repression were, in my opinion, out of all proportion to the damage done.

of the gross blunder of the Government, in proclaiming Martial Law;

The proclamation of martial law, resulting in an absolute reign of terror, during which innocent Sinhalese villagers were left to the tender mercies of the Panjábis, who, as Moslems, sided with the Moors, was in itself, I think, a gross blunder, inasmuch as there had been no single act of sedition committed against the British Government, the whole affair from beginning to end being simply a quarrel between two races and two religions; and most unprejudiced persons must admit that the summary trial and committal of the accused by Court Martial on the biassed testimony of Moors—a method equalling in injustice the practice of past ages and the use of *lettres de cachet*—was far from what would be expected in a Colony under the British Crown.

and of the proceedings of Courts Martial held in Ceylon equalling in injustice the practice of past ages and the use of *lettres de cachet*.

One of the objects of your visit to London being, as I have heard, to ask that a careful inquiry be made into the cause and means used for the repression of the recent disturbances in Ceylon, as a friend to the different races that inhabit the Island, and also as a well-wisher to the British rule, I wish you every success, and if I can be of any further use I trust you will let me know.

Believe me, dear Sir,

Yours faithfully,

FRANCIS D. STUART.